TRANSFORMATIONS

Healing Trauma with
Psychedelic Therapy

by
Dale Carruth

Transformations: Healing Trauma with Psychedelic Therapy

Author: Dale Carruth

Copyright© 2022 – Dale Carruth. All rights reserved. No part of this book may be copied without express permission from the author.

Published by 3 Feathers Books

3feathers3@protonmail.com and 3feathersbooks@gmail.com

Cover Art by Dale Carruth

Proofreading and editorial advice: Theo von Oberstockstall & Vincent Czyz

ISBN: 9780645324938 print

ISBN: 9780645324945 ebook

Subjects: Psychedelic Assisted Therapy – Healing Trauma – PTSD & CPTSD – Mental Health – Psychotropic Drugs – Entheogens – Psychedelics – Therapy – Psychedelic Research – Plant Medicines – MDMA – Psilocybin Mushrooms – Ayahuasca – Sexual Abuse – Psychedelic Therapy

First Edition, February 2022.

Printed by Ingram Spark

Legal Disclaimer

The content of this book and all concepts, ideas, facts, historical accounts and other information included in it (all hereafter referred to as "this Book") have been provided for educational and entertainment purposes only.

The Publisher and Author of this Book make no representations or warranties of any kind about this Book, including (without limitation) representations or warranties as to diagnosis, prevention, treatment or cure of any medical or health condition.

This Book is not designed to replace or take the place of any form of medical advice. This book is not intended to replace the need for independent medical or other professional advice or services, as may be required.

This Book has been compiled from sources deemed reliable, and it is accurate to the best of the knowledge, information and belief of the Publisher and Author. However, the Publisher and Author do not give any warranty or guarantee as to its accuracy and validity, nor as to the outcomes you may experience from following or using any techniques, strategies, examples or information contained in the Book, and cannot be held liable for any errors and/or omissions.

This Book contains general information only, and does not take into account the unique, individual circumstances of any reader. This Book is not intended to replace the need for independent, professional medical or other professional advice and services based on your particular circumstances. Where appropriate and/or necessary, you should consult a suitably qualified healthcare professional including but not limited to your doctor or such other professional advisor before following or using any techniques, strategies, examples or information in this book.

You agree to accept all risks associated with your use of this Book. By using this Book, you acknowledge and agree with the above disclaimers, and that you have no legal cause of action or any other rights against the Publisher or Author of this Book.

TRANSFORMATIONS

Healing Trauma with
Psychedelic Therapy

by
Dale Carruth

Other Publications by Dale Carruth and Awards

2021 – *Beating the Benzo Blues: Getting off Benzodiazepines*, an easy-to-follow guide for safely withdrawing from prescription benzodiazepines

2000 – 2021 Some forty feature articles published in various magazines

2004 – Awarded Creative NZ-PEN Manuscript Assessment (with Barbara Else)

2003 – Awarded Creative NZ-PEN Mentorship (with author Tina Shaw)

Contents

Acknowledgements v

Foreword by Julian Palmer vii

Introduction 1

Part One: Seek and You May Be Found

Chapter One: The Call of Ayahuasca 11
    How to Find Underground Psychedelic Therapy 13

Chapter Two: A Brief History of Psychedelic Therapy 17
    LSD 17
    MDMA 19
    Psilocybin Mushrooms 20
    Ayahuasca 21
    Australian Acaciahuasca 23
    The Underground 24
    The Psychedelic Phoenix 25

Chapter Three: The Trauma Epidemic 27
    Denial Is Not a River in Egypt. 27
    What Are PTSD and CPTSD? 30
    Living with CPTSD – Shannon 31

Chapter Four: How Psychedelics Heal Trauma 37

Chapter Five: Medicines Used in Psychedelic Therapy 43
    The Short-Acting Medicines: MDMA, Psilocybin, Ayahuasca & Acaciahuasca, Ketamine. 44
    The Longer-Acting Medicines: Mescaline, LSD, Iboga. 48

Chapter Six: Detecting a Good Therapist/Facilitator 51

Chapter Seven: How Many Medicine Sessions Are Needed? 55
    Psychedelic Therapy Sessions Have a Trajectory 56

Chapter Eight: 12-Step Addiction Programmes and Psychedelic Therapy 61

Chapter Nine: Microdosing 65

Part Two: Medicine Sessions—In Their Own Words

MDMA Therapy
    Cathy, 35, Journalist 73
    Barry, 50, Architect 79
    Shaz, 60, Ex-military 87
    Linda, 28, Social Worker 93
    Louise, 32, Business Owner 99
    Sandra, 25, IT Programmer 103
    Terry, 35, Veterinarian 108
    Ben, 50, Marketing Manager 124
    Paula, 36, Naturopath 131
    Paul, 50, School Teacher 139
    Stephanie, 35, Environmentalist 144
    Martin, 50, Social Worker 147
    Shannon, 46, Sales Representative 157

Psilocybin Therapy
    Stephanie, 35, Environmentalist 166
    Deborah, 26, Lawyer 172
    Marie, 56, Social Worker 176
    Terry, 35, Veterinarian 179
    Tim, 32, Business Owner 194
    Shaun 52, Artist 198
    Nic, 52, IT Specialist 200
    John, 24, Civil Engineer 203

Shannon, 46, Sales Representative 209

Ayahuasca Therapy
Natalie, 30, Medical Doctor 217
Lily, 45, IT Specialist 224
Gina, 62, Business Advisor... 227
Shannon 46, Sales Representative 232

Part Three: For Therapists and Facilitators

Chapter One: First DO NO Harm... 243

Chapter Two: Psychedelic Therapy—a Three-Stage Process........ 247
Stage 1: Assessment and Preparation 248
Stage 2: Medicine Session 250
Stage 3: Integration Sessions 259

Chapter Three: States That Can Occur During Psychedelic Therapy 261

Chapter Four: The Road to Hell is Paved with Good Intentions 269
Acaciahuasca: Initiation and Trial by Fire. 270
MDMA and Dissociative Identity Disorder 273

Chapter Five: Reviewing the Psychedelic Resources 277

Conclusion: Who's Really in Control? 285

Bibliography.. 291

Appendix 295

Acknowledgements

Saving people from a life of mental bondage, not of their own making is a calling that nobody should ever have to fear. I pay tribute to the courageous underground psychedelic therapists and medicine providers who, at great risk to their personal liberty, are brave enough to provide a much-needed, illegal treatment for suicidal and traumatised people. When miraculous healings unfold before your eyes, it is indeed a great motivator; when the truth of these healing medicines is revealed, what else can one do? They cannot simply be ignored. Thus, a calling is born.

To the brave people who allowed me to share your personal stories in this book—many thanks for the courage it took to travel the hero's journey and take matters into your own hands when all odds were against you. Only through our courage can we help change society's attitudes (and the law) regarding these much-needed healing medicines.

Julian Palmer—thanks for your help and guidance in this latter part of my life's healing journey. Your medicine may have saved my life. You certainly opened many obscured windows and doors on this mystical path through life, and what's unfolded since continues to be a magical mystery tour (I sometimes feel as if I've become a character in a Carlos Castaneda novel). By generously sharing your medicine and vast wealth of psychedelic knowledge, you fulfil a needed service on this earth.

Dr Friederike Merkel Fischer—thanks for your time, generosity of spirit, and mentorship. I enjoy our Zoom chats across the oceans and miles and greatly value the wisdom I receive. Hopefully, we'll meet in the flesh one day. You are a true pioneer and sacrificial lamb in the field of underground psychedelic therapy. I'm sorry we live in a society that imprisons gifted healers for their life-saving work, but I'm grateful you were able to write a book that so inspired me. It seems we haven't moved far from the Middle Ages, when witches were burnt at the stake.

To the people who've supported my sometimes-difficult journey through life—sponsors, friends, therapists, my mother—I thank you. You are the stars in my sky, illuminating my journey back home to myself ... one step at a time.

Foreword by Julian Palmer

Dale's book comes at a crucial time: Western society is discovering the immense power and value of psychedelics for healing, especially in relation to healing trauma. As a trauma survivor herself, Dale understands this terrain very well and, with the assistance of psychedelics, has been able to lead many people through powerful processes.

In this book Dale focuses on the substances that, because of their effectiveness for treating trauma, have been gaining the most traction in the world: MDMA and psilocybin. But she also includes ayahuasca. What is contained within this book is a valuable record of her work with clients—how they have responded and how they feel this medicine has worked for them. These records are definitely more relevant to regular people than the much-vaunted scientific studies into these compounds as any reader should be able to see clearly how these compounds work, how people experience them, and what results they themselves could actually get from them.

I first met Dale when she flew from New Zealand to attend a weekend ayahuasca event with myself in South East Queensland in 2017. She put me on the spot at that time, telling me that if ayahuasca didn't work, she would probably kill herself! Luckily it did work, and she noticed some profound shifts and changes in herself. After seeing for herself how profoundly these compounds can help people heal, she has been pursuing this path with a rare passion, fearlessness, and dedication. Along the way she faced many challenges and underwent initiations that come with sharing these medicines with others. Except for various reading materials and my sometimes quite blasé responses to her many queries, there wasn't much specific training available. Despite this, Dale leapt right into this work with a very professional, earnest, considered, and compassionate manner.

Releasing this book is a brave move for Dale. It means coming up from the underground in her own name despite the risks and red tape that presently prevent this work from becoming well-known. Dale's courage is a testimony to her desire to highlight the importance of psychedelic work and the immediacy with which it needs to be carried out. I believe this book can help guide therapists to carry out this most important work in helping to heal the millions who suffer daily from the crippling effects of trauma. This unique contribution can also help people seeking psychedelic-assisted therapy to understand what they are in for and help them prepare for and understand the processes involved in going through these most profound and effective treatments.

Julian Palmer

Introduction

'If a law is unjust, a man is not only right to disobey it, he is obligated to do so. —Thomas Jefferson

'An unjust law is one that forbids transparency, and thereby attempts to compel, coerce, manipulate a responsible adult by withholding facts, or any law that allows one person to control the actions of another (when those actions do no direct harm) is an unjust law.' —Christine Marie Mason

I'd suffered from debilitating PTSD symptoms, caused by childhood sexual abuse ever since I stopped self-medicating with alcohol. I'd tried most available therapies and nothing had really worked. I'd exhausted all options except one: ayahuasca. I was reluctant to walk down that road, however, as I was a sober member of Alcoholics Anonymous and had been for twenty years. To consume a non-prescribed, mind-altering substance would be considered a relapse. But Plan B was suicide, so what other people thought suddenly seemed irrelevant.

I assumed I'd have to go to Peru, where ayahuasca is legal, which seemed a big ask for a traumatised person. But as luck would have it, synchronicity paved the way, and I was introduced to an Australian healer by an American I met in an ayahuasca Facebook group. In early

2017 I flew to Australia from New Zealand to receive my first illegal ayahuasca treatment.

Obviously, the results were profound or I wouldn't have written this book. For the past five years, I've continued to heal, research widely, and train with some very knowledgeable people. I've availed myself of further psychedelic treatments with MDMA, psilocybin, San Pedro cactus and ayahuasca. Further down the track, I was presented with other desperate and suicidal people (not hard to find these days). My relief at finding the cure to what had ailed me along with the empathy I had for others living with PTSD inspired in me an obligation to share my newfound knowledge. The rest, you could say, is history. Healing is not just about the removal of symptoms; it's about opening up in faith to a higher force and living in its guidance and flow.

I guess I should mention, in the name of credibility, that I have a BA in Psychology and I am a certified addiction counsellor (CAC). I worked at a benzodiazepine-addiction counselling and detox service for a number of years. I wrote and delivered a training package to doctors and mental health workers on benzo addiction and detoxification and guest lectured on the subject at three New Zealand universities. I've authored more than forty articles (mainly on social issues) and a booklet on benzo detoxification called *Beating the Benzo Blues*.

Many don't know, or simply forget, that psychedelic medicines were used therapeutically by esteemed doctors and psychiatrists, in the 1940s, '50s, and '60s, to treat a variety of mental conditions within a hospital framework. They were studied, researched, and written about by credible and scholarly academics.

Like a phoenix rising from the ashes of criminality, psychedelic-therapy research is experiencing a meteoric comeback, and society is beginning to understand and acknowledge the important place they hold for the healing of mental health issues. *Psychedelics*, the singular of which simply means 'mind expanding', are not dangerous or addictive. In fact, many who have used them under the right conditions rate the experience as one of the most important of their lives. Studies on psychedelics using human subjects are taking place at universities all around the world, including in Australia and New Zealand.

While most authors would insert a disclaimer here, saying that it's not the intent of this book to promote illegal drug use or incite illegal activity, I can't in good conscience do that. I'm in full agreement with Thomas Jefferson: 'When we live in a society that criminalises the use of life-saving, mind-healing medicines, these laws must be challenged, changed or ignored.' We are compelled to rise up against the chains of ignorance and capitalism that keep our society bound in sickness and despair. I believe it's our ethical and moral responsibility to challenge anti-humanitarian laws. These medicines must be legalised, as they were in the 1940s, '50s, and '60s, and made available to all who desperately need them.

This book is first and foremost directed at people struggling with the fallout of trauma—usually diagnosed as PTSD, CPTSD, anxiety, or depression—people who struggle daily to function and stay alive. If this description fits you, please don't give up; there is a solution that truly works. Currently, it's illegal, but don't let that stop you. Find a way to do it. This book will help you. Life should not be a journey of survival dictated by the wreckage of your past.

For those already intent on psychedelic healing, this book will provide information on whether this therapy is suitable for you and if so, how you might go about finding a safe underground therapist. Hopefully, licensed therapists will provide this treatment again one day but until such time it's my sincere hope that all those in need find a safe and effective way to heal now.

This book will also serve as a valuable resource for underground and emerging psychedelic therapists and facilitators. It offers a tried-and-true treatment protocol, processes, procedures, and guidelines for safe and effective practice as well as some rare and compelling qualitative research.

Navigating the landscape of the Australian underground psychedelic-therapy scene, I quickly spotted the need for trauma-informed people to step up to the plate. It's one thing to provide these potent medicines; it's another to re-traumatise people during the course of healing. Some of my early experiences could have been less difficult had the facilitators been more informed.

Most facilitators I encountered had minimal knowledge of trauma and its fallout. Addiction knowledge was also sadly lacking. There was minimal focus on assessment, preparation, and integration. People were largely left to deal with the fallout of extreme emotional experiences, which were sometimes paradigm-shattering. Though what these facilitators offered was better than nothing—and I'd gladly do it all again—I saw plenty of room for improvement. This is my humble contribution.

Part One: Psychedelic Therapy: Seek and You May Be Found

Highlights most of the things relevant to the topic and the safe participation in underground psychedelic-assisted therapy, that includes MDMA, psilocybin, and ayahuasca.

Part Two: Medicine Sessions - In Their Own Words

Twenty-two people took part in a total of forty psychedelic therapy sessions with either MDMA, Psilocybin or Ayahuasca. They share their stories of profound and transformative healing. Using information gathered in their assessment session, I introduce them and describe what motivated them to seek out psychedelic therapy. They then express in their own words what their medicine experiences felt like, what insights were gained, and what enduring changes they've noticed in their lives as a result of doing psychedelic therapy. All names and identities have been changed to protect client anonymity. Minimal editing of client stories occurred in order to enhance the messages clarity.

The demographic is predominantly middle class and multicultural. Ages range from mid-twenties to early sixties, but most are in their thirties, forties, and fifties. By occupation, we have a teacher, a doctor, a lawyer, a university lecturer, various IT specialists, an architect, an accountant, a soldier, social workers, a naturopath, a business advisor, a salesperson, a journalist, business owners and engineers. Some had never taken an illegal drug in their lives, while others had some previous encounters with psychedelics or drugs. Most had tried a multitude of traditional therapies with minimal results.

All participants had suffered from some trauma, stemming from either: childhood abuse or neglect, domestic violence, car accidents, armed-forces events, rape, bullying, the early death of a parent, or combinations of the above. They were diagnosed with either PTSD, CPTSD, anxiety, depression, ADD, OCD, autism, or a combination of these. Half were victims of childhood sexual abuse (six females and six males). Several were suicidal.

Just two weeks prior to his treatment, Martin, a 50-year-old social worker, had booked a room on the 41st floor of a hotel—he intended to jump. Only thoughts of how it might affect his grandson had kept him from taking the final step. Just one psychedelic treatment liberated him from his suicidal ideation. He is now free from a frozen emotional state, sleeps well (after enduring years of sleep paralysis in which he'd wake up screaming several times a night), and has reconnected with family after years of no communication.

Cathy and her husband underwent psychedelic therapy to save their marriage which was about to end. With a small child, they were at their wits' end. His PTSD—attributed both to military trauma and childhood sexual and emotional abuse—caused him to explode in the presence of small triggers. He'd then go on a drinking binge to soothe the resulting shame. More abuse would follow. Cathy says they are now quite happily married, and he is pretty much symptom-free.

Part Two; is divided into three sections based on the medicine used: MDMA, Psilocybin and Ayahuasca. This provides the reader with an understanding of how these different substances work, their similarities and differences. Some clients report on multiple treatments with one, two, or all three medicines.

Trigger Alert: Some of these stories contain graphic accounts of childhood sexual abuse, rape, and other traumatic events. Suicide is also mentioned.

Part Three: For Therapists and Facilitators

Part three is directed at practising underground therapists and medicine facilitators and future psychedelic therapists. It will also prove beneficial reading to anyone considering participation in psychedelic therapy -

as knowledge indeed is power. It highlights the qualities needed to provide effective psychedelic therapy. It provides tried and tested treatment protocols and procedures It discusses the various mind states induced by psychedelics and how best to work with them. Importantly, it addresses some of the difficulties that may arise when conducting psychedelic therapy and courageously details some of the things that can and do go wrong, which most books tend to avoid mentioning. It assesses the current literature and resources that are available on both trauma and psychedelic therapy.

Overall, this book provides solid testimony to this fact: psychedelic therapy is far more effective than any currently available option for healing a host of mental illnesses. The current call for 'more psychedelic research' seems to me a deadly delaying tactic. Immediate action is needed or government policy and lawmakers will have even more blood on their hands.

I suspect that there's minimal profit in a cure. 'Mental illness' is big business for Big Pharma; their gargantuan profits depend on traumatised people taking addictive, mind-numbing pills for years on end. The standard treatment protocol for returned war veterans is a prescription cocktail of mind-numbing pills that diminish their ability to see, feel, or contemplate the horrors they've seen and done in the name of patriotism.

As psychedelic therapy appears to 'cure' many mental illnesses, at least to the degree that the person is exponentially more functional, it's unlikely they'll be legalised anytime soon, and even then, only under very strict conditions. So, if this is a life-or-death decision for you and you meet the safety criteria outlined in this book, you now have the option to take matters into your own hands.

Part One

Seek and You May Be Found

CHAPTER ONE

The Call of Ayahuasca

I was woken from my amnestic sleep not by the kiss of a handsome prince, but by the dark, bitter brew of a vine and a tree. I first heard of ayahuasca in 2014 while researching ibogaine, an African plant medicine known for its miraculous treatment of addiction. Being an addiction counsellor, I was interested in such things. I'd watched glowing YouTube reports of people who'd found relief from their PTSD (post-traumatic stress disorder) after taking ayahuasca. I'd read numerous articles and books—positive results, backed by research, was claimed for the treatment of depression, anxiety, PTSD, and addiction. While all this certainly sparked my interest, I had a major dilemma: I was twenty years sober in Alcoholics Anonymous, and taking a mind-altering substance would be considered a relapse.

AA had replaced my family, saved my life, and given me much-needed human connections. But the never-ending battle to keep my head above the vortex of murky waters that kept threatening to take me down was becoming exhausting. I was clinging to flotsam like a shipwreck survivor. While the overt symptoms of PTSD—nightmares, flashbacks, dissociation—had largely dissipated, I still struggled with hypervigilance and an extreme lack of trust in people. I still locked myself in my bedroom at night.

Ayahuasca, singing her siren song and infiltrating my thoughts and dreams, invaded my consciousness. Over the years I'd tried so many things to heal myself—counselling, psychotherapy, primal therapy, rebirthing, psychodrama, religion, sweat lodges, spirituality, prescription meds and sobriety—but the loneliness and the pointlessness of my life enveloped me like a shroud, and there seemed only one thing left to try before I checked on out. By this time, I really didn't give a damn what fellow AA members or anyone else thought: ayahuasca was my last hope.

Mysterious, synchronous, funny how when you commit to something everything starts falling into place. I joined an online ayahuasca group, and soon met an American guy who put me onto an Ozzie guy, who'd been facilitating ayahuasca ceremonies for fifteen or so years in Australia.

J.P. had a website, had written a book on psychedelics, been interviewed by media, spoken at entheogenic conferences. He seemed the real deal. Soon we were emailing back and forth. Although I confided that I was ready to take myself out, he seemed unfazed. Standard fare perhaps. He calmly answered my many questions and assured me I'd find relief. He sent details of his upcoming 'workshops'. He wasn't pushy, didn't demand money up front, and largely left it up to me. He seemed cruisy, intelligent, and irreverent without being arrogant—things to like in a person. He was currently touring South America, drinking ayahuasca with jungle shamans and attending a plant-medicine conference. I read his blog and gathered more info. Finally, I booked a flight to Oz to drink this strange medicine with a bunch of total strangers—a tall order for someone with PTSD and severe trust and control issues.

How to Find Underground Psychedelic Therapy

Until psychedelic therapy becomes legal, which is potentially a long way off (at least in Australia), how might you gain access to a safe underground therapist or plant-medicine facilitator? Sadly, the options are slim as few appropriate people are willing to take the risk, which is not to say that many inappropriate people aren't. First, do your research and decide whether this therapy is a safe option for you. The books I recommend in (Part 3 – Chapter 5), along with this one, should help you reach that decision. Then, if you still feel called to board the psychedelic train, venture forth and may the Force be with you.

Social Media are a good place to start. Within Facebook Groups search for psychedelic-related, local, national or international groups. There are many. 'Ayahuasca' is the one I started with. It boasts 90,000 members globally, which should give some indication of the immense interest in this topic. While it's pretty much a marketing tool for the legal Peruvian ayahuasca retreats, there are occasionally good discussions and a community willing to answer your questions. 'Thank You Plant Medicine Community' is another Facebook group whose page allows you to read testimonies from people who have taken plant medicines to heal. There are a few specifically Australian psychedelic Facebook groups as well. One I facilitate has a specific focus on trauma healing.

Psychedelic Groups and Societies. There are psychedelic societies all around the world. Currently, in Australia, there is the Australian Psychedelic Society (APS) in Melbourne, Adelaide, Sydney, Perth, and Brisbane. The APS holds regular social events and gatherings. This is possibly one of the best places to meet people and start up a conversation regarding psychedelic therapy. https://www.psychedelicsociety.org.au

Music Festivals or Healing Ceremonies. Music festivals are frequented by a broad array of psychedelic consumers, both novice and experienced. Within a festival's open community, you may find connections to a psychedelic therapist or plant-medicine facilitator. You might even find a workshop where the topic is discussed.

Meetup Groups. Look for groups advertising legal substances and gatherings, such as Cacao Ceremonies, Sound Healing, or Breathwork. You will possibly meet someone there who knows of someone. https://www.meetups.com

Psychologists or Therapists. With psychedelic research well underway, many psychologists and therapists are informed and may know of someone providing underground psychedelic therapy. Some, having tried psychedelics themselves, will already be converts. Most won't offer it in their practices for fear of losing their license or registration though the occasional one may. Psychedelic-friendly therapists may offer 'psychedelic preparation or integration' on their business websites and this is the clue to look out for.

Doctors and Psychiatrists. Some doctors and psychiatrists may know of an underground psychedelic therapist, especially among the few who were recently licensed to offer legal ketamine therapy for treatment-resistant depression in Australia. Marie (story in Part Two) received ketamine therapy for her depression, with positive results, prior to doing psychedelic therapy. Her psychiatrist encouraged her to seek out psychedelic therapy for her trauma-related issues. I also met a ketamine doctor at a recent Brisbane APS meeting.

Holotropic Breath Workers. Holotropic breathwork, created by Stan and Christina Grof in the late 1970s, was a response to the changed legal status of psychedelics. Holotropic breath workers may well know of someone offering underground psychedelic therapy.

Personal Network. You may be lucky enough to know someone or to know someone who knows someone who has received psychedelic therapy. Word of mouth is by far the best option because the person can offer their personal experience and their evaluation of the therapist.

Discretion is always the key. Don't ask incriminating questions on written formats like Facebook or Messenger as this leaves a permanent record. Most savvy underground therapists and plant-medicine providers are protective of their identities, for good reason, and only communicate through encrypted sites, such as Signal and Proton Mail. A face-to-face meeting is the preferred introduction as no recorded communications are retained.

CHAPTER TWO

A Brief History of Psychedelic Therapy

In the last twenty-five years, psychedelic medicines have been roused from their enforced anesthetisation, and research on their efficacy for treating mental illness is once again ongoing around the world. It's no secret that these medicines were used therapeutically and with astounding success in the 1940s, '50s, and '60s.

We don't really know exactly where the true psychedelic history began, but according to Brian C. Muraresku, author of the bestselling *The Immortality Key: The Secret History of the Religion with No Name*, psychedelics not only played a role in the origins of Western civilisation, they were the first religion. He reconstructs a history, repressed by the Christian Church, of a psychedelic sacrament, administered by women (priestesses) at Eleusis, to connect people with the divine. To be reconnected with the divine is the ultimate healing act.

LSD

LSD was the first psychedelic to be researched for its therapeutic potential for treating mental illness. Albert Hofmann, a chemist at Sandoz Pharmaceuticals in Switzerland, accidentally ingested a small amount in 1943. Visions of intense colours surged towards him, and he felt as if he'd actually died. His mind felt suspended in space as he saw his own corpse lying on the sofa. This state continued for hours, and he was probably relieved when it eventually stopped. But the next morning when he entered his garden, the world felt recreated: everything glistened and sparkled. His senses vibrated with heightened sensitivity, which persisted for the entire day. He strongly believed that LSD would offer tremendous value to psychiatry. Sandoz tested LSD for toxicity on rats and later on humans, and it was then offered for scientific and medical use.

Ronald Sandison, a British psychiatrist gave it to patients who had not progressed with traditional therapy. Three years later the Powick hospital board were so impressed with the results that they built an LSD clinic. Patients arrived in the morning, took their LSD while lying in private rooms. Nurses checked on them regularly, and in the late afternoon the patients convened to discuss their experiences. A driver took them home as they were often still under the influence.

Between 1954 and 1960, psychiatrist Humphry Osmond, who coined the term 'psychedelic,' trialled LSD in Canada in a bid to help alcoholics stop drinking. In combination with supportive psychiatry, he achieved abstinence rates of 40–45%, far higher than any other treatment at the time—or since. In all he treated 2000 alcoholic patients. One of the more famous ones was Bill Wilson, the co-founder of Alcoholics Anonymous.[1]

Elsewhere, studies of people with terminal cancer showed LSD therapy could relieve severe pain, improve quality of life, and alleviate the fear of death. Meanwhile, at Harvard, Timothy Leary and Richard Alpert gave

---

[1] Osmond, H. 'A Review of the Clinical Effects of Psychotomimethetic Agents'. *Annals of the New York Academy of Sciences.* 1957.

it to artists and writers who later described their experiences. They also gave it to students in experimental studies. But when rumours spread that they were giving drugs to students outside of a lab setting, the police began investigating. The university warned students against taking LSD, and Leary was sacked, supposedly for inciting countercultural views. This scandal played out in the press, and soon the whole country had heard of LSD.

Restrictions were placed on experimental drug use and in 1962 Sandoz cut back on its distribution. But the formula was easy to obtain and determined individuals made it with minimal difficulty. LSD's availability increased, as did the moral panic about its effects on young minds. The authorities were worried about LSD's association with the counterculture movement and the spread of anti-establishment and anti-war views. Calls for a nationwide ban followed, and as its negative reputation grew, many psychiatrists stopped using LSD.

In 1966 two U.S. Senate subcommittees held hearings and listened to testimony from both sides—doctors who claimed that LSD caused psychosis and the loss of cultural values, and LSD supporters, such as Leary and Senator Robert F. Kennedy, whose wife had undergone LSD therapy. Kennedy challenged the FDA for shutting down LSD research programmes. In 1968 LSD possession was made illegal in America and, shortly after, in England. Experimental research was still possible with licences, but LSD was hard to obtain and research ground to a halt.

MDMA

MDMA was first synthesised by the German pharmaceutical company Merck and granted a patent in 1914. It was acquired by Dow Pharmaceuticals as one of the spoils of the war. Alexander (Sasha) Shulgin was later given the rights to work with it. He tried it himself and was impressed with the results. Both he and his therapist wife, Ann, recognised its potential for helping traumatised people. Ann discovered that it expanded the unconscious material available to the clients and accelerated trauma recovery. She and other psychotherapists were using it with great success until 1985, when it was scheduled by the DEA and became legally unavailable to those who needed it. The scheduling was based on the fear generated by the rave scene and adulterated versions of MDMA known as 'Ecstasy,' which was involved in the occasional overdose and death.

Psilocybin Mushrooms

Psilocybin mushrooms have been used therapeutically for thousands of years and have a long history of medicinal use amongst indigenous peoples in many parts of the world. They were re-popularized in 1957 by R. Gordon Wasson, an American banker and mushroom enthusiast, who stumbled across an indigenous tribe using them in Mexico. He brought a sample back and gave it to our favourite Swiss chemist, Albert Hofmann, who isolated psilocybin and synthesised the drug in his Sandoz Pharmaceuticals lab. He produced 2 mg pills and distributed them for research purposes.

For the next twenty years, thousands of doses of psilocybin were administered in clinical experiments. Psychiatrists, scientists, and mental health professionals considered psilocybin treatment to be a promising aid to therapy for a broad range of psychiatric diagnoses, including alcoholism, schizophrenia, autism-spectrum disorders, obsessive-compulsive disorder, and depression.

Despite this long history of medicinal use and ongoing research into its therapeutic and medical benefits, psilocybin and psilocin were listed as Schedule I Controlled Substances in 1970. This, the most heavily criminalized category, was reserved for drugs considered to have a 'high potential for abuse', and no currently accepted medical use. There is significant evidence to the contrary on both counts when it comes to psilocybin. *(Drug policy.org)*

Ayahuasca

Ayahuasca is a psychoactive tea that has been used in Peruvian culture for over a thousand years and is an integral part of the spiritual practice of many tribal communities in the Amazon. It induces mystical experiences and is one of the most intense psychedelic experiences in the world. The original ayahuasca brew was prepared using only the vine (*Banisteriopsis caapi*) and no admixture plants (no DMT). Until the mid-1980s, this was the definition of ayahuasca that all ethnographers and ethnobotanists recorded.

According to Gayle Highpine, (in her book, *Unravelling the Mystery of the Origin of Ayahuasca*) - among many of the Amazonian tribes, the ayahuasca vine was considered 'the mother of all plants,' and a mediator and translator between the human and plant worlds.

> 'Ayahuasca vine is not visionary in the same way as DMT. Visions from vine-only brews are shadowy, monochromatic, like silhouettes or curling smoke or clouds moving across the night sky. It is because their visions are usually monochromatic that vines are classified by the colour or type of vision they produce: white, black, blue, red. Snakes, the most common vision on ayahuasca, are considered the manifest spirit of the vine. Visions can be hard to see; in fact, the 'visions' may not be visual at all, but auditory or somatic or intuitive. But the vine carries the content of the message, the teaching, and the insight. The leaf helps illuminate the content, but the teachings are credited to the vine. The vine

is The Teacher, The Healer, The Guide. The purpose of drinking ayahuasca is to receive the message the vine imparts. This is why it is the vine, not the leaf, that is classified by the type of vision it gives. 'For them (the tribes) the vine is, in truth, a living guide, a friend, a paternal authority.'

In the mid-80s, ayahuasca acquired a new definition: the combination of Banisteriopsis Caapi and the DMT-containing plant, Chacruna. Ayahuasca became by definition 'orally active DMT'. The first anthropologist to adopt the new definition seems to have been Luis Eduardo Luna in 1984. Luna associated with well-known psychonaut Terence McKenna, absorbing his perspective before beginning his own fieldwork. Since then, anthropologists have increasingly adopted this definition.

The ayahuasca-healing boom started in the Amazon in the mid-80s, largely due to Terrence McKenna and other American ethnographers. Since ayahuasca was legal in parts of South America, (Peru, Brazil and Columbia), tourists flocked to the largely American-run ayahuasca retreat centres that sprouted up in Peru and, later, Brazil. Jungle shamans were in high demand to share their medicines and healing wisdom.

Testimonies about the tremendous healing benefits of this new ayahuasca brew erupted on YouTube, in chatrooms, and on other social media forums. Canadian doctor, Gabor Mate used ayahuasca to treat addicts after his own profound experiences with it. Documentaries were made by ayahuasca entrepreneurs. A luxury ayahuasca retreat centre opened up in Costa Rica, catering to those less keen to brave the jungle. North Americans, unwilling to trek down to South America, sought to legitimize its use under the umbrella of sacred indigenous medicines, and membership in the Native American Church grew exponentially. Clandestine ayahuasca retreat centres opened up in the U.S., and shamans offering their brews started touring the world.

Australian Acaciahuasca

The serving of the Australian ayahuasca brew, often referred to as acaciahuasca—because native acacias are used for the DMT component—began in the late 1990s in Byron Bay, the Northern Rivers region of New South Wales. Byron-shire psychedelic enthusiast Darpan started an ayahuasca study group for people similarly interested. Darpan had studied under Stanislav Grof, the father of psychedelic therapy, and had also worked at a legal MDMA clinic in Holland. Nick Space-tree was the only man in the group to have actually tried ayahuasca at this time. Ambitiously, the group decided to invite infamous psychonaut Terrance McKenna to come and speak with them. Surprisingly Mckenna agreed and the rest is history.

When Terrence Mckenna visited Byron Bay he brought with him, from his own ethnobotanical garden in Hawaii, what may have been Australia's first ayahuasca vine (there are those who insist that the ayahuasca vine preceded him). Mckenna would send Darpan monthly bottles of ayahuasca to sample. Darpan was probably the first to start serving the brew to Australian groups in 1999.

Julian Palmer and his mate Dan Shreiber (now deceased) followed in 2001. The two collaborators got much of their info off the web. They began concocting and trialling different acaciahuasca brews, later serving it in groups. Julian tells me that his motivation to serve the brew was based mainly on the results he began seeing in the people who drank it. He served it for seven and a half years, charging nothing, and doing on average three to six groups a year. He wanted to keep it pure and serve it on his own terms. He trained others on how to make the brews, and they soon began serving it and charging for it. Broke and homeless, Julian started charging in 2013.

Julian says he received his instructions from the acacia itself while consuming the brew. Acacia was enthusiastic to work with him and encouraged him to serve it up in a non-traditional space without any cultural baggage, which is what inspired this new way of working. He caught a lot of flak from others for deviating from the traditional path of Peruvian shamanism. Twenty years later, however, he is still going strong and so is Darpan. Many others have since sprung up to join them, offering varying degrees of experience, motivation, and integrity. I could name at least a dozen currently serving various ayahuasca brews in and around the S.E. Queensland and the Northern Rivers region of New South Wales.

The Underground

When psychedelics were struck a legal blow, some therapists ventured underground to continue their work with traumatised, depressed, and anxious clients. Others sprang up quietly. One such example is Dr Friederike Meckel Fischer, a medical doctor and psychotherapist. Friederike conducted psychedelic group therapy for many years in her large Swiss family home. Group sessions took place over a live-in weekend. Her method of practice was hands-on, delving into the client's traumas while they were under the influence of a psychedelic substance: MDMA, LSD, 2CB, psilocybin, and ayahuasca, among others. Her treatment model combined psychedelics with the Family Systems model of therapy.

Sadly, Friederike was almost burnt at the stake after being reported by the disgruntled wife of a client, who, while in the framework of psychedelic therapy, recognised the dire state of his marriage and decided to end it. Friederike was unduly prosecuted, spent two weeks in remand prison, was given a 16-month suspended sentence, and lost her license to practise as a psychotherapist in Switzerland. As a consequence, she disclosed her underground therapy work in her ground-breaking book, *Therapy with Substance: Psycholytic Psychotherapy in the Twenty-First Century* (see Chapter Eleven).

The Psychedelic Phoenix

Psychedelic research probably started its meteoric comeback as a result of a massive surge in war veterans returning from the battlefield with PTSD and of the skyrocketing suicide rate. In 1998 the Multidisciplinary Association for Psychedelic Studies (MAPS) began research trials on PTSD in America, using MDMA to treat sexual abuse survivors, rape victims, and victims of domestic violence for PTSD. The early results were staggering: In 2010 Phase One trials showed an 83% remission in PTSD symptoms. After Phase Two in 2017, the FDA granted MDMA breakthrough status for treating PTSD.

MAPS currently train therapists to administer MDMA in controlled therapeutic contexts in preparation for its ensuing decriminalization. The MAPS therapy model involves three MDMA treatment sessions delivered a month apart and a total of fifteen therapy sessions, both before and after MDMA sessions. Two therapists, a male and a female, are always present. This is in part a safety measure due to the projections that can arise from a client.

Although Australia has been slow to jump on the psychedelic bandwagon, a breakthrough was celebrated in October 2021, when the first psilocybin trial received ethics approval. The TGA continues to resist amending the current illegal status of MDMA and psilocybin for the treatment of PTSD despite the tireless efforts of many to prove their efficacy. In February 2019 Israel granted MDMA compassionate-use status for treating returning war veterans with PTSD. Israel is also taking part in MAPS research trials. Switzerland has granted both MDMA and psilocybin compassionate-use status for treatment-resistant people suffering from mental health issues.

CHAPTER THREE

The Trauma Epidemic

Denial Is Not a River in Egypt.

Almost half of the people who tell their stories in Part Two of this book, both men and women, report traumatic incidents of childhood sexual abuse. While most of the media focus regarding PTSD is related to war veterans, many more cases of PTSD arise from childhood sexual abuse. The statistics will never truly be known, as sexual abuse is grossly underreported (it's estimated that only about 13% report their abuse), but metadata from many Australian studies show that on average one in five females and one in eight males is sexually abused before the age of fifteen. Fifty-eight per cent were under 10 when the abuse happened. Ninety to 95% of the abusers were male (*Bravehearts Australia*). Stranger danger is an exaggerated fear as is clearly shown by a 2016 ABS survey: Only 12 % of abusers were unknown to their victims; 35% of abusers were family members; 51% were known to the family. Fifty-five per cent of victims experienced multiple incidents (*Australian Bureau of Statistics*).

Sexual abuse survivors *are* the mental health crisis. They are labelled with some DSM (Diagnostic and Statistical Manual of Mental Disorders) diagnosis, but these labels often just serve to mask the truth—unbearable childhood trauma inflicted upon them through no fault of their own.

High-profile cases appear in the media: Jeffrey Epstein, Ghislaine Maxwell, Harvey Weinstein, Cardinal George Pell, Jimmy Saville, Bill Cosby, to name a few. But this is just the tip of the iceberg. Fathers, mothers, uncles, brothers, grandfathers, neighbours, Boy Scout leaders, teachers, priests, policemen, judges, butchers, bakers, and candlestick-makers are also plundering the innocent. Perpetrators are everywhere, comprising a literal pandemic, a virus of far-reaching consequences, and there appears to be no vaccination in sight.

Denial of sexual abuse can be traced back to the father of modern psychoanalysis, Sigmund Freud, the first to recognise and explore the phenomenon of sexual abuse. He deemed it so destructive that, left untreated, it had the potential to warp every aspect of the individual's development, to destroy their will and murder their soul. But his view soon changed when he was threatened by his contemporaries.

Father Jim Cogley, in his article, *The Legacy of Sexual Abuse Denial Can be Traced Back to Freud*, describes it thus.

> 'Freud uncovered an enormous body of evidence—personal, clinical and legal—that demonstrated beyond the shadow of a doubt that huge numbers of children were being abused, mostly by their fathers. The backlash he received when he began to disturb that particular hornet's nest was immediate and harsh. Many of his closest friends and contemporaries were the biggest offenders. These colleagues lashed out at him with the kind of indignation that only the guilty can muster. He was even accused of being insane. The pressure was so great that he chose to retract what he'd said and stated that the traumatic memories, which he constantly heard, were a fabrication of the mind, grounded on frustrated Oedipal desires. In effect, he said that the revelations

of sexual abuse had no foundation in reality, but were expressions of the patients' repressed sexual desires.'

This Freudian legacy of false memory syndrome has prevailed until recent times. This legacy of denial was so strong that in the 1950s, psychiatry's view was that even if sexual abuse did take place, it was unlikely that there would be any long-term consequences. How terribly wrong they were.

When a child is sexually abused, they lose their innocence, their trust, and a fundamental sense of safety in the world. They essentially lose a piece of their soul. In order to cope with the shock and betrayal, a host of distractions, addictions, and dysfunctional behaviours may erupt in a misguided attempt to regain some sense of control over their environments and bodies. When the perpetrator is a parent, the consequences are exponentially worse. The child's very existence is threatened as they now must somehow navigate living in the kingdom of their abuser. In this situation, repression of memories and dissociation seem reasonable and adaptable responses to such an untenable predicament.

A mental health system in which traumatised people are categorised, labelled, and medicated, sometimes for life, needs a drastic overhaul. It can no longer be considered functional or healthy. While the DSM is constantly changing and updating the criteria for PTSD—we're now on version 5—one criterion remains the same: The person must have experienced or had long-term exposure to a traumatic event such that their life or physical integrity felt threatened. One does have to wonder why responding with terror to a horrific or life-threatening event even warrants a psychiatric diagnosis.

What Are PTSD and CPTSD?

Recognition of PTSD (post-traumatic stress disorder) came about in 1970 and its other form, CPTSD (complex post-traumatic stress disorder), was identified in 1994. The first is generally caused by a one-off traumatic event, such as a car accident, rape, or war event. The second is associated with ongoing trauma happening over a period of time, such as living in an abusive home.

PTSD Symptoms

The most common PTSD symptoms include nightmares, hypervigilance, flashbacks and dissociation, following an event during which one's life or bodily integrity felt threatened. The following symptoms describe what a person living with CPTSD typically deals with.

1. Hypervigilance – a constant underlying feeling of unsafety. A sense of impending doom. Hyper-alertness and watchfulness. Big startle response.
2. Inability to fully relax – body tightness and tenseness, shallow breath.
3. Sleep disorders – nightmares, difficulty going to sleep and/or waking up in a state of alarm. Sleep paralysis.
4. Appalling self-image – low self-esteem and self-loathing. Shame-based.
5. CPTSD sufferers are often drawn to unavailable people, mainly because of their own inability to deal with true intimacy, which is perceived as triggering.
6. Anger and bad temper – which are really terror in disguise.
7. Paranoia – a constant, underlying mistrust of people.

8. Isolation – people are generally perceived as dangerous, so there's a need to isolate to keep safe. It's far easier not being around people because the only time a PTSD sufferer can relax to some degree is when they are alone.

9. Suicidal thoughts – people with CPTSD find life so difficult that suicidal thoughts are a constant companion. This seems to offer a back door solution if things become unbearable. It provides a sense of control.

10. Lack of spontaneity – a need for control. Rigidity.

11. Workaholism – a need for success, to compensate for feelings of self-disgust.

12. High drug and alcohol consumption or other compulsive and addictive behaviours in order to suppress and manage all of these other symptoms.

Note: throughout this book I may use 'PTSD' to refer to both PTSD and CPTSD.

Living with CPTSD – Shannon

Shannon, a 46-year-old sales representative, gives a great account of what it's like to live with PTSD. This will also explain what motivated her to seek out psychedelic therapy. Having survived multiple incidences of childhood sexual abuse she was diagnosed with CPTSD shortly after attaining sobriety in AA. When people stop self-medicating with alcohol or drugs, it's common for their PTSD symptoms to become more pronounced. What follows is a prelude in her own words to the rest of her story, which is in Part Two.

'My carefully constructed façade of success came tumbling down after my good friend and work colleague killed himself. I think I was the last person to speak to him. He was supposed to come to my place for dinner that night but phoned just as I was cooking our dinner to say he wasn't coming. Consequently, I wasn't that friendly. My last words to him, delivered in a pretty miffed tone were, 'Oh well, suit yourself then.'

When I received the news via telephone early the next morning, I was utterly shocked. A mutual friend who lived next door to him had found him in his garage, car engine running, exhaust pipe blocked, lights out, nobody home. My last words to him just kept reverberating in my mind—*Oh well, suit yourself then … Oh well, suit yourself then.* Knowing these were the last words I spoke to him truly devastated me. Maybe if I'd been less self-centred, I could have been more helpful or at least picked up on how bad he was feeling. But I was riding high on success, money, and a hell of a lot of partying.

His suicide completely undid me. It crashed me into a downward spiral of despair and excess drinking. The shock of his sudden death ripped off my mask of normality and success. It's hard to explain the shock and deflation when a friend takes their life, an act that is so contradictory to the human will to survive. The shock is incomprehensible—yesterday the person was here, tangible, breathing, and full of potential, and now they've ceased to be.

I'm old personal friends with the will to die, but something deep inside always kept me going, perhaps the belief that if I killed myself, I'd have to come back and do it all over again—and there's no way in the world I'd ever want to do that. The other thought that kept me going in times of despair is that I couldn't let those who'd perpetrated crimes against me win. How easy it would be for them if I just quietly offed myself. How very convenient. No need to live in fear of what their future might hold when the plundered child becomes an adult. Despite these beliefs, I spiralled down the well of despair and stared into the dark abyss until

I eventually ended up at the doctor's office. Upon seeing the state I was in, he immediately referred me to Psychological Services and I ended up in a Day Therapy Programme.

I arrived there one morning still half-cut from the night before and covered in bruises—I'd fallen down the stairs of the nightclub where I'd celebrated my 30th birthday. One of the nurses was the first person to suggest I go to Alcoholics Anonymous. After a few more synchronous events and two more people suggesting I go to AA, I eventually wound up there.

The real nightmares began when I stopped drinking. I'd wake up sweating and screaming in terror. Some nights I felt a dark male presence in my room, leaning over me. My nightmares were usually about a man trying to break into my house. He'd be at the front door, so I'd run to the back door, but he'd be there as well. I was running all night and there was no escape. Some nights I was so terrified of these nightmares I couldn't sleep. I'd barricade myself in my room by pulling a chest of drawers in front of the door. Some nights, insane with terror and anxiety, I felt the urge to sleep under my bed.

My kind and wise addiction counsellor sent me off to rehab. My six-week stint cracked opened a Pandora's Box of ghosts. There were clear warning signs from the start that something, apart from my alcohol consumption, was very wrong with me. One night a male warden on night duty entered my bedroom, shining his torch in my face. I woke in terror and immediately started screaming at him to get the fucking fuck out of my room. When he stated that he was just doing his job, I kept swearing louder and louder as terror fired my nerve centres. I had no idea why I was having such an intense reaction. The next morning, chastised by my counsellor, I felt ashamed and embarrassed.

A few days later a girl working through her sexual abuse in a psychodrama group triggered a massive reaction in me and I ended up sobbing and completely dissociating from my body. I had no idea why I was having these strange and intense reactions. It seemed over the top and confusing. It was as if, post-alcohol, my subconscious was leaking out, trying to tell me something.

I should mention at this point, that I could barely remember any of my childhood before the age of fourteen. When my AA sponsor would ask me about my life, I'd always say, 'Well, when I was fourteen, I was hospitalised with alcohol poisoning after drinking a bottle of Blackberry Nip. That was my first ever blackout. I was put in the Girls Home for running away from home.' He'd ask, 'But what about before that?' Weird as it sounds, I just couldn't answer him. My life seemed vague and shrouded, like a hazy, out-of-reach dream.

After my stint in rehab, I scored a well-paying sales job in another city and gladly packed up and left my hometown, where bad memories seemed to lurk at every turn. I was happy to be starting a new life—or so I thought! But I soon met a guy in AA and we started a relationship. One night while we were having sex, his face completely blacked out and I froze in terror. I couldn't see his face, even with my eyes wide open; it was just a dark shadow. I was terrified and completely dissociated from my body. I didn't know what was happening to me. I felt I was going mad. I went to a doctor who diagnosed me with PTSD and referred me to my first government-funded sexual-abuse therapist.

Freaked out, hypervigilant, easily triggered, and reactive, I had a fight with my boss, a young upstart, and got fired. My new life was not to be. I was devastated. I returned to university to finish the psych degree I'd started a few years earlier. PTSD continued to wreak havoc on my relationship—constant flashbacks, nightmares, and dissociation, especially during sex. My partner had no idea about PTSD and didn't understand my strange behaviour. Neither did I at the time, which made me feel even more ashamed.

While finishing my degree, I researched PTSD relentlessly and began to understand what was going on with me. Metaphorical lights went on everywhere, and I was grateful to the people who wrote those books - but understanding it didn't stop it.

Occasionally I returned to my hometown to visit my mother. I was usually a total wreck by the time I left. Being in my father's presence was ominous, tense, and threatening. I was terrified of him. One time after I left, I had to book myself into a motel five hours up the motorway, where I stayed locked in the room for two days in a state of total terror.

One time my partner and I had an argument while walking in the bush. I completely dissociated from my body and felt like a terrified child. I think something must have happened to me in the bush because it wasn't the first time I'd had such a weird reaction in that environment. I was dissociated for hours; I just wasn't there. My mind was away somewhere in a fog. In the end I couldn't take it any longer and, regrettably, ended our relationship.

At times it seemed easier to stay single with no one around to trigger me, but loneliness and despair starts to take you under. You can't hide from the fact that something is deeply wrong with you but you don't know how to fix it. You feel deeply ashamed of all the failures in your life as jobs, relationships, and friendships all go west. You wonder what the hell the problem is and what will become of you if you can't hold down a relationship or a job.

Through years of counselling, psychotherapy, primal therapy, rebirthing, group therapy, and assorted workshops, I pieced together a few more missing bits of my life, but much remained incomplete, lost and unhealed. There were lurking ghosts, memory gaps, weird reactions and triggers. I'd move house or change job, and things would go well for a while as they do when you have ample distractions. But wherever you go, there you are—and so are your ghosts!

I owe my life to ayahuasca and other psychedelic therapies because all my symptoms have largely gone now. I'm pretty much free of my ghosts as they've slowly revealed themselves to me during psychedelic therapies. This is nothing short of a miracle. I am finally free.

CHAPTER FOUR

How Psychedelics Heal Trauma

As quoted by Carl Jung, 'Until you make the unconscious conscious it will direct your life and you will and call it fate.' Psychedelics are the magic key that turns the lock to the door of your unconscious. They render the unconscious conscious so it ceases to dictate your life's unwitting trajectory.

Typically, under therapeutically guided doses of psychedelics, you come to understand how, why, and when your triggers were formed. You can then disarm and discharge them. You can gain access to repressed traumatic memories that were too overwhelming to deal with at the time, due to adrenalin flooding your brain or because they were just too horrific to process and that caused you to enter an altered state of consciousness. You will process these memories cognitively, somatically, and emotionally. As a result, you will no longer be activated by unconscious triggers that previously caused you to react out of all proportion to a mnemonic event. Your suppressive or distracting behaviours, addictions, and compulsions will diminish or disappear. A powerful claim indeed - but well evidenced by the stories in Part Two.

Anne Other in her book, *Trust Surrender Receive* gives a good description of how trauma effects the psyche in the quote below.

'When trauma overpowers us to the point that our organism is overwhelmed, the hypervigilant psyche moves to override the fear by putting us into a non-ordinary state of consciousness. In that condition the psyche captures the emotional and cognitive memory of the traumatic event, to protect us from the full realisation of what has occurred. The way our traumatic memories become captured, unknowable to our conscious awareness, occurs in an instant, absent of our volition or knowledge.'

In response to a life-threatening situation our psyche steps in to protect us. Something beyond our everyday consciousness shuts down the mind and enables us to dissociate from the overwhelming trauma. If and when a person is ready to gain access to and release these traumatic memories from their captured state, they will need to return to a similar non-ordinary state of consciousness by choice. In this non-ordinary state of consciousness, elicited by psychedelics, we capture, process, and integrate these memories.

This could be viewed as a classic example of state-dependant learning, a psychological term for the phenomenon whereby people remember more information if their physical or mental state is the same at the time of encoding and recall. While psychedelics all work a bit differently, their common theme is that they return us to non-ordinary states of consciousness where we can access and process suppressed, traumatic memories.

A person's presenting 'problem' or 'symptom' is usually the outward manifestation of an unresolved inner conflict that has its origin in a traumatic event. When the unconscious starts leaking suppressed, traumatic material into everyday consciousness, this generates anxiety and the brain moves to suppress it in any number of ways—addictions, obsessions, dissociation, avoidance, or repetitive behaviours. For these patterns to resolve, the traumatic event must be seen, experienced, detonated, discharged, understood in a new way and integrated. Psychedelic therapy allows us to do this.

MDMA is a gentle, entry-level medicine and a soul-soothing balm for traumatised, depressed, or anxious people. Most would do well to start with this. During a therapeutic MDMA session, an entire repressed traumatic event can reveal itself in astonishing detail, so you can experience a broader understanding of the context in which you were traumatized as well as an increased sense of compassion coupled with an understanding of the effect it had on your life.

MDMA heals at the heart level, reconnecting people with their lost or frozen emotions, self-love, and empathy for self and others. Many sexually abused people are riddled with shame and self-loathing (possibly part of the perpetrator programming to keep their victims silent). MDMA seems to eradicate shame and replace it with feelings of self-love and self-acceptance. It downregulates hypervigilance, the most prominent and debilitating symptom of PTSD.

Scientists have shown that MDMA releases serotonin and reduces activity in the amygdala, a region of the brain that deals with our fear response. It simultaneously increases activity in the prefrontal cortex, an area of the brain that deals with logical thought. MDMA increases flow between the amygdala and the hippocampus, which is believed to be responsible for long-term memory formation and retention. This increased flow between the amygdala and the hippocampus enables the excavation, processing, and integration of traumatic memories into consciousness, then into long-term storage.

Psilocybin mushrooms can facilitate an extremely transformative experience for those with mental health issues—if they're prepared for it. While MDMA enables the eliciting and processing of traumatic events, psilocybin can go even deeper, showing a person how their identity was programmed during such events (particularly childhood trauma). Psilocybin magnifies the programming that was constructed during the trauma, the deeply entrenched ideas that appear real, the constructed sense of the world that was formed early in life.

Psilocybin often induces the physical release of trauma through somatic shaking. Sometimes the physical pain of a trauma—rape, sexual abuse, violence—can actually be felt. Whereas MDMA's focus is on opening and healing the heart, psilocybin seems more intent on healing the body through trauma release and reprogramming the unconscious mind. Psilocybin therapy is not about the pleasurable experiences or interesting insights that MDMA might provide. The dismantling process engendered by psilocybin can feel somewhat destabilizing and is more likely to require some integration afterwards.

Ayahuasca: With this powerful medicine we leave the realm of evidence-based treatment into something otherworldly. Ayahuasca is a tertiary medicine and probably not the best one to start with unless you've already done a good amount of work on yourself. Ayahuasca needs minimal help from a therapist during its active state because essentially ayahuasca *is* the therapist. Drinking this brew often evokes a plant spirit teacher who communicates directly with you in a variety of ways: somatically, intuitively, experientially, visually, or with an internal voice.

How ayahuasca works to heal trauma is not fully understood. It can be an extreme experience and even quite traumatic to go through. Dr Michael Pollan, author of *How to Change Your Mind*, believes that ayahuasca works by shocking people out of their previous trauma by disrupting the default mode network, which is essentially a programme in the brain that acts like a stuck record, spinning repetitively in its trauma groove.

My experience post ayahuasca was that it dramatically calmed my hypervigilance so that I was no longer constantly triggered and reactive. I liken it to SAS training: Once you've pushed yourself to your limit (in this case, your psychological limit), small things seem less problematic because you have endured so much more; it's like an extreme form of exposure therapy.

CHAPTER FIVE

Medicines Used in Psychedelic Therapy

Mainly due to logistics and cost, the most commonly used medicines for solo sessions of psychedelic therapy are the short-acting ones, which remain active for around four to six hours. A shorter experience is more affordable for most while still offering effective relief from symptoms. It's also easier for a solo therapist to hold effective space for the shorter time period of four or five hours. The short-acting medicines are MDMA, psilocybin mushrooms, and ayahuasca. I've included a little information on ketamine because it is now available legally through a few licensed doctors in Australia to treat depression.

Longer-acting medicines such as mescaline and LSD are effective for around ten to twelve hours, which is too long a time for one person to hold therapeutic space and would also be unaffordable for the average person. Hence, these are more likely to be offered in group settings with multiple facilitators.

The Short-Acting Medicines: MDMA, Psilocybin, Ayahuasca & Acaciahuasca, Ketamine.

MDMA

Please note: MDMA is NOT 'Ecstasy'. The latter is a street drug that contains wildly differing amounts of MDMA. Some researchers found as little as 10%, plus a lot of other unknown stuff. Both amphetamines and PMA (para methoxyamphetamine—empathogens with similar effects to MDMA) are found in Ecstasy. These are more toxic to the body and take longer to work; hence, people may think it's not working and top up the dose, increasing the risk of overdose.

While not considered a true psychedelic some people do experience visions on MDMA (see Louise in Part Two). It is however an extremely beneficial psychoactive compound for treating trauma, a powerful, psychotherapeutic catalyst that reduces fear while increasing empathy. It belongs to the empathogen-entactogen class of psychoactive drugs which stimulate feelings of compassion, love, interconnectedness and emotional clarity.

Psilocybin Mushrooms

Psilocybin is nature's most available tryptamine-derived hallucinogen. Like all psychedelics the psilocybin experience is dose-dependent. A therapeutic dose is typically around 2.5 to 3.5 grams for *Psilocybe cubensis* or 2 to 2.5 grams for the stronger *Psilocybe subaeruginosa*. Higher doses are likely to lead to ego dissolution, which is not the most beneficial or sought-after experience for therapy. The experience lasts for around five or six hours.

Psilocybe cubensis (Golden Teachers) are a preferred mushroom for therapy, but sometimes it will depend on what's available. Therapists are generally best off using home-grown mushrooms rather than wild harvested ones as this decreases the risk of a poisonous mimic. Winter is wild-mushroom season in Australia, where the highly potent *Psilocybe subaeruginosa* makes an appearance. This is also a good therapy mushroom but can be a more direct and confronting experience than the gentler *P. cubensis*.

In Australia, psilocybin therapy is offered in both group and solo sessions. Solo sessions are best for deep-trauma excavation as the client is more likely to need the undivided attention of the therapist. However, group sessions are somewhat cheaper and can reveal as well as mimic powerful interpersonal dynamics.

Ayahuasca and Acaciahuasca

The modern-day Amazonian ayahuasca brew contains two or more plants, usually the ayahuasca vine (*Banisteriopsis caapi*), which contains a series of MAOIs (monoamine oxidase inhibitors) and Chacruna (*Psychotria viridis*), containing DMT. While not entirely accurate, it is usually stated that the DMT provides the visions, while the MAOI component prevents the rapid breakdown of the DMT, thus making it orally available.

The Australian brew is often referred to as acaciahuasca because native acacias are used for the DMT component. These high-DMT-containing acacia species include Northern Brother wattle (*Acacia courtii*), stiff-leaf or blunt leaf wattle (*Acacia obtusafolia*), narrow phyllode variety (*Acacia acuminata*), and gossamer, weeping, or white sallow wattle (*Acacia floribunda*). For the MAOI component, either *B. caapi* (ayahuasca vine) or Syrian rue (*Peganum harmala*) is used.

It's worth mentioning, before I'm hogtied, that *Acacia courtii* is a micro-endemic species and is considered a rare tree. It's sought after because of its comparatively high DMT content. But many thousands of trees are currently being grown around Australia, and there is an incipient trade in farmed *Acacia courtii*, rather than the wild-harvested ones. People in the Australian scene often make a big fuss if you even mention using this tree. It's also worth mentioning that the Australian acacia–containing brews are on average somewhat stronger, more vision-inducing, and more surprising than the South American brews.

Note: For the sake of simplicity, I may refer to both medicines as 'ayahuasca'. However, I'm typically speaking of Australian acacia brews from here on in.

Taking ayahuasca typically causes both open- and closed-eye visions as opposed to hallucinations and can invoke a teacher plant spirit, sometimes referred to as *Mother Ayahuasca*. This medicine works on every aspect of the body: physical, spiritual, emotional, and mental. It is purgative and can also be convulsive.

In Australia, ayahuasca is typically taken in groups on weekend retreats and consumed on Friday and Saturday night so that the client has two consecutive sessions. The effects last around five or six hours. It is occasionally administered in solo sessions by a therapist - when a person doesn't wish to, or is too traumatised to participate in a group.

Ayahuasca can be a very intense experience and is often referred to as an 'ordeal' medicine for good reason. While you can't fatally overdose from it - as aptly stated by psychedelic researcher Terrance McKenna, you can potentially die from astonishment. It can facilitate an immense shift in perspective and provide instant relief from anxiety, depression, and PTSD.

Ayahuasca is not a medicine to play with or to take lightly; a small percentage of people can become unravelled. Maybe choose a gentler option to start with, like MDMA or psilocybin. These may be all you need. If you have PTSD and decide to drink ayahuasca, I highly recommend finding someone who uses *B. caapi* vine in their brew rather than *Syrian rue*. In my experience the vine offers far more effective healing. Ayahuasca is not just a psychedelic (mind expander) it has the power to heal your body.

Look for smaller groups where experienced helpers are available or solo sessions. Australian average group sizes are around fifteen to twenty people. Some are far larger. Patiently wait until you find someone experienced and reputable. Cowboys abound in the Australian ayahuasca scene, and I assume around the world. Intentions may be good, but never underestimate this powerful medicine; things can go wrong. Ayahuasca usually calls those she wants to meet and will often kick the arses of the disrespectful. (See Part 3 – Chapter 4)

Ketamine

Ketamine is now available legally and administered by a select few authorised doctors/psychiatrists. It was first used as an anaesthetic for animals before being approved as an anaesthetic for humans in 1970 and used to treat injured soldiers on battlefields. Unlike other anaesthetics, ketamine doesn't slow breathing or heart rate, so patients don't need to be on a ventilator to receive it. Doctors noticed that the drug had powerful effects against depression and suicidal thoughts, so it was studied and, in controlled, clinical settings, administered to severely depressed people. The green light was given. The dissociative effects last about two hours. The trip, however, is not the treatment. Ketamine helps grow new synapses in the brain that were possibly damaged due to depression.

The Longer-Acting Medicines: Mescaline, LSD, Iboga.

Mescaline

Mescaline comes from cactuses usually found in and around South America and Mexico. Cactuses, such as San Pedro (*Echinopsis pachanoi*), Peruvian torch (*Echinopsis peruviana*), Bolivian torch (*Echinopsis lageniformis*), and the North American peyote buttons (*Lophophora williamsii*) contain mescaline.

In Australia it is typically taken socially in groups or on walks. Its effects last around ten to twelve hours, so it's not usually offered in solo underground therapy. Mescaline's insights seem more focused on social and environmental interaction, connection and energy. It carries out healing work on a physical (somatic) level rather than through visionary hallucinations or deep-trauma processing. It provides clarity of more current, internal and external awareness.

LSD: (Lysergic Acid Diethylamide)

LSD's effects last around ten to twelve hours and vary a lot depending on who made it and the dose taken. LSD can take the person on a journey of analytical self-understanding, giving insight into the psyche as well as auditory and visual hallucinations. It's not commonly used in Australian underground solo therapy as its effects last too long for one therapist to hold quality space.

Iboga

Tabernanthe iboga is best known for its ability to detox addicts from heroin. If an opiate user takes heroin within two weeks of ingesting iboga, nothing will happen as ibogaine resets the opioid receptors. It's also useful for personal transformation and healing. Julian Palmer, in his book, *Articulations,* sums it up below.

> *"Iboga is a plant that many people are scared of, but essentially, I think they are scared of facing what Iboga will reveal about themselves. Iboga is not there to hit anybody over the head with a two-by-four plank because it is malevolent, but only because it feels certain forms of 'tough love' will wake the human up from their unconsciousness."*

The African Bwiti tribe first used it for initiation rites. The initial psychoactive experience is considered very intense, with peak intensity lasting six to twenty hours. Iboga sessions take several days and are usually offered in a group setting by two or more facilitators. Generally, you can't drive for three or four days after ingestion, and it can take a full week to recover from the experience. These are some of the reasons why iboga is considered an endurance journey.

Iboga is definitely available in the Australian underground but is a quite specialised and expensive treatment, and one would do well to thoroughly research this option. Iboga can take a toll on the heart and body, mainly in those physically compromised. Care is essential with addicts, who can have compromised physical health due to their addiction. This is one of the natural, plant-based psychedelics that can cause death.

There are many other psychedelic treatment options available—plant, toad, synthetic—but I've decided not to cover them in this book largely because they're not considered as therapeutically beneficial for healing trauma as the above-mentioned ones. Common ones include crystal DMT, Kambo and Changa. 5 MEO DMT is a potent and often revered experience but has a fairly high-risk ratio for causing problems afterwards, mainly in trying to integrate this extremely potent medicine. I know several people who had a difficult time after consuming 5 MEO DMT. One was suicidal for some time due to the existential crisis it evoked. Another was admitted to inpatient psychiatric care; she was in active addiction and pretty unstable beforehand and should never have been offered this medicine. Clearly, the facilitator didn't undertake a proper assessment.

CHAPTER SIX

Detecting a Good Therapist/Facilitator

Few licensed therapists are willing to take the risk of conducting illegal activities because they risk losing their license if caught. So, the pickings are somewhat slim. Primarily, use your instinct. Is the person someone you trust and feel safe with? Do they have the knowledge and skill to protect your psyche? Do they display empathy and care and seem generally happy and functional? What is their understanding and knowledge of your issues? If you have PTSD, you'll want to know whether they have a good understanding of this? Do they understand addiction? Are they open to answering your questions? Do they have good boundaries?

Some counselling or psychology qualifications are highly recommended. A psychology degree at least provides some academic knowledge of PTSD as well as other DSM (Diagnostic and Statistical Manual) classifications. They must be able to ascertain your suitability and safety for participating in psychedelic therapy. It's helpful if they understand brain chemistry and drug interactions. A diploma in addiction counselling might prove useful.

Although I have academic qualifications, I'm no blind respecter of society's hierarchies or institutions. In fact, from my personal experience with certain doctors and psychologists, I can say with conviction that a doctorate is no warrant of fitness or guarantee that a person has the necessary attributes needed to be a good psychedelic therapist. Elon Musk, discussing his employment practices in a recent YouTube video, said that university degrees are no prerequisite to join any of his companies because universities kill creative thinking by training people to regurgitate the status quo. While I largely agree; having at least some qualifications shows a degree of dedication and interest in the topic.

A therapist/facilitator who has had personal experience with mental health issues and has used psychedelics to heal themselves can offer a deeper understanding and greater empathy than someone with academic knowledge alone. I generally find that sharing a bit about my own personal history of sexual abuse and PTSD really puts clients with similar issues at ease. They understand and appreciate that they're not dealing with some academic who merely has book knowledge, but with a peer who understands them on a deep, personal level. Personal sharing generally goes against the grain of traditional therapy models, but I feel it creates a deeper level of trust.

It can't be overstated that a psychedelic therapist must have extensive personal experience using the medicines they administer. How else can they navigate the territory these powerful medicines will take you through? The therapist should know the source and purity of the medicines they provide, that is, where they came from, who made them, and what they contain. MDMA should be tested for purity and the presence of other substances. Ideally, the therapist should grow their own mushrooms or get them from a reliable home-grown source to avoid poisonous imposters. They should pick, source, or grow their own plants and make their own ayahuasca brews. Purchasing ayahuasca online offers no guarantees of what you will be consuming.

Be wary if the therapist/facilitator doesn't undertake a full mental health screening prior to offering medicine. This assessment is to protect your safety. Psychedelic therapy is not for everyone and can exacerbate some mental illnesses. Generally, don't embark on psychedelic therapy if you are diagnosed schizophrenic or have any psychotic disorder. It may well unravel you. Bipolar is another condition where psychedelics should generally be avoided as they can set off a manic phase. Dissociative identity disorder (DID) is also problematic due to the destabilising capacity of psychedelics. The therapist/facilitator should understand your trauma history in order to address what may arise during your medicine session. They should be aware of any blood pressure or heart issues and what medications you are on.

Avoid people who administer psychedelics purely to make money and have no real knowledge of mental illness. These people are out there and probably not the best choice for a therapeutic relationship. I'd also avoid people who seem to help others as a way of avoiding dealing with their own issues. Psychedelic therapists need to be a long way through their own healing to avoid transference, burnout, codependency, and denial. I'd personally steer clear of anyone referring to themselves as a 'shaman' and dressing stereotypically although there are a few genuine practitioners out there who have truly fulfilled the requirements of that title. A five-to-ten-year apprenticeship in the jungle under an indigenous maestro is a rudimentary requirement or a long relationship with the plants that they administer.

Psychedelic trauma therapy requires that the therapist be present for the whole session. I know of one qualified therapist offering psychedelic therapy who just has a quick chat, administers the medicine, and leaves the clients to it. This is not psychedelic therapy, and you might as well save yourself the money. The presence, guidance, and safety measure of the therapist are what allow you to go deep and excavate your trauma.

The therapist should have a working knowledge of and abide by the standard counsellor's code of ethics. This means they would definitely not consider having an intimate relationship with you as a client. Sexual abuse is not unheard of within the global psychedelic community but it's more of a problem in South America, where ayahuasca is legal. In short, sexual activity shouldn't form any part of a therapeutic relationship. Sexually traumatised clients may look for a saviour and may want to latch on to the healer/shaman/therapist or person they perceive is helping them. This can be an unconscious replaying of trauma called a repetition compulsion. An ethical therapist would be aware of this tendency and NOT take advantage of it. Certainly, from an ethical position, intimate relationships cannot develop during, or close to, any psychedelic treatment since people are vulnerable and highly prone to suggestion.

To uncover this information about your potential therapist/facilitator, you will need to do some research and ask questions. This should occur prior to or during the assessment phase, before any medicine is given or received. Their responses will be telling. Transparency and disclosure are good signs; defensiveness, arrogance, and reluctance to answer will speak volumes. Check out their website, and references.

CHAPTER SEVEN

How Many Medicine Sessions Are Needed?

For successfully treating trauma, varying numbers of sessions are recommended by various authors, therapists, and institutions. MAPS recommend three MDMA treatment sessions with month-long intervals and fifteen therapy sessions. While three medicine sessions might be more than enough to process a one-off trauma, such as a car accident or war event, my observation is that three sessions would not be enough for someone with developmental CPTSD.

The Castalia Foundation, on the other hand, recommend one hundred self-guided MDMA sessions. In my opinion this is total overkill and definitely not required. Self-guided sessions are not as powerful or effective as guided sessions, which help bypass the subconscious gatekeeper and allow more rapid healing. Also, surrender can be an issue with self-guided sessions. It's far easier to surrender when a trusted guide is watching over you.

The nature and extent of the trauma are the determining factors regarding the number of treatment sessions needed. Chronic childhood trauma is vastly different from a one-off trauma event. In my case and others, I know, three sessions would not have been enough to process developmental trauma.

While Terry (Part Two) was able to process his car accident in just one MDMA session, he required four MDMA sessions plus three psilocybin sessions to process his childhood sexual abuse to the point where he felt comfortable in leaving it alone. He currently microdoses and plans to have guided sessions once or twice a year should the need arise. His life is pretty functional: he's able to maintain a demanding job; his relationship is intact and thriving; he's weathered considerable ups and downs, including the Covid pandemic. Marie (Part Two) had three MDMA sessions, three psilocybin sessions, and one ayahuasca session for her chronic childhood trauma and seems content to leave it at that for now.

Healing is a journey, not a destination, and can take place over a period of years. Breaks are necessary so that you can continue to live a balanced life. A minimum of one month is recommended between medicine sessions to integrate properly and for your neurotransmitters to recalibrate. To me, 'healing' means fully knowing, accepting, and integrating my own personal history. To others it might mean living comfortably in their own skin, eliminating hypervigilance and triggers, and being able to sleep soundly without nightmares.

While enthusiastic psychedelic capitalists are touting psychedelics as an instant cure-all, this has not been my experience. True, they heal mental illness faster than any available option, and you will notice an immediate change, but it's not all smooth and effortless sailing. Time and a lot of grit are needed to process a traumatic history.

Psychedelic Therapy Sessions Have a Trajectory

Psychedelics seem to work on a timeline, addressing your most pressing material first, then venturing back through your lifespan. If you've already done a lot of inner work, you may gain access to repressed material faster. If you've been traumatised, you should perhaps start with MDMA, especially if you have no previous medicine experience. This allows both you and the therapist to see how you'll react. MDMA is a relatively predictable and gentle medicine. However, people do have different levels of sensitivity and capacity to handle the intense emotions that can follow a medicine session.

The first session acquaints you with the medicine—how it feels, what it does. This first treatment is usually experienced as the most profound. The immediate relief in going from hypervigilant to relaxed is quite astonishing and extremely impactful - as most people don't realise how highly strung they were, until they have a state with which to compare their former situation. This deep sense of calm seems to reprogramme the brain and provide those few precious seconds to consciously choose a response instead of reacting explosively to a trigger. This new response needs to be practised and reinforced to break habitual behaviours.

People who've suffered years of sleep deprivation may find that after just one MDMA session, they can now sleep soundly. People with OCD may be relieved of their obsessions and compulsions after a single session. The profound sense of self-love and self-acceptance experienced on MDMA can instantly alleviate the shame that many sexual abuse victims carry. A soul retrieval may be experienced—a return to and reengagement with the body.

The second session may be experienced as quite shocking. Both Shannon and Terry (Part Two) relived repressed sex abuse on their second MDMA session. While Shannon's first session was experienced as profoundly loving, the second shot her straight into unconscious and somatic re-experiencing of sexual abuse. Terry's remembrance of his uncle sexually abusing him was as if he'd tucked this away somewhere but had known it all along. Psychedelics can catch you off guard; in fact,

I think this is their specialty. They work in tandem, the medicine and the subconscious, like a wise therapist meting out what you can handle.

Irrespective of the dose, the second MDMA session can feel a bit disappointing to the odd person, compared to their first. My observation is that this seems more likely to occur in big consumers of alcohol or marijuana. Fear of surrendering to the medicine and what may be revealed may be a factor. Even if the effects don't feel as strong, internal issues can still be addressed and behaviour patterns understood with the help of therapeutic intervention.

The third MDMA session can be surprising. When a client is comfortable with the therapist and the medicine, they are more likely to surrender. Once the conscious mind has surrendered, the subconscious can reveal itself, hence this session may well be the one where a repressed memory emerges and is re-experienced.

Memories may return in various forms: somatically – the body acts out and replays the event, jerking rhythmically as if a rape is occurring; emotionally – releasing emotions unable to be experienced at the time of the trauma, hyperventilating in terror, intense crying; cognitively – full details and pictures of the repressed event; sensorily – re-experiencing smells and tastes. Memories may emerge in pieces with clues and details arising in different sessions or in full, vivid detail.

Depending on the progress made with a particular substance, I would suggest moving to psilocybin after three MDMA sessions, if needed. Psilocybin requires a deeper level of surrender, and the experience can be more difficult, but it can offer a more powerful and transformative result.

Following the medicine sessions, memories may continue to emerge, along with the accompanying emotions, which can feel a bit painful and overwhelming, so it's important to engage in integration counselling and space the medicine sessions out so that life doesn't become hard work and no play.

Challenge yourself to try out new behaviours and reinforce them through practice to break out of old habits and comfort zones. If you normally react angrily to triggers, maybe choose to respond differently, with the few precious seconds of grace afforded you by the medicine. If you're prone to isolating, maybe join a group, go to social gathering, or attend an AA meeting if that seems appropriate.

So, in answer to the question - how many medicine sessions are required - I would say as many as are necessary to feel a sense of resolution. The difference is, that now, after just one psychedelic treatment, you'll gain a sense of hope that you've finally discovered the magic elixir. With a good therapist guiding the process, the results will be exponentially faster than any currently available legal treatment. That I can almost guarantee.

CHAPTER EIGHT

12-Step Addiction Programmes and Psychedelic Therapy

Traumatised people often reach for substances to anaesthetise their psychic pain and suppress traumatic memories, so it's not surprising that many end up in 12-step recovery programmes, such as Alcoholics Anonymous (AA) and Narcotics Anonymous (NA). AA and NA members are increasingly finding their way into the psychedelic healing community; Shannon, Martin, Gina, and Grant, who tell their stories in Part Two, are members.

Addiction often forms part of the standard trauma sequela and while the 12-step programmes work well to address the addiction and keep people clean and sober long enough to address their trauma, it doesn't provide the solution for healing PTSD. Minimal healing can occur while people are still self-medicating. Sometimes psychedelics remove the desire to self-medicate, but not always, and even when it does, my observation is that it's unlikely to last long term without the ongoing focus and attention that 12 step programmes provide.

Herein lies the problem: 12-steppers who use psychedelics for healing, face being ostracized or judged because taking a non-prescribed mind-altering substance is usually considered a relapse—despite the well-documented fact that Bill Wilson, the co-founder of AA, underwent LSD therapy back in the '50s. He did this to treat his depression, which lingered long into his sobriety. But many in AA simply choose to ignore this inconvenient truth—a prime example of the power of denial.

It took immense courage and three years of research for me to finally take the ayahuasca plunge after twenty years of sobriety. The fear of being ostracised from my AA tribe was overcome only by my desperate desire not to kill myself. The risk paid off; it fast-tracked my healing and flicked a switch that finally gave me a connection to a Higher Power. I have no regrets except maybe that I waited so long. I'm not as attached to AA as I once was and have since discovered more fun tribes, but I still attend.

While the 12-step fellowships are not perfect, I'm drawn to the focus on spiritual principles and even consider the 12 steps a great integration tool. It provides guidelines for ethical and functional living and self-improvement; it empowers us to take responsibility for our own behaviour. A typical slogan you might hear is, 'When you point the finger, there are three pointing back.' The serenity prayer, seen on banners at meetings, encourages 'acceptance' of things we can't change and 'courage' to change the things we can—namely ourselves.

12-step fellowships also provide a much-needed sense of community and support for members who are often estranged from dysfunctional families. Meetings provide human connection even if a person just sits in the room and listens. Isolation is one of the main causes of the devolution of mental health in traumatised people. Research studies show that isolation is worse for a person's health and life expectancy than obesity or smoking.[1]

---

[1] Holt-Lunstad, Julianne; Smith, Timothy B.; Baker, Mark; Harris, Tyler; Stephenson, David. 'Loneliness and Social Isolation as Risk Factors for Mortality: A Meta-Analytic Review'. First published March 11, 2015. Find in PubMed https://doi.org/10.1177/1745691614568352

After his psychedelic treatment, Bill Wilson strongly believed that psychedelics were the way forward for those who felt disconnected from a Higher Power. He even advocated for their inclusion in the 12-step programme. It would have been a hard sell for poor, old Bill to say the least, and his attempts were thwarted. But I sense a kindred spirit, smiling down from the great beyond, about to be proven right all along. [2]

Engaging in psychedelic therapy for trauma healing should not be treated as any different to taking an antidepressant for depression, which many people in AA do. Legalisation would make these substances valid treatment options and thus dissolve the need for secrecy. It would enable people to continue going to meetings without feeling shame if they should wish to. Secrecy, based on fear of stigma, can undermine the efforts of recovering addicts who take psychedelics. Some may decide to move on and find other communities, but that choice should be theirs. I'm not saying one should blatantly share their psychedelic experiences in AA meetings as this would be confusing for newcomers trying to gain sobriety, but one should feel comfortable to talk freely with their sponsor and selected others.

Progress has been made. An American group of like-minded people calling themselves Psychedelics in Recovery has emerged to accommodate 12-steppers who use psychedelics for healing. They host international Zoom meetings as well as face-to-face meetings in some cities. Unfortunately, some PIR members include marijuana in their accepted list of therapeutic plant medicines and this to me is a red flag. I've seen way too many people deluded by this idea. As an addiction counsellor

---

[2] Kurtz, E. (1989). 'Drugs and the Spiritual: Bill W. Takes LSD'. *The Collected Ernie Kurtz* (1999). Wheeling, West Virginia: The Bishop of Books, pp. 39-50.

and recovering person myself, I definitely don't consider marijuana a necessary plant to include. I view it as an addictive drug. If you're in recovery from addiction and want to take psychedelics to heal trauma, you need to set very clear boundaries and intentions about why and how you do this. Yes, marijuana certainly has benefits for pain relief and other applications, but recovering people should generally steer well clear of it. There are plenty of more suitable options.

Psychedelic therapy will emerge as a sanctioned treatment again one day, but until that time, opting to do this therapy remains a massive decision for 12-steppers. Traumatised members should not have to wait until they are suicidal, and yet that is often the case. Last year a woman I knew from AA took her own life after 20 years of hard-won sobriety. She had CPTSD. After she'd seen the massive transformation in Martin (story in Part Two), we'd discussed the possibility of her trying MDMA therapy. Unfortunately, she was on prescription meds and struggled to get off them, so sadly, I couldn't help her. It pains me greatly to know there is a solution but not to be able to scream it from the rooftops. Hopefully this book will carry the message to those who need to hear it.

CHAPTER NINE

Microdosing

Microdosing refers to the ingestion of a small amount of an entheogenic substance: typically, a tenth of a full dose. Microdosing is considered for various reasons. Common applications are to replace antidepressants, improve motivation, or aid creativity and lateral thinking. Microdosing can be beneficial for people detoxing off prescription meds, particularly antidepressants and benzodiazepines. A microdose is a sub-perceptual dose. By definition it can't consciously be perceived except for maybe a slightly higher level of 'energy' and motivation, and brighter and sharper visual perception.

James Fadiman and Paul Stamets are the two best-known experts on psilocybin microdosing. They have slightly differing approaches to microdosing protocols. Mushroom god Paul Stamets suggests a dosing protocol of five days on and two days off. Fadiman recommends a dose followed by a two-day rest. Fadiman is currently undertaking a massive, online, self-reported research project on microdosing. His is my recommended protocol (www.psychedelicsurvey.com).

A microdose of dried *P. cubensis* mushrooms is about a fifth of a dried gram (0.2gs) and with *P. subaeruginosa* about a tenth of a gram. (0.1g) As with all psychedelic compounds, you will need to experiment and test for your own sensitivity. The optimal dose depends on your personal brain chemistry. Previous use of prescription meds or heavy alcohol and marijuana use will impact your neurology. People on long-term prescription meds often require higher-than-the standard recommended microdoses to receive any benefit.

Psilocybin microdoses can offer an effective replacement for prescription antidepressants as they don't have the horrible side effects attributed to prescription antidepressants—loss of libido, weight gain, suicidality, and aggression. Prescription antidepressants usually take three weeks to become properly effective, whereas a psilocybin microdose has an almost immediate effect (within twenty minutes of consumption), so it can be taken as required.

If you currently take prescription antidepressants or benzodiazepines, microdoses won't be very effective unless you substantially increase the microdose as these medications decrease psilocybin's effects. It's actually better to wean off meds before microdosing. Find a trusted detox protocol. My booklet, *Beating the Benzo Blues,* provides an easy-to-follow and well-tested benzo detox protocol. For antidepressants you can find an online programme for a slow-taper regimen. Harvard University have one and it's the one I opted to use some years ago.

My Microdosing Experiences

Psilocybin Mushrooms

I'm quite sensitive to psychedelics, possibly because I hadn't consumed any alcohol or drugs in the 20 years prior to using them therapeutically. The first time I microdosed *psilocybin*, I didn't weigh the dose as I had no scales. I just ate a whole dried mushroom. I felt great—happy, joyous, and relaxed. The second time I felt a bit depressed, and the next day I was wobbly and vision-impaired. I thought I shouldn't take any more. I later tried for a third time but took a bit too much and felt on the verge of an immersive experience. That night I woke up screaming and felt something poking me in the ribs. A weird, vibrating light was above me. I was later told that magic mushrooms have a history of alien-type encounters.

After taking a full dose of *P. cubensis* (2.5gms), I microdosed again and this seemed to be the key. I had heard from others that it was better to microdose after taking a full dose. In terms of the effects, things were visually clear and sharp, and I was infused with a motivating energy.

B. Caapi Microdosing

Before participating in my first ayahuasca session, I'd come off a 14-year stint on antidepressants. After an intense ayahuasca session some months later which elicited a lot of emotional pain, I felt quite depressed for a while. As luck would have it, I happened to visit a local plant-medicine nursery. After chatting with the owner, he gave me some *B. caapi* (ayahuasca) cuttings to microdose. He told me to scrape the bark off the twigs with a potato peeler and just eat it, or put it in a capsule and swallow it. You need only a small amount.

I experienced body relaxation and calmness like being in a post-yoga state of meditation. I felt quite insular like I wanted to keep to myself but was happy to be in my own company. It was thought-provoking and mindful. Later I drove to a gathering where people were sharing their personal stories. I felt empathy toward others and was super-sensitive and quick to cry. On the downside, it made me a bit wobbly and clumsy on my feet. I later fell over while walking the dog, so it's probably not safe to drive for a couple of hours after dosing.

Some entrepreneurial psychonauts from the Amazon jungle make *B. caapi* tinctures and sell them online. Alternatively, you could buy a *B. caapi* vine from a local medicine plant nursery and grow your own. They are available in Australia.

Tabernanthe Manii.

Tabernanthe manii is a plant species in the same genus as iboga. A microdose is usually between three to ten drops of the tincture. While similar to iboga root bark (it also contains ibogaine), its effects are somewhat smoother than the bark. Be warned: Just a few drops of this stuff can be incredibly potent. Five drops evoked feelings of intense anger in me to the point of rage. I decided to stop microdosing for fear of losing impulse control, an example of its amplification properties.

The second time was magical and funny. I was supercharged with energy and displayed a lot of witty humour. The third time, the manii spirit warned me off social media and made me see clearly how I was giving Facebook strangers free rent in my head. It showed me how senseless and unnecessarily stressful all the arguing on Facebook was and how obsessed I'd become with provocative statements that I or others had made and how much headspace and time was taken up with the resulting ruminating thoughts.

On other occasions it has made me more aware of my diet. It's given me superabundant energy—to a point where I actually had to go running and I'm definitely no runner. I returned to yoga to discharge my excess energy. All this from a few potent drops. Manii is an intriguingly powerful, kick-arse teacher and people receive great benefit and insight from microdosing with it. As it affects the opioid receptors, I imagine it to be a good microdosing option for people detoxing from prescription opiates.

Iboga Root Bark

I've felt no inclination to microdose iboga root bark, but others do, so I'm drawing on Nick Sun's *Medium* article for info as this is more his domain.[1]

The microdose is around 40 to 80 mg of dried root bark; three days on, three days off. According to Sun, iboga, in both full doses and microdoses, helps break old habits and establish new ones. It can increase willpower and curb procrastination. It can decrease the volume of ruminating thoughts and connect you with your internal wisdom. It illuminates awareness of your thoughts and the resulting behaviours. Iboga can invoke knowledge of ethical behaviour and make it harder to act inappropriately, hence motivating you to do the right thing in challenging situations. One of the ways iboga teaches is by amplifying your maladaptive patterns until you become extremely aware of them, so things that trigger you will trigger you even more. In other words, as well as breaking addictions, it can amplify them to show you more clearly their hold over you.

Microdosing iboga root bark should be quite safe, but if you plan to take it over a long period, it's worth getting your heart checked out with an ECG. Full doses of iboga have caused the occasional death but usually in unhealthy people or drug addicts with compromised health.

There are many contraindicated medications that should be avoided with iboga as alkaloids accumulate in your system and you can have an adverse reaction if you combine any of the following: MDMA, amphetamines, prescription stimulants, cocaine, opiates, MAOI's,

---

1 Sun, Nick. 'Microdosing Iboga Root Bark'. *Medium*. December 2020.

steroids, beta-blockers, anti-depressants, anti-psychotics and other psychiatric medications.

LSD

I've not microdosed LSD, nor have I felt drawn to use it at all (apart from a few recreational experiences back in my early twenties). Twenty micrograms is considered a standard LSD microdose. According to some sources, it's the second most popular substance to microdose after psilocybin. In 2020 LSD microdosing was proven by the Beckley/Maastricht Research team to reduce the perception of pain and increase pain tolerance by 20% (the same as opioids like oxycodone and morphine), so I imagine this to be a good option for people detoxing from opiates.

Part Two

Medicine Sessions—In Their Own Words

MDMA Therapy

Cathy, 35, Journalist

Looking in from the outside Cathy's life looks idealistic; she and her husband have well-paying, interesting jobs and own a lovely home in a 'good' area, and also have a healthy child. But Cathy suffers from anxiety, insomnia, stress and exhaustion and had been on antidepressants for the last year. She came off these a month prior to her MDMA session.

Her husband, an ex-army veteran with PTSD, attributed to both, military experiences and childhood sexual and emotional trauma, recently underwent MDMA therapy to heal. Although his treatment effectively healed both his PTSD, and OCD, their marriage was still under severe strain and on the verge of collapse, because of what he'd previously put Cathy through. She was unable to move on from her resentments. But because a young child is involved, they are both strongly motivated to solve their marital problems.

Although nervous at the prospect of taking a drug, Cathy witnessed the incredible transformation of her husband and at his prompting, decided to try a treatment for herself. She needed help to relieve her anxiety, insomnia and fatigue and hopefully save her marriage.

Cathy - First MDMA Session (125 mg)

Cathy's words

As the medicine came on, I felt free to express myself with no hesitation or fear of the consequences. It felt fascinating as I found both problems and answers I didn't have awareness of prior. The feelings of pain were heightened, as were the feelings of release, self-love and healing. I felt free to do and think whatever I wanted or needed, without any judgement or self-consciousness.

I found lots of repressed pain and an incredibly damaged heart which required healing. Overall, it was a very healing experience. It was very visual and the entire session was spent inside my chest. I had a vision of my heart for the entire session as it went through various formations: from broken and wilted, to whole, full and pulsating.

I realised I had taken full responsibility for my husband's emotions and trauma. I was so burdened by his behaviour and feelings I actually felt weak and sick: physically, mentally and energetically. It was as if I was suffering from his pain more than he was. I sucked it all up, like a big giant sponge.

I felt responsible for how he behaved and the feelings he felt. I had let his experience of the world dictate mine – if he wasn't enjoying the beach or a social event or whatever, it would trap me and although I'd pretend to be enjoying it, I wasn't – because I was with him and all his negative emotions. When he felt happy, I felt amazing! I loved it when he was happy. I couldn't wait for the next 'hit' of him being happy. It seemed he had control of me in a weird and complex way.

I had tried to manage my behaviour around him to keep things calm and safe. I thought I could 'manage' or 'soothe' him as needed, and I did this at my own expense, if and when necessary. I had learned how to do this when he was drinking alcoholically. I was scared of him and I feared he could hurt me or our child. I would never have admitted this prior to this medicine session.

I realised that I resented him for hurting me in the past when he was alcoholically drinking and for never speaking of it again or apologising to me. He hasn't taken any responsibility for it or ever expressed remorse. He doesn't even think it's significant. I felt so much repressed anger for those experiences with him as a young woman in my early 20s. Those experiences changed my life. The pain and hurt he introduced me too was far more than I'd ever been exposed to before in my former life, so it was very significant and overwhelming. But I pretended it wasn't. I kept a cool façade. I didn't want to lose him. I never confronted the shit.

Before meeting Mark, I had no experience with alcoholism, anger or depression. I never realised how scared I was by it. I wasn't able to love him purely or authentically when I was scared of him. But I didn't feel I could leave him either. I felt we had to be together. I didn't want to separate and be a failure like my parents who were divorced multiple times. Mark signified an exciting, shiny future for me in my mind and I overlooked anything that didn't support that. I realised that because I was scared, I was difficult to love. I'd become reserved, distant, robotic, weak, and cold. I was nothing like my former self. I had lost myself and my vibrancy and beauty and it seemed like it was taking forever for me to find who I really was, in the medicine session.

I had lost the closeness I once had with my friends and family. I knew I had to let go of Mark's pain/anger/control/negativity, but I feared if I let go of it; I would have to let go of him and the parts of him that I love. And so, it was really hard to let it go at first. I even gently put it down, like a little fragile feather. It amazed me that I wanted to handle his pain and anger with such tender care. It had caused me much hurt and yet I was still protecting it. This is still very confronting and strange for me. I feel like there is something significant in this that I need to understand.

Under the medicine I realised that I had a very safe and stable childhood, life, and previous romantic relationships prior to meeting Mark. I was completely fearless and free. I loved that me. When I found the 'real' me in my mind's eye, it was the me, before I learned of Mark's trauma, burdens and anger. She was very innocent, open and naïve – a child version of me. I felt this incredible need to create boundaries to feel safe again and to let that little girl free.

I felt a need to release any pain that wasn't mine and to never ever let another person's pain burden me again. I needed to stand up for myself and protect myself for once in my life! I made a very bold and distinct separation between my heart and my emotions, and my husband's. Once I processed all of this, which was very confronting and sad, I spent the rest of the session building up my heart; it's size, colour, and strength. I switched between the warrior woman I needed to be, to release the anger and create strong boundaries, and the open, loving, fun, sweet innocent child that I wanted to be again. I could vividly see my face as a child and she was so lovely. I wanted to be her again ... and I did. I wanted a full healed heart again too and I healed it, slowly but surely.

The next day I felt sad because I thought that these realisations could mean the end of my marriage if my husband wasn't prepared for big changes and to hear this confronting experience. I feared he wouldn't cope with my medicine experience as 'he' was the 'pain' I needed to process. He despises 'blame' and I feared he would see this as all blame.

He is responsible for the threatening drunken experiences and the anger that my child and I have endured. But I feel completely responsible for my narrative, for staying, for not communicating, for not confronting the problems, for playing a victim for 10 years. I wasn't sure if he would be open to, and respect my boundaries, and I felt sad about that. Sad, but calm and wholehearted. I wondered if it was possible for us to change and fall in love again.

I didn't feel his anger in my body any more. I felt a distinct separation between our emotions. I am healthy again. I didn't feel anxious. I listened to relaxation music and I visualised my full, undamaged heart which calmed me when I feared what the future might hold.

The next day, I felt headachy, tired, and emotional. I'm scared my marriage could end, but I knew I couldn't go back to being lifeless and scared after the experience I just had. I know a happy future is ahead. I hope it is with my husband.

A week later and I feel light and only responsible for my actions and emotions. I feel calm (I haven't felt any anxiety). I feel AMAZED by the complex underlying narrative that I uncovered, and I would never have expected myself to play such a victim role. I really thought I was much stronger than I was. I'm still in awe of everything I found, both the pain and the resolutions. There is still a long way to go, but it was an incredible head start in the right direction.

This has been an amazing experience and I highly recommend it to others. I have referred about five friends to the therapist who are also struggling with their marriages. I was very nervous before the MDMA session, but the therapist, the environment and the setting were wonderful and very calming. I'm so very grateful for her kindness and compassion. I felt my story was important when I was around her and she provided a beautiful space for me to explore what was happening and why it mattered - why I mattered.

Cathy emailed the therapist six months later

I have experienced such a beautiful shift since my session. It wasn't instant, as it felt like such a cathartic experience, like I had to release so much pain and resentment first. And then I had to organise it all in my heart and mind, to make sense of what the hell had just happened! But now I feel clear and open, and transformed. I know who I am and what I stand for. My heart feels full. When I put my hand on my heart and listen to relaxation music, it takes me right back to the beautiful resolution I experienced in my session, where I felt healed, whole, and powerful. I also have become more spiritual. Not religious, but I sense the earth and energy in a way I didn't before.

I'm also more aware when I'm off track and I know what to do to get back. That's been grounding for me. The earth on my feet feels more connected. It's amazing. I can't really explain it. My husband is well too and we are both happy. I think I speak on behalf of both of us, that the sessions were difficult but life changing with incredible learnings. I know I'll be back for another session one day, when the time is right. For now, I'm great and for that, I want to thank you. I'm so grateful my husband convinced me to try it. One of the best decisions I've ever made. Expect to hear from me again one day in the future!

Barry, 50, Architect

Barry has one of the worst child-hood, sexual abuse histories I've heard and that is saying something. It includes several violent rapes, one by a convicted paedophile who is currently serving jail time for similar crimes, another by a known paedophile who has since been murdered. Another perpetrator was a scout master. Barry suffered a violent rape and beating by a cousin. He endured abuse at the hands of his mentally ill mother, who, sexually, emotionally, and physically, abused both he and his brother. Sadly, his brother committed suicide.

Not surprisingly, Barry has avoided any intimate relationships; they would be way too triggering for him. He was diagnosed with depression 25 years ago, but wisely avoided taking antidepressants which he intuitively sensed wouldn't help.

After a trip to Peru five years ago where he had his first ayahuasca experiences, he was sold on psychedelics healing abilities. He drank ayahuasca in Australia a few times between 2017 – 2018, hoping it might heal his long-standing issues around his childhood abuse and growing up in an extremely dysfunctional family environment. He took fresh psilocybin mushrooms around that time which seemed to help him more. His desire to try MDMA therapy is because he feels nothing else has really worked that well for him. While ayahuasca had helped him somewhat, it didn't take him right down into his pain and trapped emotion or help expel it. He's looking for catharsis. Many people think that catharsis is the answer to healing their trauma but it's not that common for MDMA to heal through catharsis. It tends to work in a different way. Healing doesn't have to be painful or traumatic.

Barry's First MDMA session (125 mg)

Barry's words

Ayahuasca has taken me into fear states and has worked heavily in opening me up and clearing my body. It prompted me to begin meditation and yoga; but it's never managed to pierce the thick wall that separates me from a lot of pain that I feel is deep down inside me and has to come out for me to feel better.

When I take ayahuasca, I feel it inside me, trying to pierce through areas where there are energetic knots and blocks. Energy flows in through the soles of my feet and often makes me shake. It then moves through my body like a needle or dentist drill trying to pierce through blockages. It seems like some kind of internal operation is taking place. I know they are blockages because I've experienced a sense of relaxation and release when some of these operations are successful. Some of the places it tries to pierce through, are the places where the chakras are located. It always tries to pierce a hole into my heart area and also in my solar plexus. It feels like a lot of emotion is behind both these areas, because I have felt waves of sadness and grief rise very briefly during these internal "operations." For some reason, however, it never manages to actually get through. It's not a very pleasant experience; it feels like it's doing something to help me but I never drive home from an ayahuasca session feeling like I made a huge breakthrough or feeling any better, like something has shifted inside. It's more that I notice it's action in other more subtle ways, like how it prompted me to start meditating.

Psilocybin mushrooms are better for me it seems. I've had dried mushrooms a few times and felt like it was getting closer to my pain but it was only a huge dose of fresh mushrooms with a glass of Caapi Vine tea beforehand and soft beautiful music that made me really connect with a lot of the pain trapped inside me. This pain came directly out of my solar plexus area. I bought a keyboard afterwards and reconnected with my musical past again after letting it go for decades. Fresh mushrooms are hard to get though and involve picking them directly and taking them within 48 hours. The Caapi tea makes them more powerful. Fresh mushrooms are much stronger than dried and I had a massive dose. At least it showed me that psychedelic medicines can help me which was really uplifting. I'd concentrated on ayahuasca before that because I thought it was the strongest and also because it is the most accessible. But after I cried for hours on the huge dose of fresh mushrooms, I realised I would probably do better to look for other things. An ayahuasca facilitator I know recommended I try MDMA therapy, as he thought it would be more healing for me. So basically, I want to see if MDMA will help me more than ayahuasca.

As the MDMA was coming on it first seemed to make me still and quiet and then I felt an influx of energy through the soles of my feet coming up into my body. Unlike ayahuasca the energy was not intense and harsh but gentle and soothing. It was like a blanket of peace coming up and gradually taking me over. It was like my mind was gradually being anesthetised with a sense of calm and gentle peace so that I didn't really care what was happening.

At one point I started to feel gentle pressures inside me especially near my solar plexus and heart. I noticed it was going about the same work as ayahuasca but in a much gentler way. It was moving around inside me trying to open me up. The gentle pressures inside me were like a slow rolling wave gently pushing through blockages and tensions rather than piecing through harshly like ayahuasca.

I felt a huge release in my solar plexus area after one 'push' and then a deep sense of peace right in the middle of me. It then came up into my chest and loosened all the tightness and anxiety in that area. Then it went up through my chest and spine into my brain and really filled my mind with more peace. At this stage I felt like I left myself for a while. It was like a kind of disassociation, like I drifted away on a cloud. When I came back, I noticed that it was pushing against my heart in the same place that ayahuasca had, during all the sessions I had previously. For a few seconds I felt a tiny bit like crying but then it receded again. It was also giving me a deep sense of peace in my solar plexus area.

Then I drifted away again, and when I came back, it was like I was separated from myself but in a safe, calm state. It was like nothing was a big deal or worth getting worked up about. It was okay to just not worry about anything or try to understand anything. The best thing to do was just be still and enjoy the floaty, quiet feeling. So, I did that.

Then gradually some thoughts came wafting up into my awareness after the therapist prompted me to envisage the house I grew up in. My house appeared, the one I grew up in, where all the trauma occurred, and I looked at it from above, then at the yard, then inside at the rooms. It was like a kind of survey of the geographical place where everything happened. I have had years and years of dreams about this house, of being trapped under it, and not being able to get out. I knew it was the medicine getting me to look at this house and the life I had there, even though I didn't really feel like it and was content to just feel peaceful and do nothing.

I then remembered my family and the continuous upheaval that occurred in that house. The constant screaming of my mother, my father with a beer in his hand trying to ignore her and focus on his horse-racing form-guide, and then him going to the pub to get away from her. I remembered getting older and growing up in it, and how it went on for years and years, just a totally toxic household. I didn't feel any pain looking at all this however. It was just a sense of considering again something that once happened. I realised how screwed up it all was, but I considered it dispassionately, like it wasn't a big deal now.

I remembered the sexual abuse me and my brother experienced and the constant, never-ending screaming and hostility of my mother. Again, it wasn't a big deal. I didn't feel any emotion. It was like I was looking at it from a state of quiet. These thoughts of looking over everything globally from above and surveying the past continued for a long while until the thoughts stopped coming and I just stayed in that state of quiet and peace until the medicine started to wear off. The only other thing that happened was that at one point in the session, in the middle when the effects were strongest, I drifted into a feeling of bliss for a few brief seconds, but then it receded, and I just felt the peace again.

The main insights I got was realising that my mother was mentally ill and not just an angry woman, but someone who had a severe personality disorder while she raised my brother and I. I realised before this session that she was ill but this time was able to look at it much longer, remembering and going over more detail of how she behaved. Without any sense of pain or emotion I recognised she was very sick.

I also recognised she was lost in her own world and needed help but never got any help. It was the 1970s and there just wasn't the medical/psychological infrastructure to deal with her. She was left to raise two kids alone without any help and she was sick. My father didn't love her and regretted marrying her and having kids with her because he now knew she was crazy. He did everything he could to be as far from her as possible. He was rarely at home. My brother and I were left alone with her. It was like I was removed from her and the situation I was in as a boy. I was just watching her scream and yell and slam doors. She constantly berated my brother and I and expressed her profound anger and hostility in lots of different ways, but without any sense of involvement.

I thought to myself, 'no wonder I'm messed up,' having grown up in that environment. But it was without any sense of self-pity. All the insights and thoughts I had were with a sense of detachment like what I was thinking about was not important anymore. My final thought was that it was all over now and that it was long-gone, like it wasn't a big deal. This was the main thing I got from the session; that it was something that was finished long ago.

The next day the medicine was still working in me. I felt a sense of peaceful detachment all day and it was hard to do anything. I listened to more of the music I had been listening to during the session and just thought about things, although to be honest, my mind was empty for long periods of time. It just felt like I was having a rest from everything and there was no motivation to do anything other than sit around and relax.

The second day after the session, I felt more back in the world and more back inside my regular self. I feel some small lingering sense of quietness, but it is more distant now. I haven't noticed any enduring effects so far other than the sense of quietness I felt, but this is receding as time goes on.

I would definitely take it again. I have had plant medicines but this feels totally different from the others. I am intrigued by it. I feel it was doing something similar to ayahuasca, mushrooms, and cactus to some extent at least, in the way it opened me up to an inflow of energy that worked to push through blockages, but it did so in a totally different way. It was like it put my mind into a state of gentle peace first, like it was an anaesthetist putting a patient out before the surgeon gets to work, and then it did its work inside me trying to open areas inside me. The more it opened me up and the more peaceful my mind and body became, the more it felt like I was getting further away from myself, more removed from myself. When I was really detached it began the survey of my childhood house and what happened there. It was an action completely unlike other plant medicines I have taken. It was a beautiful feeling and so gentle.

The facilitation was great; the talk at the beginning of the session was good because it orientated me to what I wanted to deal with which was sexual abuse in my family. The medicine went beyond this, however, and looked at my whole family life. It was taking the lead and I was just a passenger so even though I wanted to focus on sexual abuse only it went wider than this. I realised more clearly it wasn't just the sexual abuse that messed me up but the years of living in such a horrible environment. I knew this before but again, this time I was going through everything in a lot more detail and for a lot more time because there was no pain or reaction to what I was thinking about.

The therapist was great because she was not intrusive and I was not distracted from the experience by having to talk when I didn't feel like it. At one point I felt a little talkative and talked for a little while but it occurred by itself and happened naturally rather than through effort. After this short period the desire to talk petered out again and I drifted off again into the state of peace. I think for me, just letting the medicine do what it wanted to do was the best thing. I have talked about my issues with therapists before, long ago in my twenties and it doesn't do much by itself. I know what happened to me. There are no uncovered secrets to come out. The problem is on the feeling level.

I know that when I want to talk a lot it happens by itself. I had a really powerful healing experience on magic mushrooms once where I really cried hard for a few hours and so a lot of pain came out. I was with a friend during this and naturally, by itself, I started talking about myself, blurting things out, as I cried all the pain out. The words came out with the emotion.

Maybe it will be different in other sessions, but the first session was all about staying with the medicine and enjoying the peaceful, quiet feeling, and drifting away for a while; then thinking about things as thoughts came, all without having to focus on other things going on around me. I feel like I don't really understand much about MDMA. It feels like it works in a very different way than the plant medicine I have taken. There are some similarities I noticed related to the inflow of energy and in how it tried to open me up but there are more differences than similarities between it and plant medicines The whole thing seemed soothing rather than traumatic. There was no bad bit before the good bit. No fear and anxiety and then release of emotion.

Maybe I will experience more emotion in further sessions; maybe I won't. I don't know because I really don't understand it. I know mushrooms make a lot of people cry and release pain. A huge dose of fresh mushrooms was the only thing, so far in my exploration of plant medicine that made me really cry out a lot of pain and feel better afterwards; but I don't know whether coming directly into contact with pain and crying it out is important to how MDMA works.

I feel better after this first MDMA session. I didn't cry or feel any emotion during it at all apart from a few seconds when the medicine was pushing around my heart. It feels like something really happened but on a level that I can't understand. Maybe whether I cry or not is not the way to judge how this medicine works. I just feel like I really don't know how to assess it yet because it is so different from what I have taken before. I just feel based on my first experience, that it is its own thing and works in a way that I don't understand. It was just a beautiful deep experience.

Shaz, 60, Ex-military

Shaz was referred for MDMA therapy by her psychologist, whom she'd seen regularly for the last seven years. Her psychologist had undergone MDMA therapy herself, and recognised its many benefits and thought it would help Shaz.

Diagnosed with PTSD seven years ago, after a car accident in a foreign country, Shaz believes she probably had it long before that. At the time of the car accident, she had argued with the taxi driver about the route he was taking. Distracted, he crashed into another car resulting in his death for which Shaz blamed herself. Some years later another traumatic incident occurred at work that triggered her unresolved PTSD to a point where she had to leave her job.

A cold and emotionally barren childhood left her with abandonment and neglect issues. At the age of five, she was raped by a visiting family 'friend' and spent some time in a hospital afterwards possibly as a result of the rape - she can't remember exactly. Her family rarely visited her in the hospital ward; she was largely left alone, which just served to enhance her feelings of abandonment.

Coming from a military family, Shaz followed in her father's footsteps and joined the army at seventeen. The cold confines of the army barracks offered up several more extremely traumatic experiences. Shortly after joining, she was drugged and gang raped by a group of older army guys. I might add here that Shaz is definitely not the first female soldier I've spoken to who confessed to suffering abuse at the hands of her own troop. Another who'd served in Afghanistan told me she was far more afraid of her own troop than she was of the enemy.

Another army incident which left a deep scar on Shaz's psyche occurred when she helped a young girl attempt to escape from the army. The girl could stand it no longer so Shaz helped her hatch an escape plan. But the girl was subsequently caught, charged with desertion, and imprisoned. Barbaric to say the least. After serving her sentence, on the day of her liberation, a friend picked her up from the jail gates. Driving home a tragic accident occurred and they were both killed. Shaz felt somewhat responsible saying that it wouldn't have happened had she not helped the girl escape.

Shaz's accumulated traumas have left her feeling isolated and bewildered. She lives alone, is unemployed, and her only solace is her animals, her garden and weekly visits to see her psychologist.

Shaz - First MDMA Session (125 mgs)

Shaz's words

I was diagnosed with Complex PTSD and major depression and medicated with Seroquel and Prozac but stopped taking these prescription drugs about seven years ago. I now microdose magic mushrooms for my depression.

During the active effects of MDMA, I became increasingly more relaxed the more I allowed myself to surrender to it. I felt very aware that my equilibrium was in flux but I felt safe and calm as much as I am able when trying something new.

My thoughts are directed by a new self-voice that now incorporates the knowledge of all that is hidden and the patterns of behaviour and thinking that has been constantly caught in the dread-filled fear of being exposed. This voice comes from a larger, deeper well and has a tone and texture of surrender and acceptance of everything that has brought me to the here and now. It's a perspective that has brought my conscious awareness away from being inside the trauma, viewing reality to moving outside the trauma and seeing reality differently from this perspective and how I am in it. There is a feeling that there is more of me available to experience the moments of my day.

I can visualise the keeping of my traumas hidden from a very young age; beltings, emotional abuse, going to hospital, being molested, the fear of rejection and abandonment. This fear began early and built the shell wall that keeps me locked up within myself unable to be comfortable in social settings. This shell has been forged and maintained by years of added trauma resulting from repeated patterns of behaviour. This first MDMA treatment feels like it has put cracks in the shell. There feels like a release or surrender, a laying down of it all and giving it up. A freshness seems to be seeping into the feel of my thinking.

The next day I felt wiped out, relaxed, but still processing and noting the subtle differences in my thinking. The following week I gradually felt more and more settled but still feeling subtle shifts in perspective which does grab my attention because it's new and so I'm navigating it with a larger awareness.

I will take it again to build on the insights and the calmness it brings to my sense of self. I would recommend this treatment to someone who is suffering from trauma or are in need of finding inner peace. The setting was wonderful, it was very supporting and comfortable - not to mention the great view.

Shaz - Second MDMA Session (120 mg)

Shaz's words

After getting through a very difficult and emotionally painful week following the treatment, I now have a very real sense for the first time that I am getting better and that there is a very real power directing this healing. I think part of the success of this medicine, is that there is a therapist who directs you to look at your traumas. Once the medicine and mind combined on this it almost felt like it took me hostage while it began to obliterate all my emotional defences over the next seven days.

Where the first treatment felt like it put cracks in the fairly impenetrable fear-based shell surrounding me, the second has ripped it wide open and it hurts. But now I sense for me, that that's how it had to be, because being saturated in that pain showed me how to understand the true nature of it. In the end, all the traumas of my life have been bound by the one common thread, I needed to protect myself. I learnt to hide as a toddler, it's been an inbuilt, go-to-survival strategy that I have developed and maintained as if it were second nature. I have survived. This is what I am guilty of and even though I do still feel it in my stomach a bit I know there is no shame here.

During the week following the treatment I would have told you I am not ever doing it again. Two was enough and never again. But that's not right for me now. I want to do this third dose because this time I have a clear intention and the one thing I couldn't even say before without feeling intense pain; I'm ready to work with this medicine one last time to surrender and forgive myself. So, I thank the therapist once again for the journey so far and I look forward to working with her again.

Shaz - Third MDMA Session (125 mg)

Shaz's Words

For the first two weeks after the session, I felt severe depression from consciously witnessing the damage caused by my traumas and how it has impacted the way I think, how I interpret the world and how I interact in it. I see it as mental illness. I feel a bit lost in that the impact of this feels overwhelming to me. I feel tired with little strength or Will left to keep trying to overcome a lifetime of ingrained patterned behaviour.

After sitting with this for two weeks and having some integration sessions I started to accept that this is something I have to accept and I'm going to have to be aware of it and begin to guard myself against negative self-talk and judgments. This feels lighter. Having the awareness to catch my thoughts either before or after they have taken hold, immediately lightens the negative feelings and thoughts and that in and of itself is a blessed relief.

The medicine works on the mind in such a way that it bypasses your conscious programming and shows you objectively how the thought patterns emerged and the consequences which result. Seeing it, knowing it, understanding it, and then feeling it when it shifts is a huge sign that healing is taking place. A very big thank you to the therapist for walking the path you walk, as you work to heal. I hope you will always be protected.

Therapist notes: During this third session Shaz regressed and started reliving the rape she had experienced whilst in the army. She had not previously accessed this because she was drugged at the time it happened. She now relived this rape, including smelling the body smells and remembering the humiliation she'd felt when her rapists taunted her about her undeveloped chest. Her body jerked rhythmically as if she was actually physically reliving the rape. MDMA helped her remember and also release the terror of this trauma.

The therapist then took Shaz back to the scene of her childhood rape and she could now remember everything she had experienced as a five-year-old. She particularly remembered feeling abandoned in the hospital afterwards when she was left in a hospital ward alone and nobody came to see her. She can't remember exactly why she was in the hospital but suspects it had something to do with stomach issues and bed wetting, possibly as a result of the rape. It was a very intense session and testimony to the power of this incredible medicine.

After three MDMA sessions, spaced four weeks apart, Shaz was able to leave therapy with the psychologist she'd been seeing for seven years. According to her, MDMA therapy was life changing and definitely the thing that had helped her the most.

Linda, 28, Social Worker

Linda was diagnosed with anxiety and PTSD and recently had to leave her job because of stress related physical and mental health issues. She grew up as an only child with a self-absorbed, alcoholic mother who had a string of violent, alcoholic partners. She felt isolated, scared and alone; especially when witnessing the frequent and frightening domestic violence occurring in her home.

Dismissive of Linda's emotional needs her mother was quite volatile and occasionally physically violent. Linda's mother probably had undiagnosed PTSD as result of her childhood sexual abuse according to Linda. Her own mother (Linda's grandmother) was alcoholic but is now a long-time sober member of Alcoholics Anonymous. Linda has an enmeshed and co-dependent relationship with her mum, essentially acting as her caretaker.

Linda's biological father left when she was two. She was sent to stay with him for a month when she was four. She doesn't remember much about it except that he fed her Twisties for dinner and was always at the pub, usually taking her with him. He cut off her long blonde hair because he couldn't be bothered to brush it. Linda says she hates her father and hates men in general as they scare her.

There's a question mark around an uncle who took her into his bed while babysitting her when she was around six. She remembers being naked and he having underpants on. She thinks he was just comforting her, but isn't sure. She has no bad feeling about him, but often wonders if he's looking at her sexually.

A few weeks prior to her MDMA therapy session, Linda participated in an ayahuasca ceremony to address her anxiety, panic and general *fear of life. She found the experience quite traumatic and didn't feel safe with the male facilitator who seemed chaotic and self-absorbed.*

Linda's First MDMA Session (100 mgs)

Linda's words

My intention for this MDMA session was to address my anxiety and PTSD, and hopefully work through my past traumas, and alleviate my severe panic and hypervigilance.

When the MDMA started working, I felt really good and very calm. I then went into a familiar trauma response where I become freezing cold and tired. I still felt calm enough to speak about past traumas that would normally elicit a panic attack in the past. I would never have been able to discuss this stuff without becoming emotional, upset, and angry.

I was really able to talk about things from my past that had previously been too traumatic for me to speak about. I've never talked about this stuff because it just felt too painful to go there; particularly some events around my mother and how she treated me. There has been a lot of pain, deep wounding, and difficult emotions. I hadn't ever really allowed myself to go there, acknowledge it or talk about it. Realising that my mother had a drinking problem was a huge insight. Obvious as it seems now, I'd not twigged to this at all, prior to the session until the therapist pointed it out to me. This had a huge impact on me. It also allowed me to see and feel the terror I felt when my mother's boyfriends and my stepfather were violent towards her. So much screaming, arguing and violence. I was often scared for her life.

The day after the session I felt a bit tired and somewhat in my head, processing what came up. Other than that, I felt fine, definitely much calmer and more relaxed in my body - much less panicked. A couple of days later I felt a bit sad and down, likely due to all the stuff that arose in my session around mum which is painful to feel.

Over the following week I noticed that my hypervigilance and panic had greatly improved, less fear and anxiety in my body. Generally, I feel less angry and frustrated and much calmer. I find it much easier to make decisions without panicking; decision making was very stressful for me. I'm not as emotionally reactive to people or situations which would have previously made me really upset and tearful, or angry and frustrated. Overall, I am more able to cope in situations that previously would have overwhelmed me.

The effects have started to wear off somewhat after four weeks. The anxiety, panic, and hypervigilance seem to be returning though to a lesser degree and I'm back to overthinking. I'll continue with MDMA therapy to work on my PTSD and associated symptoms. My goal is to feel safer in my body and in the world, to heal from past traumas, and to navigate my relationships with the people who have hurt me and to hopefully find forgiveness for them and myself - to have a deeper love for myself and others.

I'd definitely recommend this treatment to others. I already have. The therapist created a very comfortable and safe space and I felt totally at ease with her. She was so supportive throughout the session and able to create a safe space which enabled me to revisit places that would usually have been difficult for me. I felt safely guided by her support. She reached out and offered me comfort at times which really helped when I was upset. She had the wisdom and knowledge to educate me which helped me to understand things I hadn't seen before, by the questions she asked and what we talked about.

This work has created some massive shifts and is allowing me to process and work though deep inner wounding that has needed addressing for ages. I talked through nearly the entire session; bless her for getting through all that with me and helping me make sense of everything that I blurted out. I'm so grateful to her for offering this treatment that allows such deep healing. If only this was available to more people. I hope so in the future. For now, I'm blessed to be able to access this treatment. Thank you so much.

Linda - Second MDMA Session (100 mg)

Linda's words

When the MDMA came on it felt similar to my first session; although this time I experienced a period of anxiety when remembering some past sexual assaults and talking about them. My heart was racing and I felt scared, anxious, and stressed, which continued until the end of the session and even for a short time after. The medicine brought up some past traumatic experiences that were very frightening and this was the first time I'd ever discussed them with someone.

I remembered details of a rape I experienced as a young teenager which I'd almost completely forgotten and other sexual assaults I had endured. I remembered they had happened but it was like I'd buried them away and had never previously talked about them in therapy. This explained a lot of my anger towards men which has been an issue my whole life - and a pattern I believe that stems from my father. I then had further insights about my father and how I felt being around him as a child – scared, unsafe and cold. I remembered things that happened to me when I was with him and how much I hated the smell of alcohol that he always reeked of. I felt so much anger towards him. The journey then leads me into the sex work I did in my teens. I've felt so ashamed of this. Even discussing all this made me feel sick to my stomach - like I just wanted to vomit. I feel a real sickness in my body when I think and talk about these instances with men.

The next day I felt a bit anxious and a racy in my chest. The second day I felt calmer. The following week I was calm and more relaxed with a decrease in my anxiety and hypervigilance. I slept so much better. Overall, I feel calm and relaxed and able to reflect on and process what came up without being distressed or triggered like I previously would have.

As with the first session the therapist was fantastic! She was so supportive and because of her, I was able to go deeper and remember and process some really frightening things that happened to me which I've never spoken about with anyone. She was so kind and empathetic in her approach and supportive throughout the session, and also in our integration sessions after.

Linda - Third MDMA Session (100 mg)

Linda's words

Just prior to this session I'd been really triggered while staying at a friend's place. I was so worked up I had to have a counselling session. During my stay my friend's husband was abusive, demeaning, bossy and loud. This mirrored events that occurred at home when I was young. I hated my mother's boyfriend who was always yelling and violent towards her, and my friend's husband reminded me of him. I was definitely symptomatic of PTSD, having nightmares and night terrors. I also felt really angry at my mother for exposing me to all that.

When the MDMA came on, I felt calm and very relaxed. My whole body which usually holds on very tight, just released. I went into the response where I feel physically cold and grind my teeth. For the first time, I had some somatic releasing of my body with shaking. It felt really good. I then had insights relating to abuse from my father and the terror and fear I felt being with him. I had the physical response of going cold when I talk about him - feeling yucky, afraid, and unsafe. And this was when my body began shaking. I felt nausea while discussing other horrible situations I'd been in with men; my uncle, sex work, and my stepfather. More shaking. They all reminded me of dad.

I realised that I never had a safe home environment. How unsafe I felt with my unpredictable mother. I didn't have a happy childhood where I was actually able to be a child and do the things I loved. My life focused on mum and her issues, or what partner she had, and her bringing abusive men into my life. I have a lot of anger towards my Mum; this has come up strongly since the session, anger at her for not protecting me or caring about me and always putting her own needs first. I wasn't safe. I had no power. I had to go along with what she wanted.

The next day I felt great, so happy and clear headed. The following week, grief and anger arose as I processed what had come up during the session. I wasn't in a terribly low mood, just feeling the emotions that arose. This MDMA work has allowed me to capture and process painful memories and has opened my eyes wider to the trauma I've suffered. I now truly see just how dysfunctional my parents and family are. It's massive stuff. The veil has lifted.

It's really enabled me to love myself - to really see and comprehend all that I've been through, and to finally acknowledge my own pain and suffering, because I never have. I am kinder and gentler with myself and I don't feel crazy anymore for thinking that this stuff really hurt me.

Louise, 32, Business Owner

Louise suffered from mild anxiety and depression. She'd been taking St John's Wort for five months but stopped a month before her MDMA session. Although she's never taken any illicit drugs, she enjoys the occasional drink. While her marriage ended two years ago, neither she nor her ex-husband had been able to let go of each other, and move on with their new lives. They still lived together and owned a business together. The sexual chemistry had gone but the struggle to let each other go was intense. They met in college and still feel love for each other. They have both met potential new partners but because of the COVID-19 restrictions, were unable to travel to be with them. Louise wants to understand why they can't sever their attachment so she can move on into her new life.

Louise's father, a busy professional, provided his family with an affluent lifestyle, but not all was smooth sailing. Louise's mother died when she was just ten years old. A few years later two close school friends committed suicide. Louise found all the deaths traumatic. Her older brother and sister went completely off the rails, becoming drug addicts. Louise was the youngest in the family, but felt it her job to look after everyone else and keep the peace.

Her decision to never take drugs was based on witnessing the resulting carnage of her sibling's drug addictions. Nervous and ambivalent leading up to her MDMA session, Louise was on the verge of cancelling. She received some needed encouragement from the friend who had referred her and finally decided to take the plunge. She was rewarded with an unusually powerful session - a highly visual journey with spirit guides present.

Louise - First MDMA Session (120 mg)

Louise's words

My intention was to clear feelings of overwhelm and regain confidence in who I actually am. To remove feelings of staleness, sadness and help find answers to my current life situation. As the medicine came on, I felt a tingling and warmth from my legs, rise and settle in my heart, where most of my journey was felt. The warmth across my chest felt comforting. At some point that warmth spread up into the left back of my brain. Once I let go of resistance to what was happening inside me, the journey really began there.

My journey was super intense and amazingly visual. I followed, but actively participated in, what I know was my soul's journey through my whole life and beyond. I felt safe participating in this journey, which felt like I was inside my body, and inside my mind at the same time. My spirit guide was a big white horse and although sometimes I was scared and shaking, the white horse galloped me past screaming faces with fiery torches in the dark, only to reach a place of pure peace and blissful serenity which was felt immediately. Everything was felt in the moment, like a baby who can go from crying to laughing in an instant.

My spirit guide horse took me to places in my mind and body that I didn't even know needed healing or uncovering. When I was most scared but had to surrender was when I was thrown through a door into my brain. I was seeing all the dead connections light up again with brilliant colours. I was made to watch as I was pressed against the inside of my forehead. I remember the sticky feeling of my back and hands against the wall inside my head.

I experienced intense grief at times when confronted with loss. My mind and soul fell so quiet once during the experience that I watched myself die on my journey, but I never felt troubled or anxious about it. I had a choice to wake up or not (not wake up to the 'real world' but wake up in my journey) at which point I felt intense peace and stillness.

During the journey, I felt happiness many times, wandering through gardens alight with colours and small animals. Some would illuminate when I touched them bringing on a sense of childlike fascination and awe of my surrounds. Three significant figures accompanied me at times during my journey which added to my sense of safety. These were all very special people, including my mother who had passed on 22 years prior. I felt extreme comfort when she hugged me and we sat rocking our legs on the clouds together with my best friend and now partner.

Overall, I felt I completely trusted the experience and had to go through the scarier moments of the journey to reach the end feeling of peace. All the chaos of my childhood was removed. Hanging onto my husband, as he is my sense of 'family,' and not letting him go, will continue to make me so sad that I will die from that, but also die with that feeling of sadness and remain cold and limp. So, I have to wake up and let him go.

The message was: Keep running past the people that are trying to grab onto you and use you for their happiness, you need to be strong and gallop on. If you can't even stand up, you can't water the plant and it will not grow. Shed the big cloak of responsibility and then you will walk tall in your own garden. I am not responsible for other people's happiness; they are responsible for their own.

Everything in my whole life now makes sense, everything that has happened, and some things that will happen. No more chaos or confusion. Now I have a still mind free of clutter and a warm sense of peace throughout my chest. An experience through my inner self that is so awakening, yet confronting but the end result is bliss. Not caring about the little things anymore. I now have clarity.

I felt extremely tired the day after but peaceful and warm in my heart. Mostly in-appetent, only eating small amounts. The night of the session I had the best sleep I've had in a month. I would definitely take it again to experience the beauty of going within again. I would highly recommend it to others. I felt safe, guided but not over stimulated by the facilitation. The music was phenomenal and resonated strongly with me.

My MDMA journey truly was the most profound experience of my life. It tapped into parts of me that needed awakening and release so I can move forward. I knew that I trusted my journey and what had happened. This was made real to me when I found a four-leaf clover straight after the session, the one I was looking for towards the very end of my visual journey.

The session definitely enabled Louise move on with her life; shortly after the session she moved interstate to be with her new partner. A year later she returned to have another MDMA session in order to get more guidance on her future endeavours. She had another extremely visual and insightful session.

Sandra, 25, IT Programmer

In her early teens, Sandra was diagnosed with bulimia, generalised anxiety, panic disorder and depression. She had been taking antidepressants up until six months prior to her MDMA session. With a history of co-dependent, rescuing relationships, it was with some relief that both she and her current partner underwent MDMA therapy simultaneously, to address their dysfunctional childhoods, life issues and to help their relationship blossom.

Raised in a devout Christian environment, Sandra endured intense religious indoctrination and the accompanying guilt and shame. Her parents divorced when Sandra was ten and they rigorously fought over she and her sister, which made Sandra feel owned. Her mother is still heavily involved in the Christian church where Sandra's grandfather is the minister. Her father left the church, shortly after they divorced. Although there was no physical abuse, there is a question mark around sexual abuse which Sandra didn't or couldn't enlarge on.

Sandra describes her current issues as: self-loathing, fear of financial insecurity, carry over guilt and shame as a result of her religious indoctrination, irrational fear of making a mistake, and trouble spending money on herself. She currently experiences problems with her job and feels like her employer owns her.

Sandra - First MDMA Session (125 mg)

Sandra's words

My intention for the MDMA session was to heal from anxiety and childhood trauma and to gain some more coping mechanisms for dealing with adult life.

The MDMA made me feel calm and it was really easy to access old memories. I really enjoyed breathing in and out slowly and lying on the couch. I felt very sure of myself and who I was. I wasn't over-thinking. My insights were around feeling "owned" by my job and realising that it came from feeling owned by my parents through childhood and particularly during their custody battle.

I'm feeling the weight of the re-programming from church brainwashing that was still going on. I thought I was past it but there's still lots of work to be done here. I'm feeling undeserving and unworthy of money because of my low self-worth. It really highlighted these things to me and brought them up to the surface so that I could see, feel, and deal with them.

The next day I felt very emotional. I cried a lot, but it felt really good to cry and release the emotions. There were no come-down effects. I just felt lighter and even though I was more emotional I felt better in myself, as I wasn't scared of the emotions anymore, I've since found my job to be far more manageable after the "ownership" insight I had.

The following week I felt up and down emotionally and there was a lot of processing going on. I felt lighter, less anxious, calmer and better in myself. I felt like myself, but I also felt like a four-year-old child again, in the midst of my parents' divorce. I feel like there is more to process and work through: my parents' divorce, the church brainwashing, self-worth, among other things which I may not remember consciously.

It's a lot faster doing MDMA therapy than traditional therapy or trying to manage on my own. There are much larger insights to be gained in a short amount of time. It is also much gentler than ayahuasca but still has a massively positive effect. I think everyone should do it, as everyone goes through some kind of childhood trauma and would benefit from it. I'd only recommend it to people I trust and who I feel are ready for it. I don't want to publicise it as it's still illegal.

I really liked the facilitation. It was calm and quiet. The therapist was easy-going and had a great energy. The whole space felt very fluid and safe which made it easy to go deep into my issues. I feel thankful for such a great therapist and that she was willing to facilitate these sessions. We need more people like her doing this work. I thank her for giving us; both me and my partner the opportunity to do this. We are so grateful and can already see really positive effects in ourselves as we continually integrate old emotions and childhood trauma. I'm looking forward to the next session in about a month.

Sandra - Second and Third MDMA Sessions (125 mg)

Sandra's words

It made me feel so many different emotions all at once which was a bit overwhelming. It also gave me lots of clarity in terms of what I had been through in my life. It brought up memories I'd forgotten and gave me more of the puzzle pieces of my life. It made me feel good and whole.

I recovered memories of childhood sexual abuse which explained why everything in my life was the way it was, more or less. It gave me so much clarity into why I was struggling so much. It was the missing piece of the puzzle and the root cause of my anxiety. It also opened my eyes to lots of my coping mechanisms. I clearly remembered my grandfather, (the church minister) sexually abusing me. I'd previously blocked this out. He told me he was punishing me for something I had done wrong. This is why I get so extremely anxious when I think I've done anything wrong. It happened at his house while my parents were staying there in between houses. My grandmother was cooking dinner at the time. Afterwards we all sat at the table for dinner. I remember Wheel of Fortune being on TV. I refused to eat. I think this is probably when I developed an eating disorder. I don't feel like having sex now and am worried my partner won't understand.

I felt really out of it the day after the second session; I couldn't stop crying all day. After the third session I felt calmer and surer of myself. There were no come-down effects but lots of heavy emotions came up. I definitely felt down for the days/weeks following the therapy. It just opens the box on your emotions and shit, and it spills out everywhere. I felt very down, fragile, and terrified, but also grateful, calm, and lighter in a way. At least everything is out in the open now. Very up and down – like a rollercoaster not knowing what was next.

But I feel a lightness and clarity. I've been working through letting go of coping mechanisms, doing self-love, and reprogramming myself. It's been a period of seriously integrating what I learned in these therapies. The therapy itself is powerful but it's the counselling and integration of the emotions and trauma that really has shifted things for me. Being aware of what came up and then changing what I was doing and learning how to heal from it. You could say all those effects are from the MDMA therapy in a way. It shines a magnifying glass on areas of your life that you need to see and focus on. I'm learning to forgive.

I feel like I am entering a period of deep integration and learning. I just want to integrate what has come up and work on practicing self-love and getting stronger in who I am. Maybe down the track if I had further issues or struggles, I would consider it again, but I don't feel like I need any more at this stage. Three sessions were the right amount for me. I need a rest!

I recommend it to others, but only if they're ready. I would tell them to only do it if they feel called to do it (same with ayahuasca). It's not an easy thing to do – it has been one of the most challenging things I have done in some ways – because you face your fears and all the shit you've buried deep inside. Some people are not ready for that yet. And being ready for it doesn't make it easier – because you have no idea what is buried inside.

The facilitation was good – I liked doing it in a home with a dog. It was nice to lie down with pillows and blankets but also have room to move and stretch if needed. I am so grateful to the therapist for facilitating these sessions. It has been a very difficult but necessary journey for me and I'm so thankful for having the opportunity to do it.

Terry, 35, Veterinarian

Terry was referred for psychedelic therapy by his psychologist, who had herself experienced psychedelic therapy with both ayahuasca and MDMA. Terry had been her client for the previous eighteen months. He originally went to her for around his difficult marriage to his now ex-wife - who had alcohol and PTSD issues. Terry's primary role as her caretaker had left him angry and resentful.

Four months prior to his MDMA referral Terry was diagnosed with PTSD after a terrible car accident in which two people were killed. A guy speeding in an SUV, hit a motorcyclist and sent him flying through the air to land directly in front of Terry's moving car. The SUV driver then hit the median strip, flipped and landed on the car directly behind Terry's, killing the driver of that car as well. When the motorcyclist came into the path of Terry's car, he swerved to miss the SUV and ran over the motorcyclist. Terry now constantly flashes back to the sensation of running over the body. He constantly ruminates about whether he killed the motorcyclist or whether he was already dead beforehand.

At the moment of the crash Terry thought he was about to die and constantly flashes back to this as if in a freeze frame. He hears his partner screaming as the SUV flies through the air towards them. He is constantly hypervigilant, scanning for ways he might die. Driving is now a trigger. He has nightmares and stressful dreams and feels unrested, numb and cut off from his emotions. He expends a lot of energy just trying to be OK. His alcohol consumption has increased to three or four drinks a night and more on the weekend; all classic symptoms of PTSD.

Further assessment reveals that Terry has a porn habit which happens routinely, every couple of days. There is significant guilt attached to this, possibly stemming from his previous religious background as a born-again Christian during his teens. He says he doesn't believe in anything now and just feels angry at God. He is self-reflective, has good self-insight, but very poor eye contact, which I sense indicates a deep sense of shame.

Terry's mother has always suffered from anxiety but was never medicated. Sent to boarding school as a child she had a cold and distant relationship with her mentally ill mother. Terry's father was orphaned as a toddler but eventually got adopted. There was no physical or emotional abuse but when asked about sexual abuse, Terry admits to having an uncomfortable, foggy memory of an uncle who creeped him out. He's not sure why and hasn't seen him in 20 years. Statements like this are often a red flag and I suspect that more will be revealed.

Terry's intention for his session is to get relief from his debilitating PTSD symptoms caused by the accident. He opts not to wear an eye mask as it made him feel restricted. In such instances the person usually just closes their eyes.

Terry's First MDMA Session (120 mg)

Terry's words.

As the MDMA started to activate, I felt wavy in all of my senses, as if I was in a pleasantly rocking boat. My sight and hearing felt gently overcome in waves of amplitude or volume. I would alternate between being very aware of my senses then having an insightful moment of positive emotion in response to this input, then sliding back to a purely sensorial experience. At the beginning, this feeling wasn't linked to any emotional or cognitive insight, it was purely experiential. This was extremely welcome as my PTSD had left me feeling completely numb to any emotion at all - except an over-riding anxiety that something bad could happen at any moment. But under MDMA I became aware that I was relaxing deeply in a way I hadn't since the car crash; in fact, I was relaxed to a degree I don't recall ever having been in my life.

The insights predominantly centred on the car crash but there were also some overarching realisations of thoughts, feelings, and beliefs that in the months since the crash I'd become unmoored from. One of the strongest was a deep feeling of love for my girlfriend who was also involved in the crash. I realised how much I love her and wanted her to know I do; in ways I hadn't felt or been able to articulate meaningfully since the crash.

I also remember feeling a deep and profound understanding of how fortunate I am not only to be alive after the near-death experience of the car crash but a larger sense of privilege that I have loving friends, family, a relatively successful career, and no unmet needs in my life. This feeling gave me a sense of responsibility to take hold of my life and live it fully given the level of fortune and privilege I have, not only to be alive but to be safe, well, loved, and well-positioned. Given the depth of feeling I had, of the chaotic pointlessness of life before the session, this was a fairly abrupt turnaround that I felt deeply thankful for, even at the time.

The primary realisation I had about the car crash, was that it wasn't my fault; that anyone in my position would have done, could only have done what I did. My mind had been preoccupied by re-visiting whether I could have done anything different to avoid the body I ran over so that perhaps the person wouldn't have died. But I realised that this was cyclical thinking with no real answer and was never going to get me anywhere. This event was definitively not my fault; I was just in the wrong place at the wrong time.

What I realised was that I never left the side of the road that night; that I was still basically stuck by the road staring at the crash site, as I did for so long that night, trying to figure out what had happened. In shock and trying to figure out what any of it meant. Before the session I thought the most crucial moment in the crash was when I saw the car flying through the air towards us and explicitly understood I was about to die. I was annoyed that this was how I died.

This had caused me to start thinking of the universe as pure chaos. I understood that in the face of such sheer dumb luck (for me) and tragedy (for the deceased) that nothing about human existence really meant anything. But in the session, I realised there was another way to look at this that took a less nihilistic approach. I realised that if I wanted to take hold of the good things in life that I needed to understand that this wasn't my fault. I didn't do anything wrong.

I also began to access the feeling that while my old ideas of spirituality were incapable of encompassing and making sense of this trauma, that didn't mean there was no spiritual dimension to it at all. I began to see that perhaps death wasn't purely negative. Instead, there were aspects to the possible spiritual dimension of the crash that I was unaware of and incapable of seeing or comprehending. This conception of the crash opened me up to less fraught and cyclical thinking. I feel like this insight was just the beginning and during the session I only picked up a thread of this idea.

The most crucial thing that happened was accessing a clear memory of the thing I'd repressed since the night of the crash. Since then, I'd avoided actively thinking directly of the event despite the intrusive involuntary thoughts, feelings and nightmares. During the MDMA session I was able and willing to think through events, step by step, without any internal emotional resistance that had built up since it happened. Instead, I freely and easily remembered that on the night of the crash I thought the body on the road was the driver or a passenger from the car that almost killed us.

During the moment of the crash my partner thought she saw the body fly out of the car so in the aftermath I sat for hours by the side of the road hating the body as the perpetrator who'd almost killed me. My guilt over hating the body had since ruled my thinking in unconscious ways. I don't know yet how much this has affected me but, in the session, I realised I had edited the event to change this narrative and avoid the guilt of what I understand now to be a very understandable thought process.

The morning after the session there were no come-down effects but I woke with a significant amount of tension in my back, shoulder and neck. I had a significant pain and restricted movement so I sought a remedial massage which helped dissipate the tension. Beyond this I continue to feel relaxed and reflective, filled with a sense of love and care for myself and my partner in ways I'd lost touch with before the session.

I felt fine for the first five days after the session; relaxed, open, more at peace with the realisations I'd had. But on day five a small annoyance at work triggered a deep anger. This relatively unrelated work grievance opened a deep chasm of roiling rage that felt undirected and with which I could do nothing. I thought of the perpetrator of the crash fleetingly, imagining inflicting violence on him as retribution for the psychological damage he has caused. Mostly though my brain feels unwilling or unable to continue the work of directing this anger anywhere productive or resolving it in any way and it remains bubbling under the surface. This is where I feel stuck now, but even so, it feels remarkably different and better than the place I was stuck before.

Prior to the MDMA session I had stressful dreams and nightmares every night and woke numerous times during the night. Prior to the crash I slept deeply through the night. In the morning, I woke with distinct memories of traumatic feelings and events. But since the session I am sleeping deeply through the night again, without negative feelings at all.

Apart from the anger I mentioned earlier, I've regained some motivation that my PTSD robbed me off. I feel like being active, outside in the fresh air, talking to people, engaging lovingly and meaningfully with my partner. Beyond the profound level of relaxation, I felt perhaps for the first time in my life the medicine allowed me to access and face memories, thoughts, and feelings, I was becoming increasingly closed off from.

I wish the numerous people I know with PTSD could access this treatment. The domestic space and the ability to look outside was really helpful for me during the session so I could look out at open air and not feel trapped. It was great for me to feel the warmer feeling of a lived-in space that was less clinical. It was also great to have a comfortable couch to lay on. I also really valued having the pre-session consultation in the same space so I could picture the space I would be in before the day of the MDMA session. This is desperately important work and I feel fortunate to be able to participate in it.

Terry's Second MDMA Session (120 mg)

Terry's words

My intention was to get to the bottom of my anger. I began to feel relaxed to a degree that I never do at any other time. I felt wavy and emotionally open. I felt talkative and excited to continue, in the hope that I could talk through my trauma and anger.

There are some things about the session I'm not ready to write. But in brief what began as a discussion about my parents kicked off realizations about myself and ultimately about my memory of childhood. I thought I needed to address my feelings of anger and resentment towards my ex-wife but I actually needed to understand why I was attracted to her in the first place. Thinking about this, previous relationships and attraction to women with traumatic backgrounds allowed me to start 'connecting-the-dots' of my feelings and unconscious motivations in ways I'd never been able to.

Predictably I attempted to talk and talk and talk through this, but the therapist asked me to go internal. As with the first session I was resistant to this idea but unlike the first session a greater part of me understood the need for this and so I agreed, closed my eyes, and lay down. As I started to connect the dots of how my parent's relationship had shaped me, I thought about my ex-wife, and other relationships I'd had and realised I was attracted to them because of their trauma, and in some cases because of their histories of acting out sexually because of that trauma. Under MDMA I was self-honest enough to admit that I was aroused and attracted to this acting out and also jealous of it, how they carried their trauma so actively and close to the surface. Ironically, it's also the thing that made them ultimately unattainable, unreachable, unlovable or unbearable.

I then remembered the night I began a relationship by betraying my best friend at the time and what feelings motivated me in that moment. In that train of thought I was ultimately able to realise these motivations, this jealousy, connected back to the recesses of my mind and a memory I had locked away and repressed since I was young. As I approached this realisation, I began to squirm on the couch, my right leg began to tremble and shake. As I recovered the memory I'd been repressing for over 30 years I squirmed and shook. I remember the therapist checking if I was OK and willing for this to happen and I was. Throughout I was guided by my own detached voice of awareness that understood and knew what I then told her through clenched teeth, 'Yep, I'm OK, this is good.'

I realised that this 'blocked off' corner of my memory that I'd been aware of for years; the knowledge that I didn't like my estranged uncle, the memory of only parts of a childhood visit to a beach, were all because I'd repressed the memory of my own sexual abuse. When I was young, my uncle did things to me in the toilets that have affected my whole life without me even understanding what was happening.

I don't want to write the details here but I talked through the specifics with the therapist. Suffice to say that in this MDMA induced state, I relived the abuse in detail through my own eyes as a child. I was squirming and recoiling on the couch because I was reliving the event. The specifics matter and I have and will continue talking through them, as I understand that those specifics have changed so much of my internal thinking for most of my life. Overall, I was left feeling powerless, scared, confused, afraid, alone, helpless, and dirty in ways that I've been reacting to my whole life.

When the event was over, someone came into the toilets and things were over as abruptly and as grossly as it began. No one had come to save me, and I remembered being left alone to wash my hands and walk back to face both Mum and Dad, the rest of the family, and my abuser. On that lonely walk I now remember staring down at the dry brown grass crunching beneath my feet and deciding and knowing that I couldn't say or do anything. I had to arrive unbothered, calm, normal, and acting as if nothing was wrong and nothing bad had just happened. It was a long lonely walk. I've been walking that same walk my whole life since that day.

I realise now that I learnt about how to 'act' from Mum and Dad; that meant I internalised the maelstrom of emotions caused by the abuse, to the point that I repressed the memory altogether. I never remembered anything until this session, and I don't remember deciding to forget, just that I walled off a section of my brain. I think this repression is something I did quite quickly after the event. I have spent time since this MDMA session having memories and feelings of events I felt and experienced as a child and understanding them as the 'outlet' and 'reflex' to this repression.

Coming back 'up' through the same dot-connecting process, I didn't blame Mum and Dad. I simply understood what had happened in my brain during that walk. I realised that a series of 'short circuits' in my brain have unconsciously guided all of my thinking from that day onwards. As I came back from the repressed memory, I realised that both myself and my parents were victims of circumstance, that we weren't ever very emotionally honest with ourselves or each other due to their unfortunate life circumstances. I even had a glimpse of understanding of my uncle and his motivations as to why he might have done what he did; but honestly, fuck him. His job as an adult was not to do what he did, despite whatever was done to him.

I felt guided to debrief the therapist on what had just happened. My first question was how long I'd been 'under.' What turned out to be about three average songs length of time was what I now understood as having just done 'years of therapy.' After I debriefed, she encouraged me to go internal again, to meet the small boy that I was, as the person I am now. When I went back down to that memory, that boy that I was, I realised I could help him. Not in actuality, I couldn't stop what happened but under the MDMA I implicitly understood that I could go back into the scenario and counsel myself as a child.

As an adult I intercepted my boy-self outside the toilets, telling him I didn't have to go straight back to the family. I walked with myself down to the beach. There, on the sand, I hugged and talked to myself, not a lot of words but a deep expression of the shared sorrow and grief, I now understood I've been carrying my whole life. I told myself that it was OK; I was here now and safe. I took myself for a swim in the water, washing myself clean of what had happened, feeling the positive sensation of saltwater on my body. I swam to clean away all the residue of what had happened and understood why I'd strove so hard to feel clean my whole life. We swum and dived under the waves for a while. And then as we stood in the shallows together, we screamed at the horizon. We screamed at the whole world together; me and myself, screaming with anger and release at this finally being open. I told myself that it was OK now, that I am an adult, I am here now, and that we're safe.

This second internal session was so pivotal for me to carry into the following weeks and months. Without it I'm not sure how I would have carried the raw feeling I was left with. Knowing I'd been able to have and guide that vision gave me the confidence to keep going in the weeks after when the whole feeling seemed too big to even deal with. As I came back up from this vision I saw with startling clarity and insight how this event and its repression had dictated basically internal thoughts and decisions in my life. I realised that without uncovering this, I was stuck in a pattern of self-sabotage that I was doomed to live out for the rest of my life. I was so excited that now I didn't have to.

I realised that I have a pattern of blowing up my life emotionally every 5-10 years, and don't have to do that anymore. The ever-heightening levels of attraction I have to other women, were a symptom of all this shit and that knowing why now changes my relationship to that struggle. I could think and therefore act differently to behaviours, thoughts, instincts that have made me question, 'Why are you like this?' I don't have to be a victim to myself or anyone else anymore.

Like the previous MDMA session I saw again how deeply fortunate I am to have this weird and wonderful life, and now, with this newly expanded awareness of myself, I'm in a better position to have a great and meaningful life. I left the session feeling so much lighter and relieved. I thanked the therapist profusely for changing my life. I remarked how important this MDMA is for healing and how criminal it is that it's not a recognised treatment.

The next day I just felt shock. No comedown effects, just shock at the memories I'd recovered. Given the magnitude of the memories, the shock continued for two weeks. I kept trying to figure out ways for them to not be true. But I kept coming back to the unshakable understanding that it just made everything in my life make so much sense. Given what I uncovered, I've felt incredibly raw and angry, but I understand that this is part of the process. I know it's possible to move past this. I felt unsettled in every way, restless, with nightmares most nights. Having said that, I have also felt 'open' in ways I find hard to explain. I can see things in the world differently and understand people's motivations in a slow considered way.

These insights have been profound in understanding myself in new ways. I've spent a month understanding so much more about my life-long thoughts, feelings, emotions, behaviours, motivations, in ways that have been exhausting, staggering and yet strangely and deeply satisfying. It gave me a calm peace and self-insight that I've never felt before or understood.

I know so many people with trauma who need this therapy. The domestic setting was calm and relaxed with no distractions which was great. The facilitation, insightful and wise – encouraging silence and me to go 'internal' to let myself and the MDMA 'do the work.' In some ways this was the worst day of my life, since the day of the memory I repressed, but it was also the best/first day of the rest of my life, so I'm thankful for that. A new understanding of myself has been opened which is horrible to know, but simultaneously an incredible relief and a profound opportunity to grow and move forward emotionally.

Terry's Third MDMA Session (120 mg)

Terry's words.

As with the last two times, I began to feel relaxed to a degree that I never do at any other time. I felt 'wavy' and 'open' emotionally and very talkative. I went into the session with an intention to address the deeply raw feeling of anger I had been feeling, since the revelatory experience of my previous session.

Once the MDMA really came on I didn't feel the raw anger I'd been feeling for the previous month. At the therapists prompting to go back into the memory I'd recovered in the previous session, I began to push and punch my abuser away. I punched and kicked and pushed into the couch and cushions. Along with this action, I began to grunt and shout "UGH", "NO", "GET AWAY," culminating in a few large cathartic screams into the pillows. Large guttural screams that began from my stomach and burned my throat. I don't know if I was concerned that it was loud or that it felt a little silly but I remember feeling surprised that the screams became wails but then stopped pretty quickly as well. I think I have more of that in me but something wrapped that part of proceedings up pretty promptly and I don't really understand that yet.

I did some stretching and as I continued to feel the effects, I felt like doing a lot of talking, but it felt important to feel and experience my body laying on the couch and stretched out on the floor, rather than talking as a way to avoid this. I see now I wanted to (and always want to) stay cerebral rather than emotional and certainly rather than somatic.

I realised that I've never felt like a man. Because of the abuse, I've always felt arrested in my development - a boy. Which is why it was important for me to realise I could literally and figuratively stand taller than I usually do. I stood up with my head held high and my shoulders back, feeling strong and tall and proud. I felt like a man. This was an incredibly crucial insight for me as it began a new path to discovering who I can be now as a man.

I came into this session having had a session with my psychologist this morning which was a great way to prepare me and to focus on my intention for this session. I realised I was angry, scared, terrified even, of getting better because I didn't even know who I was without this baggage weighing me down. Carrying this baggage for the last 30 years has defined the man-child me and consequently I don't know who I am without it. What I found under MDMA was a vision and sensation and a literal posture of the man I know I can be.

The other key insight I had, was what it actually felt like to be fully relaxed. I had a clear realisation that I've never been relaxed for as long as I can remember. But now I felt relaxed, positive, and excited for the future all at once. I remember saying, 'Is this how people really feel? Can it really be like this?' What I realised is that I wake up every day with dread and one question on my mind: 'What do I have to deal with today?' But I now saw that those people who are excited about the day are not faking it, they just aren't burdened with what I've been carrying. I felt this was possible for me too.

I had a new version of the vision I had during the last session. Like last session, I as an adult, tended to myself as a boy on the day of my abuse. Last time I felt I couldn't change what happened so didn't intercede during the abuse. But this time my adult interceded afterwards. I walked back to the beach where my parents were. I strode as a man and punched my uncle in the face and threw him to the ground. I kicked him in the stomach, the balls and the face. I yelled at him that he was a piece of shit. I dragged him by the collar to the footpath and called the police. As an adult I told them what had happened and helped myself as a child explain to the police what he had done. They took him away.

Coming out of this vision I realised what I had done, the way I'd held myself and acted as an adult in the vision could be the new me. The way I could be now as a man is free from the burden of this dark repression that had been so heavy it literally weighed down on my shoulders and back for my whole life. The vision showed me who I could become now.

At the therapist's suggestion I went 'back in' to a last internal session to see if there was more work the MDMA could do, and to my surprise, I 'corrected' the vision. This time while most of the vision played out the same. After I punched and kicked him to the ground, this time I didn't drag him out to the footpath. Instead, I stayed as an adult and explained to the whole family why he was the piece of shit he is, what he'd done, and what was going to happen next, to help set things right for myself as a child. I stood and called the Police then and they came to the beach. Rather than 'saving face' for the family and surrounding families, I intentionally 'made a scene,' not for drama but to bring things out into the light for everyone; to set an example and to release myself as a child of any burden at all of pretending to be OK.

In this vision justice has been sought in full view. Horrible shit has been called for what it is, for everyone to see, so that we may begin to shed forever the cover of secrecy and shame that covered not just me and my family but others as well. These two visions, particularly in my developing understanding of their pivotal differences, were and are the models for who I can be now that I don't have to carry this burden. I can stand tall and speak up.

I felt calm and clearer the following day and many days since. I didn't have any come-down effects, I just had the usual ups and downs of integration. I felt a new resolve and positive sense of hope for the future. With the insights I described above I now have a vision of the man I can be. This is what allows me to stand taller and walk with a new freedom and positivity. I think I'm beginning to see how it can help me work through half-realised thoughts and feelings that have plagued me my whole life.

I have strongly sense there is more work to be done. I'm wondering if ayahuasca is something I'm ready for, whether it may offer me the next 'opening up' that I need. I think it very interesting that I've barely cried about this. I sense that I have a lot of crying and grieving to do.

In considering whether to disclose my recovered memory with my Mum and Dad. I've realised that Mum will not be able to 'deal' with it. I'm torn - as I recognise that by not telling them, I'm repeating the same decision I made that day as a boy. Thinking through this has me feeling that there is more to uncover in terms of emotions and ramifications that this trauma caused in shaping my relationship to my Mum and Dad during my childhood.

As Christmas nears, I've felt the trauma resurface. The original trauma happened at this time of year, so I think my body is on a cycle and is experiencing its own memory of the event. At least now I understand why this time of year fills me with dread; why large family gatherings leave me in a melancholic state.

Ben, 50, Marketing Manager

Ben was diagnosed with anxiety and depression shortly *after his marriage ended. He'd recently seen a psychologist whom he described as helpful with practical things to do with his recent separation but not the deeper internal issues which still felt unresolved. After reading about MAPS trials and having experienced MDMA before, he believed that taking it in a therapeutic context would help him.*

His marriage to an Asian girl seemed rather codependent; she wanted money and a beautiful house and Ben supplied both she and her family with that and more. He gave her expensive gifts and paid off her debts and lost a substantial sum of money after buying a stupid investment at her encouragement. She cooked and supported him practically but offered little emotional support.

Bens' parents divorced when he was eight. He stayed with his sisters and mother until age 16, then was sent interstate to live with his father who he describes as cold and unloving; a selfish man who didn't look after or nurture him. He was emotionally abusive at times, teasing Ben and played tricks on him. Ben felt his mother had abandoned him but now realises that she had thought he needed a male influence in his life. Ben was also bullied at school.

His assessment revealed that Ben has an alcohol problem and is self-medicating. He drinks a bottle of wine three or four times a week, has blackouts and hangovers and often takes benzodiazepines to sleep. On the plus side he's into health and fitness. As a teen he was stoned every day. He tried ecstasy once 20 years ago and again last New Year's Eve, resulting in an intimate encounter with a female friend which he now regrets. He recently had an alcohol induced liaison with a neighbour who also later rejected him. He is upset over these rejections and blames himself. Exploring this further he was able to realise that these rejections may not be indicative of anything lacking in him as both women had recently been in quite traumatic relationships.

The main issues he seeks to address in his MDMA session are around his sleep issues and getting off sleeping pills and his sense of acute dislocation and despair after his recent marriage break up.

Ben - First MDMA Session (120 mg)

Ben's words

When the medicine came on, I felt an overwhelming sense of joy and happiness and love for myself. I felt a complete break from the sadness and lack of caring I've felt for my own existence for so long. I felt like I could stick my head above the grey clouds and see the sun. It was such an amazing and enjoyable experience.

The most fundamental insight I had was clearly seeing the impact of being raised by my mother had on the person I am today. I was so hard on myself due to recent circumstances; feeling that there was something wrong with me and somehow, I wasn't normal and that I needed to change. This experience made me realise that this was all false. I don't need to change. My mother raised me to be a very caring and loving individual and I'm thankful for that. I can now see that if something doesn't go the way I want it to, I shouldn't look at myself to be at fault. I feel so much more connected to myself again. I was totally disconnected prior to the session. I felt lost inside. I do not feel lost anymore.

I had a very powerful recollection of just how strong my mother's love was for me. I could actually feel the feeling that I had when I was young.

I could see my mother as she was back in the 70s looking after three kids. It helped me to reflect on my current relationship with my mother. There is often frustration and impatience on my behalf when it comes to interacting with her. The day after the session I had two really nice phone calls with Mum. Today I had another one. I've made a plan to spend some time with her on Thursdays. I had never thought of fixing this relationship with my mother as a way of healing. The MDMA took me there and showed me what I needed.

The other insight was about loneliness and being alone. Since my separation I have felt a need to replace what I lost. I no longer have my wife's support as we no longer communicate. I was in a hurry to build a new relationship and was trying with anyone that came on the radar because I didn't like being alone. From the session I realised that it's OK to be alone, that I don't need to have someone to fill any voids. I can be alone and not feel sad or that something is missing.

The next day was an interesting day; I felt a little solemn at first. I think internally I was absorbing all the insights from the MDMA session and restructuring my belief system somewhat. Shortly after that feeling I started to feel calm. I binge watched Seinfeld for most of the day and belly laughed through most of it. I didn't feel like I needed to reach out to anyone but it was OK to just be with me. In the afternoon I had two close friends visit me and had a swim and chat. It was really nice to have people around for a little while. But after that I was alone again and still felt perfectly fine.

During the week afterwards I am still feeling so much better. I went out for breakfast alone and felt totally normal. Prior to MDMA, I would rarely go out and eat by myself. I am still feeling good about myself. I almost cried spontaneously when driving home and even as I type this. I have found myself again. I love myself again. The darkness is gone. I feel happiness, acceptance and understanding of who I am. Reconnection to self. Renewed love for my mother and focus on strengthening that relationship.

I believe there is still some work to be done. I still have a sense of regret for decisions made in my past. I still am unable to let them go. There is still some sort of a bond there to that decision I made to buy that investment that ultimately changed my entire life. I want to let go of that. I want to be able to let go of things that make me sad. I'll learn to see things differently so that I don't look so hard at myself to blame. I think that I did make some progress in this, but I am curious whether MDMA can help in this regard.

I would recommend this to others who have any sort of mental health issues that have been unresolvable through conventional means. This one session did more for me than all of my other psychology sessions have done. The facilitation was perfect. The music selection incredible. The connection I had with the music and lyrics was amazing. I could actually feel the emotions that the author had, through the lyrics. I really enjoyed the frankincense and whatever else was burning. Thank you sounds so inadequate. This therapist has a real gift and I'm thankful from the bottom of my heart for the session. I'm not sure if she truly realises the huge shift she facilitates through these sessions. I really don't know how to thank her.

Ben - Second MDMA Session (120 mg)

Ben's words

I felt there was additional work to be done after the last session. There were some amazing changes in my life subsequent to the first session, in particular repairing and strengthening the relationship with my mother and recently reconnecting with my father. But I was still spending a lot of time living with past regrets and being fearful about the future. My intention for this session was exploring this further with a view to finding a way to manage it better. In other words, to stop the regrets and fear about the past and future.

As the medicine started to take effect, I tried to focus on my intention. But I found it harder and harder to do so. I was really unable to focus on anything at the time. This was a stark contrast to the first session where I had so much mental clarity of past childhood events and had quite a few unexpected insights during the session. I think I told the therapist that I was having trouble focusing and she helped me to relax and surrender to the medicine by breathing.

At the point I started to relax and let go, the experience changed. It became one of pure bliss. I took several extremely relaxing and peaceful 'journeys', for example, I remember flying over a very green field, the sun was shining brightly and there were black and white cows grazing on the grass and mountains in the background. Possibly a scene from my trip to Austria last year.

On another journey I was flying through space. I remember stars and planets. The important thing during these journeys was that I was 100% in the present moment. I suspect in total I had two hours or so in this state. In my normal life it's almost impossible to attain this state; to be totally in the moment and enjoying life at that point in time; not tarnishing existence by reliving past regrets and living in fear of the future.

The main insight I had was that the answer to my current suffering is learning to live in the now. I have started reading 'The Power of Now,' a book I read many years ago that helped me a lot the first time I read it. It's been a really good read so far and I did have some successes in the week after therapy in practicing what I've been reading. However, it's not an easy thing to do and I've had some bad days when I was totally absorbed by past events.

The other insight I had was around when I left mums at 16. I remember feeling sad that my mother wanted me to go. You see, the plan was that I go to live with my father. Up until that point I had had such a wonderful time growing up with my mother, sisters and teenage friends. I didn't want to go to live in another state, but both my parents encouraged it. I'd never been close with my father. I didn't want to go but felt like I had to - because mum said it would be good for me and that I should. The insight I had here was that this was the first time I felt rejected by my mother. She had always been so loving with me up until this point and then for some unknown reason she told me to leave. This could possibly explain why I have such a hard time dealing with rejection in my relationships with women.

The next day I went out with my female friend for a relaxing picnic by the river on the same night after the session. I don't know what went wrong or what triggered her but immediately after the dinner she said she wanted to go home to contemplate (by herself). It was really rushed to - like she had to get home ASAP. This really wasn't what I needed, given the way I was feeling at that time. I was quite shocked by the whole thing.

The next day I was feeling a little bit down about it, but then started to realise that I shouldn't have relied on her anyway. Perhaps I put too much stock in our relationship. I also realised that she has some significant emotional damage from her ex-marriage and therefore I really need to be careful in relying on her (which I've since stopped doing).

The following few days I felt much better. I've been meditating twice daily and enjoying reading 'The Power of Now.' I've also made some huge headway with getting off Zopiclone. I didn't have any from Monday night until Friday - five days in total! The more I read the book and start to practice the suggestions, the better I've felt. I also had quite a successful week at work. I've been journaling and giving gratitude on a daily basis as well and I'm finding that to be very therapeutic. It's good to record feelings and emotions from each day, whether good or bad.

I'm still reading my book as often as possible. I've changed my whole evening routine now, watching far less TV and spending as much time as possible reading my book and meditating in my meditation space. My sleep is much better as well. Five days without Zopiclone was incredible for me. I hope to repeat something similar this week. This therapy has helped me so much. The facilitation was excellent as always. The setting was at my home and I loved it. That room has now become my meditation space where I meditate daily. There is so much positive energy in that room. I love spending time there. I'm thankful for another amazing and enlightening session. I'm continually surprised by the versatility of the medicine and the therapist's adaptability.

Paula, 36, Naturopath

Paula, a petite European with English as a second language was diagnosed with anxiety and depression in 2014. Though she's not currently taking prescription medication she supports herself with vitamins, minerals, and herbs. She has PTSD stemming from sexual abuse that occurred in her early teens.

Her intentions for doing MDMA therapy are fourfold: to lessen her guilt after recently leaving her husband; to release herself from a belief that she owes him something and has to wait for him to be happy in order for her to move on and be happy; to break the feeling of mental control he has over her; and to help control her anxiety related to the custody battle over their son. Her ex-husband has predominant custody. Paula picks him up after school, has him on weekends and when the ex-husband says she can. She believes he is using their son as a pawn to control her. Because she felt guilty for leaving him, she allowed this to happen. She'd tried both ayahuasca and psilocybin a few months ago with the intention of relieving her debilitating anxiety.

Paula - First MDMA session (110 mg)

Paula's words

I felt the medicine move through my body. It came on abruptly, forcing itself on me. In the past I've always fought. I experienced physical discomfort: hot and cold flushes, tingling, muscle heaviness, and cold extremities. I felt like taking an antidote to make it stop. But then I thought - just give it a few minutes, it'll get better.

As I was waiting for something more profound or significant the experience started to take shape. I was in complete darkness then a big, dark blue, metal locked gate presented itself to me. I knew I had a key. I was staring at the door that I wasn't quite ready to open. Somehow, I inherently knew there was someone in there. Eventually, I put the key in the door, waited till I was ready, then unlocked the door. However, I knew I couldn't open the door. He had too. He allowed the door to open and opened it telepathically.

I walked through the door to what I perceived was almost complete nihilism. In the nothingness was a small 2' x 2' wall. It was dark blue marble, almost black. I felt a boy child hiding behind it. I saw a head poking out from behind the wall, coming in and out in fear hiding to see who entered. I felt myself become very quiet and peaceful so as not to invade his space. Approaching slowly and carefully - every step towards him was with his permission and trust and time. He was like a scared animal. He was sitting with his back to the wall. I could see from the side and perceive in different perspectives. I decided to sit with my back opposite to his, back-to-back but on the opposite side of the wall.

Before, when he was poking his head out, I could see his eyes were full of fear and sadness. We started communicating telepathically. I knew I was responsible for him. He said, 'Why did you leave me here alone for so long?' I said, 'If I knew you were here, I would have come earlier.' We spoke some more, but I can't recollect what was said, 'I came here to release you. I can take you with me? You can come with me.' But he didn't want to go. I said, 'It's full of fear and sadness here.' He said, 'This place might be full of fear and sadness, but it's familiar to me and that gives me some comfort.'

His whole existence doesn't know anything else. I knew I wouldn't be able to convince him with words or thoughts, so I opened my heart and felt my energy radiate towards him. A pure radiant love. Slowly, he came over to me. I held him tightly in my arms with his head on my chest. I was welcoming him in with the love radiating from me. Once he was in my arms, I realised the love flowing out from me was motherly love. It felt like he had never received any before. When he allowed himself to absorb my love, he was peaceful and calm - no longer scared or fearful.

While absorbing my love he merging into my chest. When he merged fully, I could feel him in my heart. A permanent place in my heart. Even now I feel him there. Even though I knew he was now a part of me, I mentally stuck around in his landscape so that he knew I was around. He asked me to take care and protect him. I felt like I'd lost him and now I had found him. He forgave me quickly. So that promise is important. I have to take care of myself in order to take care of him. If I'm happy with myself I don't really have to do much, as he will feel it when he reaches my heart and visualises it. I only realised I was missing something when he came back. I felt complete and right and at ease; Relieved.

I was sexually abused when I was moving into my teenage years. Before the medicine kicked in, the therapist had asked me, 'What was your parent's reaction to the situation?' I said my dad made a strange face and said, 'I knew the guy was a little bit weird.' I exactly remember his words and that facial expression. My mom was a nurse and she met the perpetrator during some sort of medical procedure. He offered us free weekly math lessons. She never questioned why the doors were locked when we were studying, or why he was kissing and hugging us so much. She got very emotional, upset and angry when my sister told her that I was sexually assaulted for years. She was screaming that I was making it up so I didn't have to study. After that the matter was never discussed again. My sister who was also abused by him told him to never come back or she'd call the police. He never did.

My understanding of the experience is; when I was going through this horrible time my Mum wasn't there for me. She didn't believe me. She didn't show motherly love and she didn't provide the protection I needed at that moment. I was scared, ashamed, and sad. I didn't deal with my feelings - I just put them away; behind 'the wall,' where they remained hidden for all those years.

In my MDMA experience I knew that the thing hiding behind the wall was the representation of how I felt when it happened. I wondered why it was in the shape of a little alien. But it doesn't matter. What matters is what it represents. I finally found it in the deepest and darkest corner of myself. To be able to release myself from that sadness and guilt, I had to come as a mother and bring my motherly unconditional love, faith and compassion and whatever the mother has to protect and care for her child. I never blamed my mother for her reaction or the lack of an appropriate one. She didn't know what to do with that information. It was so taboo back then. She probably hid her feelings behind the wall just like I did.

When I finally found the courage to leave my dysfunctional marriage, months passed and I would still feel guilt that I'd left. I questioned whether the emotional abuse that I'd experienced from my husband was a good enough reason to leave. It's like I didn't believe myself. I didn't trust myself that I was making the right decision. Standing up for myself was so foreign to me. Now I feel in control of whom and how I want to be. I feel I have the power to decide for myself. I believe that if something doesn't feel right, I'll investigate and protect myself from it, instead of feeling crushed and overtaken by it. Now I feel strength. Nowadays dealing with my ex-partner is so much easier because the emotional load and guilt are not present. I feel space. I don't feel him in my chest and in my thoughts constantly.

After the session I felt very fragile for a day. I wanted to rest and be surrounded by people with good energy. I could clearly feel how much bad energy my ex-husband brings. I have to protect myself from it, if I want to maintain the inner peace I'd achieved during the session. It took me three days to digest and process everything and another to see how the experience had transformed my interactions with my ex-husband. I saw the effect he has on me - or more precisely the effect he doesn't have on me.

I would consciously go back to my MDMA experience and practice to maintain that inner peace. I had one anxiety attack about 48 hours after the session. I felt like the cloud of anxiety was trying to get back into my chest where it lived for many years. It took me about 50 minutes to remove it from my body; to again maintain my inner peace and space. It's been a week and it hasn't come back, but if it does, I feel equipped to not allow it to. It now feels like I have a space and time to deal with it before it enters. I've done it once; I know I can do it again.

The noticeable and enduring effects are that I'm very much less anxious, more equipped, and prepared. I will take it again because I believe in it. I still have some issues I want to deal with. I would absolutely recommend it to others. The therapist was very kind in supported my needs during the session; mainly of being gently touched, holding my hand, caring for me and having good intentions. It's so sad that this medicine has been unavailable to us for so long. It's sad that there are people out there who fight for this medicine to remain illegal. What a shame.

Paula - Second MDMA Session (122 mg)

Paula's words

My intention was to address my eyebrow plucking, (trichotillomania) skin picking, and nail biting when I'm anxious.

This time the medicine made me feel physically uncomfortable with a body ache throughout the session and strong heart palpitations when it kicked in. This lasted about 15 minutes. Compared to my first session the sensations and memories of the experience are not so clear. I remember bits and pieces. For instance; I got to feel how my skin feels when I'm anxious. I remember my skin was screaming and I felt actual physical pain which I can't really remember now. It was very painful, but I can't remember the physical sensation. I remember very clearly most of my first session: what happened, how it happened and how it made me feel. The memories of my feelings from the session help me comprehend the experience, its meaning in my life, and changes I want to implement.

When the medicine started to work, it immediately told me to pay attention to my skin. I felt the skin which covers my entire body is really thick and heavily layered, specifically my arms and hands. I found it very heavy. My skin and I didn't know of each other's existence - similar to my feelings of sadness and fear that were hidden away behind the wall in my first session. My skin and myself, were a separate entity; we didn't know we are supposed to be one. The skin was attached to my body, but we were surprised to find out that there is more than just 'us.' For me and my body, the skin is something other than just the skin.

This time there was no telepathic communication; I could only feel. The skin let me experience its physical pain, during my anxieties. I thought no wonder the skin looks for a way to release its emotions somehow. I felt under my skin a very strong throbbing, and tingling sensation. My whole body was undergoing some sort of scanning which was painful. I lay flat on my back and allowed it to happen. The scanning would start at my feet go a few centimetres up, return back to my feet, and go further up each time. Just as it reached my throat, I felt the medicine wearing off. It felt like whatever was being removed from my body didn't get released completely - it got stuck at my throat. (For three days after the session, I had a sore throat.) Later, I saw myself laying down in front of me - just my skin, (no body), with my face shape, hand shape, toes and such. It was unzipped from the top to bottom on the left side of my body, just lying there. More happened but that's all I can remember.

People have the inner power and knowledge to heal themselves from the inside. I'm talking about emotional healing. Many diseases originate from an unbalanced and heavily disturbed emotional state. This is a good place to start to address other diseases. I hope I expressed myself accurately.

My skin had the memories of my physical and emotional abuse trapped in it from my entire life. I acknowledged my skin's existence and its pain. Now I have feelings towards my skin. I see it as a living and feeling part of my body. I will care for it. I remember looking at my skin in front of me. I think my old skin was slipped off and was replaced with a new one.

After this session I was able to speak to my friends right away and wanted to go to the nearby beach – unlike my previous experience where I felt really unwell and didn't want to be looked at or talk for hours. I had low energy and was rundown. It took me two days to sort of recover. The next day I felt tingling under my skin, and it felt very heavy.

It's been four days since the session and amazingly, I haven't touched my eyebrows. I went to a beauty salon the next day. I felt I wanted to physically look after myself and treat my skin with some good relaxing touch. Anxiety has not paid me a visit yet; I've not even had the warmth in my stomach or unwanted thoughts. This feels really good. I need more time to decide if there's any need for another session. I've learnt a lot about myself. Perhaps this knowledge will be enough to keep working on and looking after myself. The therapist gave me everything I needed to feel safe and cared for. I was not ashamed or uncomfortable to show what I felt and experienced during the medicine. I knew she would understand my behaviour.

Paul, 50, School Teacher

Eighteen months ago, shortly after his marriage had ended, Paul was admitted to a psychiatric ward in a drug-induced psychosis after an alcohol and marijuana binge. He was diagnosed with depression, anxiety and CPTSD and prescribed Olanzapine (an antipsychotic). He attempted suicide shortly after this and believes it was the medication that made him suicidal. He hasn't been on any medication for over 12 months. Since his release from hospital, he changed track and started focusing on health and fitness. He lost weight, eats healthily and goes regularly to the gym.

Raised in a strict Mormon family, at the tender age of 18, Paul met a girl from his church and fell in love. They married two years later and quickly started a family. His wife has been his only ever partner. They eventually left the church and moved interstate. They started smoking marijuana regularly and drinking quite a lot. Since his marriage ended Paul has struggled with ambivalence about rekindling the marriage and the desire to truly find himself - have some adventures and maybe relive some of his lost youth.

Prior to joining the church both of his parents had been big drinkers, possibly alcoholic. Paul had experienced childhood sexual abuse from three different male perpetrators; a cousin, a neighbour, and a stranger who came to one of his parent's parties. Paul's intention for doing the medicine session was to overcome his feelings of low self-worth.

Paul - First MDMA session (155 mg)

Note: The initial dose of 125 mg was increased as it didn't seem to be having a strong effect.

Paul's words

During the active effect I felt nothing - no joy or pain or anything for that matter. I just felt fully present. I felt loved and an overwhelming sense that everything was OK.

At one stage I felt the need to call out to the therapist but didn't even know why. She intuitively guided me back into one of my sexual abuse memories that we'd discussed in the assessment session. I didn't realise that it had impacted me so much; I didn't realise there was still so much pain around those childhood and teenage events that obviously hadn't been healed. My head told me, "I'm good," but this wasn't the case, and I didn't even know it.

I find it difficult getting out of my head. It's been my normal for as long as I can remember. I have been thinking into the future and living in the past so much that it has become my default mechanism. I have been searching for happiness as quantified by a particular milestone or event, primarily based around things of monetary value. My family was poor compared to my wife's family and I have been comparing a part of my self-worth as a husband and father on what I couldn't give them financially. I would say, "I did good," but deep down I felt a failure in that area. I have come to realise this perceived happiness has not been in actuality the happiness I received as a result of attaining those milestones and events. In fact, it's been fleeting at best and has led to depression.

I realise that the traditional medical professionals don't have the necessary tools, knowledge or experience to assist me. I don't have to listen to everyone's advice no matter how many accolades, degrees, and experience they have. And I don't have to think 'I' know stuff just because I've read a book and can remember stuff.

I can be present by staying in the now. I can actually be happy now, in this moment. It's weird in a way because it goes against the ingrained worldly programming I have been brought up with; but it's also very liberating.

The next day I had zero come-down effects. I stayed in bed for three hours this morning and just read my journal and listened to calming shamanic instrumental music. I contemplated the insights I gained and this sense of peace I now have. The words in my mind say, "All is well, all is well."

I want to do ayahuasca next because I have all these unanswered questions and it feels like I've been searching my whole life for something. It feels like I kind of don't fit into this reality. It feels like something is missing. I am frustrated by things. I have placed value and significance on tangible things, but they never bring the perceived joy I would have assumed would have come and that I thought would have aligned to my feeling prior to the gaining of that 'thing.' It's like I've been programmed to expect happiness from tangibles and I need to let that go; but I don't know how. I would definitely recommend this to others. The facilitation felt right; the prayers, the incense, the music, the guide. I'm so very glad I found her and I thank her so much for doing this work.

A journal entry I made immediately after the session while still somewhat under the effects.

Thank you for opening the door. That little boy is loved, thank you. We always had him; you just couldn't feel our love for you. You were always loved. I love you. This experience of pain and feelings of worthlessness and not believing in your dreams. Your separation from your sweetheart, of trying to end your life, the hell you went through, it forged your beautiful heart. Through your hurt you loved others, it humbled you.

It broke you in many ways, but it softened your heart. Your heart remained soft through adversity. I know you wouldn't change a thing because who you are, this is, right here, right now. The therapist said you have superpowers and she meant it.

It's your time, Paul. It's your time. You have always done the best you can with the resources available and now you are prepared too truly live. The plants are calling you. Keep going. I have so much to show you and share with you. I love you. Your world is changing quickly for your good, just keep moving in the direction of that beautiful heart of yours. You have such a beautiful heart, Paul. You are such a beautiful being. You will realise more and more, how much you have to offer the world. Do not doubt, dream and Be. Create and Be. You are so loved. I love you so, so much.

You saw the therapist when you opened your eyes, and she was so beautiful because you actually saw into her. You are loved. You are worthy. You are beautiful. You saw her angelic-ness and her pure beautifulness because that's possible only through truly loving yourself. All you have to do today is relax. Don't jump on your phone. Don't think of work or family or anything for that matter. Just be here with me. I got you, Paul. I got you. I love you and I will never tire of saying that because it is what it is.

I was guided to call my big sister; we haven't spoken since Dad's funeral. I needed to tell her I love her and share the experience I had with my beautiful guide. She cried. She wished she could have been there for me, but I explained it was for my good. My heart would not have been softened and my capacity to unconditionally love and be present when someone is sharing wouldn't have been there.

My adversities have made me who I am. I love me - therefore I love you T (one of my abusers). I love you and I forgive you. It's OK. Let he who is without sin cast the first stone. I don't think people need to go through child abuse to get to a place of love (eventually), it was my lot to have. I don't have all the answers but I'm OK with that today. I love me completely. My journey has begun.

A little boy cried but nobody heard. The little boy couldn't hear himself cry either because there was no noise. His soul cried. Then days turned to weeks, turned to months and to years. That little boy is now 50 years old. He is lost, has been lost all these years. How can the 50-year-old man explain his hurt? He doesn't know it, but the crying soul does not relent. Then he finds an angel and this beautiful angel guides the man back to comfort the boy. And he heals himself.

My soul is at peace. The little boy is loved. I got you, I got you little Paul, it's OK, I am here now. It's OK. I got you. I love you little Paul. I'm here now. The angel embraces us. Why should we mourn or think our lot is hard? Tis' not so, all is right. May the Lord of peace himself give you his peace at all times and in every situation. Let the peace that comes from Christ rule in your hearts. For as members of one body, you are called to live in peace.

Stephanie, 35, Environmentalist

Stephanie suffers from depression, anxiety, and PTSD. She takes CBD oil for health purposes but stopped a week prior to her MDMA session. She is vegan and lives a healthy, active, sporty life. She doesn't drink or take drugs recreationally.

Stephanie had a very difficult relationship with her mother who was emotionally abusive and cold. She would give Stephanie an A4 list of chores to do from a very young age. She also had to work part time from age 14 and would start her job at McDonald's at 4am. Her mum sometimes hit her in the face and called her a slut and eventually kicked her out of home. Her mum was very overweight and Stephanie believes that this is what caused her own issues with food; because she didn't want to be like her mum.

Her father (not married to her mum), left when she was seven and died when she was seventeen. She has abandonment issues around him leaving her and says she went off the rails around this time. He had four other children to four different women. From ages 17 to 22, Stephanie had older boyfriends, went a bit wild and got into drugs. She later straightened herself out and went to university. She distrusts and dislikes men and says that some decisions need to be made around her current relationship and other issues regarding her relationships in general.

She'd done considerable research on psychedelic healing and her motivation for doing this therapy is that she's just known it was right for her for some time and believes it will allow her to access solutions from within herself.

Stephanie - First MDMA session (135 mg)

Stephanie's words

I know I need to heal my past trauma to become a better person. I don't know how to other than with MDMA because I've tried everything else. I want to forgive myself, trust myself, love others, learn to forgive and trust others. I want to feel comfortable in my body and ultimately (after I address my trauma), discover who I really am.

During the active effects I felt my voice move from my head to my neck. I felt it in my neck and stomach; a fluttery opening. I felt realisations come to me one after another like a train. I didn't consider anything, they just landed on me. I felt open, receptive and curious. I could feel my jaw quiver and my palms sweat. I realised I had a lot to uncover in my day-to-day life before I could go deeper. I was deeply concerned with control. I didn't trust myself, and that is why I don't trust others. I forgave my mother and felt some empathy for her. I finally found out her motive for her doing some of the things she did to me, particularly kicking me out of home. I agreed with her reasoning.

I discovered that I did trust my partner and I do want to be with him; a question that has caused me great concern for over a year now. I didn't know I wanted to come and solve that with this session, but I ended up with that resolution. Also, I discovered that I had only felt connected to a previous partner because of my strong need for financial security and a family. I realised that the only concerns I really had with my current partner is around the lack of those two things.

I realised my feelings of inadequacy were linked to my lack of trust in myself. My lack of trust came from some damaging decisions that I made from the age of 17 to 21 years old, that I can't understand at all. I still don't know how I made those really bad decisions. Possibly, that's why I don't trust myself. I discovered how much I wanted to be loved as a child when my father left. How much I needed my Mum to fight for me, and how much hatred had come from the fact she didn't fight for me. I also realised I'd been selfish at work. I need to think more about how I can improve that. I realised I am a protector.

I couldn't sleep until the early morning, around 1:00 AM, but I took the medicine at 1:00 PM. In future I would like to take it earlier in the day, so my workday isn't impacted. I didn't feel like eating, but did eat because I knew I needed to. I had no comedown effects or negative feelings other than sadness that the realisations had stopped flowing!

The noticeable enduring effects are, that I feel I have more empathy and a desire to talk to others and reach out to people more. I would like to do this therapy again as I feel like I've only scraped the surface, which was very needed. My initial desire is to heal this lack of trust in myself, this fear of security, and learn to forgive. It's a very profound medicine, very effective, and the only tool possible to heal yourself inside.

The facilitator was wonderful; I felt comfortable and secure, both spiritually and physically. She let the medicine pick the path and ensured I stayed on it. She guided my thoughts to see things from multiple angles and it's obvious she has walked this path before, herself.

This medicine must be available to people! There were times I was far more desperate, more alone, and more damaged. I have made it through and am doing this now from a fairly good place. I wish I could have had this when I needed it the most, rather than now, when I just want it the most.

Martin, 50, Social Worker

Following a Hepatitis C treatment five years ago, Martin's depression had spiralled down and was getting increasingly worse. Martin grew up in a low socioeconomic area, besieged by drugs and addiction and by the age of 23 was a heroin addict. At age 26 he was diagnosed with alcohol and benzodiazepine dependence; and seven years later, anxiety. He says he's suffered from undiagnosed CPTSD for years. Martin had been on a cocktail of medications from a very early age; Methadone for 20 years until 2009; different benzodiazepines and antidepressants between 1990 and 2009. He's done exceedingly well to get off all these prescription drugs; particularly Methadone and benzodiazepines which are a far more tenacious addiction and a harder detox process than most, (if not all), street drugs. Methadone's nickname is liquid handcuffs for good reason. Currently Martin is free of all prescription drugs and has been completely drug free and sober for five years. He attends AA meetings.

For many years Martin has suffered from debilitating sleep paralysis where he wakes several times a night screaming. While he's tried most psychedelics in the past, it was never in a therapeutic context. His motivation for doing psychedelic therapy, is his desperation and suicidality; in his words - his inability to bring himself to take the last three steps off a high-rise hotel in June 2021. Just weeks before his MDMA therapy session, he had booked a room on level 41, with the intention of killing himself. He took the fire escape but while up there, he'd become conflicted about his five-year-old grandson and what it might do to him if he jumped. He said that afterwards, he felt like the walking dead, doomed to suffer for eternity. So, his motivation is to get some relief or eventually kill himself. Despite some reservations around his emotional state, I felt compelled to help him.

Martin - First MDMA session (135 mg)

Martin's Words

The prayer for beautiful blessings from whatever power holds our Universe so perfectly and gently in its soft, glorious, silken, feather-like hands; the smudging, the incense, the words, the soft sounds and the venue; I simply have no words. All I can say is that even though I had not yet taken the medicine, I felt safe, loved and protected. The whole thing woven together was unlike anything I'd ever done before. I think that made it just so perfect because it was brand new for me. I'm usually so analytical and formula driven, so much so that everything must be boxed, labelled, stacked in just the right place, the right colour, the right size. I must know exactly what's going to happen because to not know, to be in something unusual, is very frightening to me. Paradoxically, here I was, everything contrary to everything I usually know, feel, believe and do - yet I felt completely safe. The therapist created such an amazingly unexpected, unknown, unexperienced, unjudged, unconditioned space. What I'm saying is that it created a brand-new open space; a blank context on which to build something new.

I took the medicine - we talked for a bit and then I put the eyeshades on, lay down and tried to relax - to give myself over to whatever was going to happen. The music started - the shades were drawn. I sensed some smells from the incense, and I just lay there with my eye shade on and with all my heart, handed myself over to Mother Universe and asked that she take me home and hold me gently.

The active effects I first sensed at around 20 minutes; from there it's difficult to judge because time truly lost meaning. But I'd estimate I jumped in the deep at around the 45–60-minute mark. My first sensations were of a warmth that seemed to grow from within my throat. It moved up towards my shoulders then down across my back and my spine, right through my thoracic region, and it just seemed to flow; ebbs and flows in and out. It was a feeling of familiarity. It was a feeling of being protected and loved no matter what, of gentleness and kindness. Today was to be about healing, about protection, about unknowing it, about self-acceptance and self-love.

The music, the smells of the incense, the seal of the room, everything that happened in this space was integral to the experience. It made the whole process happen in ebbs and flows, as if I would spiral in and then spiral back out, allowing me time to be confronted, then to look, to feel, to settle, not so much integrate, but to just join some dots. It was so incredibly gentle. The way the music would change, the smells would change, the sounds would change. The feel of the room was so integral in the journey. The way I experienced it, felt organic and natural and wavy. It just kind of weaved its way, like it was weaving a beautiful garment and joining all the patches of my life; my experiences, thoughts, emotions and feelings into a continuous, beautiful, synchronistic, blanket.

About 45 minutes after taking the medicine, I was feeling loved and protected but I was wondering where this was going. That's when things started to happen. Suddenly I saw my five-year-old grandson looking at me with his little eyes, beckoning me to come with him. His look gave me a feeling of trust and love. I felt safe, like he wanted to show me something. It was as if he was taking me through tunnels of my life and through my mind, joining dots that I never saw or knew existed, burrowing under and through things in my mind. The best way to describe it, was that he led me through a house, a house of many rooms, and told me to let go of any preconceived ideas, any judgments, anything I might think was anywhere. He said just leave these things and come with me, and so I did. Each frame seemed to hide a part of my life and experience; it was as if I kind of knew or expected what might be in there, but I wasn't sure.

As I approached the first door with my grandson I was scared, very scared, but he told me it would be OK. He told me I should come in with him and eventually, after much comforting from him I went into that room and he came in with me. When we opened the door and I looked inside I couldn't believe what I saw. I expected to find something scary but it wasn't at all, the fear wasn't real, because there in front of me, sitting on his upended calico schoolbag was five-year-old me sitting in the backyard of my house in 1973, my first day at big school. But I was crying. I was scared. My grandson ran over to me and put his arm around me and started laughing and playing with the five-year-old me. They talked and whispered, they laughed, they looked back at me as if to tell me that they loved me, they weren't laughing at me, they weren't talking about me, they were me, both of them, each one different and yet the same.

The medicine had allowed me to see beauty in myself, because I could see it in the little 5-year-old me. I normally hate the sight of myself, but to see the five-year-old me there with my beautiful little grandson, I could not do anything but love myself. The medicine was able to make me have compassion for myself. The insight was that, I'm not horrible, I'm not ugly, I'm not dirty, I'm not disgusting, and I'm not a fraud. There was a beautiful little me there, a curious, beautiful little Martin, looking, wishing, hoping at the curious world, wondering what would be, what would I become, what would I do, what fun would I have, who would I meet.

Suddenly I had a feeling of foreboding, a realisation that life isn't going to be all sunshine and happiness, that there are scary things that happened too. I sensed that we're about to leave this room and I was right - we were. My grandson left, he told me he'd be back. The five-year-old me now took my hand and we moved down a hole towards still more rooms. As we moved down the hole, I sensed all about me ugliness, despicable things, dirty things, horrible smells, as if thin white sheet was holding these things back and there were these merging, disgusting, despicable shadows all about, there were horrible muttering words there was stench and despicable smell everywhere. It was horrible.

I was so frightened, but the little me just kept looking at me and said don't look to the side, you don't need to know that stuff, just follow me I'm not going to hurt you. It's going to be OK. I felt like weeping. I felt like crying and suddenly I realised I felt a deep feeling I've never felt before. I have never felt anything before. My life has been numb, full of numbness and now I feel something that is tragic and beautiful and divine and ugly and scary and glorious and amazing and wonderful and unending and it's going to hurt me and it's going to save me and it's going to kill me, and it's going to love me.

It was a mix of everything, of opposites. I have no words just yet to describe it. The thing I realised is that my whole life, I have felt nothing. I never understood emotion. I could never have it in the right place. I was good at acting emotions. I was good at looking like I knew what was wrong; looking like I understood or I could read the situation, but I could not. I never felt like I was feeling the way I should at any given moment. I was confused by these things my whole life.

So, the little 5-year-old me and I, we approached another room. I didn't want to go in this room. I felt a deep resistance. I was really scared and I remember all my muscles tensing up physically as I lay on the couch. I remember trying to hug myself or squeeze myself. I remember pushing my face into the couch. I didn't want to go in there and I remember trying to push myself away from the door, but the little me said it would be OK. The little man said he would come in there with me, but he said he couldn't take me all the way through but there are many others inside, someone that I loved would be there.

So, with much trepidation, and with a little help from the 5-year-old me, we opened the door. I thought I knew what would be in there; I thought it would be something dirty, something horrible, something I could point out and blame; it's your fault, you're the reason for all of this. And what I saw in that room was five-year-old me again, but a different one and I was screaming - I was yelling at God. I was yelling and screaming at the universe, 'Why are you doing this to me - why did you make me suffer like this? I'm only a little boy. Why did you do these things to me? What did I do wrong? What did I do to deserve this?' I felt like a fraud. I had this realisation that I could never accept anything you could have given me, anything, and I would never have felt, because I didn't understand or know anything. I felt like I was never meant to be anywhere. These were very confusing realisations and as I was screaming out, I was screaming please don't ever let me be like my dad. I never want to be like my dad. I hate my dad he is a ******* I don't want to be that man. I hate my father.

Now the five-year-old me said, 'You need to go into this next room and you're going to have to go in there alone. I can't go in there with you now. I can't go in there with you but you need to.' I didn't want to go in there. I thought I knew what would be in there and I didn't want to see it. I didn't want to know it. Let it be there, let it stay there, keep it locked up there. I don't need that to heal. Then I felt the mother universe - that she loved me, that she wouldn't let anything in that room hurt me; that I should look in there and it would be OK. So the mother universe opened the door for me because I couldn't.

Once the doors had been opened, I saw what was in there. I was floored, my mouth ajar, as if I had just fallen backwards off a cliff. I couldn't believe how beautifully wrong I was. I had screamed at God that I didn't want to be whatever it was, I didn't want to be. I didn't want to be that anger, that violence, that horrible, that despicable thing. I didn't want to be that stuff. I begged God not to make me that stuff, and so he didn't.

He gave me exactly what I asked for. He made me the opposite of that. He made me gentle. He made me beautiful. He made me love. He made me kind. He made me funny. He made me smart. He made me caring. He made me small. He made me quiet. He made me whole. He made me OK. The mother father universe gave me everything I could have ever wanted and everything I asked not to be. It gave me that and more but there was a price to pay for those things and it wasn't a punishment; it was as if to know how beautiful I was, I had to experience how ugly things can be.

I had a realisation, that I have always looked at the world so analytically it's either; black or white, up or down, in or out, good or bad, accept or reject. How wrong I was. The answer to that question doesn't lie at the extremes, at the edges, it's in the middle, it's not black or white it's a blend, it's not right or wrong, it's both. It's not love or hate, it's connection; two sides of the same coin.

That was my realisation. Nothing in this universe is wasted, everything is perfect, everything is just as it should be. If we look at the small details of things, they may appear imperfect - like a beautiful quilt. You can look at one little imperfection and think, 'oh dear that's a mistake.' But when we look at the whole quilt, it's so beautifully imperfect. My realisation was that God made me perfectly broken so that I might discover what it is to repair, to love, to make, to break, to not be at a destination, but to just be, just to be together, nothing is in isolation, life is a beautiful blend of serendipitous synchronicity.

I had no come down effect what-so-ever it just gradually eased off. I got home about six hours after taking the medicine. I felt fine, perhaps a little woozy but happy and loved. I had a shower and got into bed, and slept for nearly 12 hours, no nightmares, no sleep paralysis, no screaming, just a beautiful, beautiful, restful sleep. I went to bed at about 8:00 PM and was asleep by about 8:30 PM, and I didn't wake up till about 8:00 AM the next morning. I was completely refreshed, no hangover whatsoever.

During the following week my mood felt relieved. It was like there was no cloud hanging over me. But toward the end of the first week, I started to feel as if I was slipping back down somewhere, into somewhere dark. Then I caught a virus, it felt like a cold, or a respiratory tract infection, but I had this sense about me, that it was meant to be, that the mother medicine was making this happen, that this was about being regenerated like a chrysalis, it was meant to be. I spent nearly two weeks sick in bed.

I never normally journal, but during this thick sickness I made voice recordings because for those two weeks, as I was sick, it was like I was on a journey like a dream, like I was on a two-week trip. And in that time, to me at least, it felt as if I was being renewed. This virus was breaking me down and renewing me. I had some amazing insights during those two weeks - dreams, incredible things. It was like the MDMA experience. It was like the psychedelic experience was a key and it unlocked this beautiful doorway and I could never have imagined where it took me. The journey has been so profound. I feel as if I've emerged from The Cave a truly new person - a softer, kinder, gentler soul; someone that's able to say things.

I would see not coincidences but synchronicity everywhere. I see it everywhere I look. Now I see purpose and I see reason, unconditional purpose, unconditional reason. I see abundant love. I feel abundant gratitude. This is beyond my wildest dreams. This last month I was convinced I was going insane, surely my life couldn't change like this, not like this, because this is beautiful. I'm a new person and I can feel things now. I can truly feel things now. I can weep and I can cry and I can honour experiences for other people, especially my beautiful wife. She has been and is so much alongside me and now it's my time to honour her so that I might transmute the pain she's experienced with me, as an expression of love for her, because she is truly amazing; as am I.

I am truly amazing. We are all truly beautiful and amazing. It feels like a fairy-tale. My life seems like a fairy-tale now, the whole world seems like a fairy tale. I feel a connection like I've never felt before. Had the therapist told me that this was how I would feel, I would not have understood it. She could not have told me this because my mind wasn't capable of comprehending. I feel like I've discovered a brand-new language, that I was initially put on this earth with the wrong instruction manual, the wrong language, the wrong everything, even perhaps the wrong gender. Now I'm not saying I want a sex change or anything, what I'm saying is that I love this beautiful feminine gentleness, this quietness, this beauty. This is truly a gift. I am overflowing with abundant love and gratitude.

The more I talk about this, write it down, talk to myself, or another person, it's as if it can move on and new stuff can come through and the coincidences and the synchronicity are amazing. I'm able to use all these experiences I have. They just seem to flow into every day. It's like a magical story I never imagined possible, like this is, it's just so wonderful.

I would take it again. For a while I didn't think I would need to, but realised that this process is so beautifully gentle for a reason; it's like layers of an onion, that get removed so gently. Sometimes we just need a key to unlock another little door in another little room in this house of stories that is my life.

I would absolutely recommend this to others. I have such trust for the therapist. She brings a gift to the world. The setting and the facilitation were perfect beyond description; the way I could look out over the ocean when I got there just gave me this sense of renewal and a refreshing. I felt so safe there; the smells of the incense and sounds of the music, I don't have the words to describe it. It all just beautifully mixed together and synced perfectly. I felt loved. I felt safe. I was never scared. I could be vulnerable without being hurt. Not once did I panic. It was amazing. What she does here is an amazing gift, such a beautiful selfless gift. I am forever indebted to her. If I had a billion dollars that wouldn't be enough to pay her for this. What she's given me, is my life. I feel like I've just been born, that I've just arrived on this planet.

Shannon, 46, Sales Representative

Shannon was diagnosed with depression as a teen but managed to avoid taking antidepressants. She self-medicated with alcohol and drugs and eventually ended up in AA at age 28. She was diagnosed with CPTSD shortly after getting sober. She started taking antidepressants at five years sober and came off them 10 years later in order to safely drink ayahuasca, by which time she was sober for 15 years.

She has a horrific history of sexual abuse: including incest from her father; sexual abuse by a neighbour; an elderly man from her pony club; and a stranger down at her local playground. She has large memory blanks of her life before the age of fourteen.

Shannon grew up in a middle class, volatile and unpredictable home. She says it all looked good on the outside but was pretty horrific on the inside. Her father, was an ex-military man with possible PTSD and alcoholism. He was physically violent, abusive and controlling towards her mother and the rest of the family. Shannon would attempt to stand up to him when he was berating or hitting other family members but usually paid dearly for her efforts.

She describes her mother as codependent - an indoctrinated Catholic who married young and quickly had four children. A woman who believed you stayed married for life through thick and thin – come hell or high water. Her mum was highly invested in maintaining good appearances for the neighbours. Although she cleaned and cooked and looked after their physical needs, she was not supportive emotionally. She was highly critical of Shannon and intolerant of her frankness and push for autonomy.

Shannon began running away from home at age thirteen and was put in a girl's home for a few months at age of fourteen. She spent a couple of months in a hospital ward for psychological medicine and was eventually kicked out of home aged fourteen – but says she gladly went.

Her intention for this MDMA session is to gain access to repressed memories from her childhood and fill in some missing gaps in her life, prior to the age of fourteen. She has previously had ayahuasca and psilocybin therapy to treat her CPTSD, prior to this MDMA session. (See - psilocybin and ayahuasca)

Shannon - First MDMA Session - 110 mgs

Shannon's words

I never thought I'd take MDMA being in AA recovery, but I'm so glad I did. It truly was lifechanging even after the other medicines I have experienced. It was such a powerful experience. I think MDMA gives you clearer and better access to your repressed memories than any of the other medicines.

It took about forty minutes to come on and WOW - I just sank into a truly remarkable gift; my body felt held in the tender hands of sublime love. I felt so relaxed, possibly for the first time in my life. The music was a scintillating grace to my ears and I felt a deep sense of peace and the presence of pure divine love. Though my relaxation was profound and deep my mind was fully alert and completely in the present moment. I experienced a full presence in the here and now and a peace so sublime. I luxuriated in this indescribable bliss for hours.

I didn't care much about anything. I just kept repeating to myself; 'I love you; I love you; I love you, beautiful girl.' I felt such a deep sense of love for myself and the deepest relaxation. Such deep peace and healing. I hugged myself and massaged my arms. There were no revelations or insights, just profound love.

Sometime later after the medicine wore off, I took the dog for a walk to the beach. I felt fully present in my body like my soul had been retrieved. I felt grounded and part of the community, not separate or dissociated. I sat on the waterfront, relaxed and alert, watching people happily. I conversed easily with a couple of dog owners. Back at home, I watched the movie, 'Glass Castle,' and cried trying to remember a happy memory with my father. I really couldn't. Everything was tainted with his need to dominate and control.

There were no come down effects. Two days later I was still feeling the afterglow and still feeling very relaxed. I knew I'd witnessed a miracle and had discovered something incredibly special. Compared to the other medicines I've tried; (Ayahuasca and Psilocybin) MDMA has been the gentlest and most effective healing for my PTSD. It wasn't re-traumatising like ayahuasca and needless to say, we trauma survivors really don't really need any more trauma. The plant medicines are super intense but MDMA is gentle yet still incredibly effective; though some people might need a stronger encounter with Ayahuasca to break through their defences.

Shannon - Second MDMA Session – 130 mgs

Shannon's words

It started out lovely to begin with, similar to last time - but then, just as my body started to deeply relax, I started having involuntary jerking movements, rhythmic movements, like someone was having sex with me. I felt young and was whimpering like a child. It felt like I was having a full-on body memory. I was an adult observing myself as a small child, transported far back in time. This jerking went on for what seemed like ages.

Although I was relaxed, I was deeply shocked at the same time, after my first beautiful session. I hadn't been expecting this and was glad I had someone with me, although it was a bit embarrassing to have someone witness this; I think it would have been like witnessing a child getting sexually abused. It's still a little bit unclear but that's what it felt like.

Once again, there were no come down effects and I felt very relaxed afterwards. But now there is a bit of anxiety and shock. I feel that my subconscious has revealed something shocking - but not shocking; something unexpected but not unexpected and there's now an ambivalence and fear in me of knowing. It's like wanting to know - but not wanting to know at the same time. But you can't make this stuff up. It's so visceral and real; so deeply imbedded in your body's memory.

Shannon - 6th MDMA session – 135 mgs.

Shannon's words

This was a big one. When it came on, the MDMA took me straight into a memory and provided crystal clear details of my father's sexual abuse of me. I have always had faint, clouded memories of this incident and had mentioned it to previous psychologists, but until now, it was just a picture, absent of feelings, so I was never 100% sure if it was completely true. But this time I knew it was, because the details were so stark and clear and so were the feelings.

I was at home alone from school, sick in bed. Dad came home from work. He worked as a travelling salesman. He bought me an ice-cream; I remember that, because it was unusual for him to be kind to me. He told me he was feeling sad. When I asked him why, he said that mum couldn't be a proper wife to him because she had asthma and that there were certain things adults did together and she couldn't do them anymore. My benevolent and innocent child self, came up with a great idea. 'Maybe you could do to me what you do to mum.' I had no idea what I was even saying. I think I was about seven. What a fucking trap.

He took me into their bedroom and got me to lay down on the end of their bed. He took my pyjama pants off. He said he wouldn't hurt me. But he lied. He eventually forced himself into my small child's body. The pain was so excruciating; my spirit fled my body in shock. I cried and begged him to stop, but he wouldn't. He wouldn't stop and it hurt so very much. I was stunned, shocked and devastated that my father could hurt me like that. His brutal betrayal was truly beyond a child's comprehension.

Afterwards he blamed me. He said I'd asked him to do it - that I was bad and dirty. He told me to go to the bathroom and clean myself up, then get back into bed. He went back to work. I was left at home alone to deal with the shock; the shock of what had just happened to me.

I lay in my bed, tears streaming quietly down my face and running into my ears. I distinctly remember the feeling of the tears running into my ears. I was so completely stunned, I'm not sure I ever fully returned to my body after that. I think a piece of my soul departed that day.

Mum came home later from her work, with my favourite cake. It had three layers of coloured sponge; pink, yellow and brown, pastry, jam and cream filling and chocolate icing on the top. I was so lost; I ate that cake as if in a dream. Joy left my life that day. I just went through the motions. Mum didn't even notice that anything was wrong. How could that be? My world had just fallen off its axis and she just acted the same.

Another time, I remembered on this journey; I'd walked the short distance home for lunch, as I sometimes did. Dad came home from work for lunch that day as well. It happened again on the end of my brother's bed. I was dressed in my school uniform. He returned to work. I robbed my brother's piggy bank and bought lollies with the money on my way back to school. I got my first ever migraine and spent the afternoon in the Sick Bay. I think I was eleven.

The week following this session, I felt so intensely angry. This MDMA session bought up so much emotion afterwards. It wasn't a come down effect - just the effect of processing all the horrible shit that was revealed in my session. Feeling your repressed emotions is extremely difficult but ultimately healing, I guess. I've come to learn that processing my emotions with someone afterwards, stops them from coming out sideways. But I didn't do this initially; process my journey with the therapist - and my emotions just all came out sideways, manifesting in anger and overwhelming sadness.

I was so extremely angry at everyone: AA. people, men, car drivers on the road, shop assistants, people I knew. I had arguments with people on Facebook. I just felt so angry at life in general. I was angry at myself for so blindly sabotaging my life and not really understanding why, or how to stop doing it. Angry I've been alone for so long. But I guess it's no bloody wonder really; if you can't trust your own fucking father, who the hell can you trust?

Reading *"Brave,"* a book by Rose McGowan, brought up another rampage of memories from the time I lived in Los Angeles. The many men who took advantage of my 23-year-old, devastated, broken and drunken self: An audition at Zoetrope studios where the director got me drunk and screwed me on the casting couch. Cliché, I know. An Iranian I met at my work (a nightclub in Beverley Hills) who locked me in his bedroom for three days and just fucked me when he got home from work. A Motown Records manager who I met at a Casino in Lake Tahoe, asked me to meet him at an LA pub, then got me in the back of his family car and fucked me, then probably drove home to his wife. The many men who just fucked my numbed-out body without a care in the world, for my young, troubled mind, and broken spirit. They broke my heart a bit more each time.

I was angry at my mother for not protecting me, but mainly angry at my father for what he did to me. He poisoned my innocent mind with his filthy sickness. He made me feel so bad, so sad, so very ashamed, so broken, tired and devastated. He blamed me, a seven-year-old kid. He constantly put me down, played me off against my mother and alienated me from the rest of the family. He killed all my pets and took my horse off me when I ran away from home and gave it to my sister. My beautiful horse - my only source of comfort and joy. My father was warped and sick and he wrecked my fucking life; I've spent my whole life healing from this vile shit.

A statement I read recently best sums up my post medicine state of mind. "Regression in the Service of Transcendence." Writing down my truth for the first time ever, feels radioactive. Just seeing it on paper frightens me; breaking the long-held code of silence. I can barely breathe. Can I really commit this to paper without deleting it? I have a habit of deleting things, as if something deeply embedded in me is programmed to delete the truth. In the face of overwhelming evidence, I still want to delete the truth. I still don't want to believe it.

My family would completely alienate me if they read this; they pretty much already have, so I'm used to it, but it's hard to endure. They would hate me for telling our family secrets and I understand. But it's not their shame either. The shame belongs to one person only - the perpetrator - our father.

These words are ugly and hard to read; but it is the truth – my truth, and the truth of what goes on in this world, behind far too many closed doors, in our 'nuclear' family homes. In the many years I've been in A.A. I've heard stories like mine too often. Many have confessed their shameful truths to me.

Why do we carry the shame - we invisible ghost people, quietly killing ourselves or drinking and drugging ourselves into oblivion, because this is our unpalatable, too painful truth? But I can't stay silent any longer. Our families want to silence us, to hide their shame. Society wants to silence us, hoping we'll quietly die and take our unbearable truths to the grave. I almost did. Telling my truth so publicly, for the first time ever, feels like the bravest and scariest thing I've ever done.

And why are these healing medicines illegal? They are the only thing that have ever worked for me and I have tried almost everything. This is so very wrong.

Thoughts on Forgiveness

Forgiveness - this topic seems to arise repeatedly. Should one forgive their sexual abuser. I see 'forgiveness,' as a religious and biblical topic - part of our brainwashing agenda. If forgiveness means taking no action, being silent and allowing paedophiles to continue their destructive ways, the forgiveness is not for me. If forgiveness means forgiving yourself, loving yourself, undoing the brainwashing that was inflicted on you to hate yourself, then that to me is forgiveness. To live with a heart full of hate is destructive. To remain silent and allow others to be abused is also destructive. Paedophilia is an addiction and chances are it won't stop with you. True forgiveness can only come after admission of guilt, apology and change. I never got any of this.

Psilocybin Therapy

Stephanie, 35, Environmentalist

Stephanie had an MDMA therapy treatment prior to this. (Intro in MDMA section) Her intention for this session was to further heal from past trauma and to become more self-loving and able to live without fear, distrust and hatred.

Stephanie - First Psilocybin Session (2.5 gms *P. Cubensis*)

Stephanie's words

During the active effects, I felt the same chest/heart-warming feeling as MDMA. I lost connection between the words in my head and what came out of my mouth. I thought a lot about my partner and how he would cope on mushrooms as he needs this healing as well, but has never taken any drugs before, nor done any research. So, I tried to imagine these feelings for someone who didn't have any context or experience with them. I felt this level of intensity might be too much for him. If you've never felt drugs and how your body responds, imagine losing your ability to speak - that could be scary.

Time seemed to lose meaning. I realised that the therapist had asked me a question and I hadn't answered, even though I had intended to, I got distracted by time. The music moved the objects around me, which became colours. I couldn't agree to fall back into it until I checked if the therapist was okay. I tried to hold off for ages, knowing I should focus on me, but my heart said, 'Once you check, you can go.' I couldn't speak easily so I tried to sign language, 'Are you okay?' She was, and I wondered why I had these compelling feelings that I needed to check.

I asked that and almost started crying. I'm not sure why. I knew I had asked her questions she felt she needed to answer but couldn't. I felt I made her uncomfortable with my silence but I couldn't respond because I was long gone by the time I finished saying something. Then I agreed to let go.

Before then, behind my eyeshade, I had a dance with the universe. I could leave that and come back if I took my eye-shade off. It wasn't a normal world, it was impacted by the colour, movement and music. I was in the depths of the universe with the mushroom divine feminine. I don't know if this is accurate, but the therapist moved the paintings around, danced, and turned into a bird. I thought that was time to fall back, because that obviously wasn't accurate. Even if it was, I wasn't here for that. I needed to go. I closed the shades and agreed to go wherever I needed to. I was dancing with the Universe and my feet flew up over my head and behind me (in my mind - I hadn't moved from the couch). I wrapped like a pretzel and broke. I wasn't physically whole anymore. I was laying while a mushroom divine feminine goddess danced over me, healing me, and showing me, she had always been there.

I realised that the connection we have with each other and the Earth is the solution to all the pain in the world. I should move more in nature, and swim in the ocean in the morning. I saw the sun shining through the ocean as I looked up from diving in. I saw the sand move and felt the fresh water and freedom. It also told me to do more yoga in downward dog. It showed me doing these things and the beauty that it held. I felt warm and loved and connected, that the world had hope. I smiled and knew there was a chance to heal the world. I felt overwhelming joy.

I was worried I would fight the mushrooms like I had with the MDMA and asked the therapist for a higher dose in that case. She offered me another half gram but I didn't need it. I appreciated the offer. I meant to say, 'Yes,' but instead, I said, 'I'll keep going instead,' so I trusted that. Then I found myself crouched and buried under an ancient tree in a huge old forest. I stood up from under the roots. I had never stood before. My wings unfurled. I was my mother, grandmother, and my entire family line. They had never accessed this world, this healing, this learning. I was coming out to the world for the first time, for my family.

Then I was deep in the ocean and I felt the pain, suffocation, and distress of all the marine life. They were connected with humans and the earth, but knew humans weren't connected with them. They are dying. I had intense pain in my chest, not on the inside, but like a pressure bearing down on me, pushing me, and I knew I just had to breathe into it. I felt like crying - they were all so saddened.

I knew that no matter what, I could go back to my breath. I smiled and thanked all the research I had done, people's trip reports, thanking them that this was the normal path, and I was safe. I couldn't move. I badly needed a drink. I was sweating and so hot but couldn't speak or move. I felt my body was burning and maybe it needed to. I knew if I tried to drink water anyway, I'd drown, because I wasn't solid anymore. I kept bringing myself back to my breathing and my intention: to forgive and love myself.

I travelled through time and knew I had an Indian goddess supporting my healing. I had a connection to India, which I've been to many times. I spent almost a year there. The jungle and its animals also came forward to heal me.

At times there was intense pain all over my body. I still couldn't move in those times, I just focused on my breathing. I tried to move my hand once to test it. It moved, so I took that as good news. The couch was pressing in on my shoulder and I felt that represented all the men annoyingly still holding us all back. It had been pressing on me for eternity and it was a familiar fight. I laughed at how familiar the fight was and wished I could tell the therapist that the couch and I had been fighting for eternity. I wished I could lay flat, go to the floor, but I felt that if I tried to roll off the couch I'd fall and fall forever.

I realised we were living in a simulation we had constructed. We're now stuck in it. Nothing is making us work nine-to-five, Monday to Friday, our whole lives, racing against each other, sick, and sad. We actually made it all up and were now trapped in our own fantasy. We could break free, but only with that connection.

Every time I left and came back from a theme, I went back to my breathing and felt like I was returning to my own team. This teamwork and returning felt wonderful, like I had my own back. We could do anything together. 'I' was now 'we.' I could be trusted, and I was showing myself that.

In between each of the themes, I'd go there, experience it, and then the mushrooms said, 'OKAY, now you need to die.' I trusted the mushroom and my team (me), and willingly fell, open armed, smiling, backwards into the death each time. Sometimes I didn't realise it was time to die until I was half stuck in the darkness (death). My reaction was then, 'Oh, yes, you, familiar death. Okay, let's go.' I did it with love and trust and faith in me, and knew I needed to die. That happened so many times. It felt like I may never come back, but that was okay, it was time. I considered I may never be able to walk or speak or work, but that was okay, as that was just how it had to be.

I was still so deep I wasn't sure if I could come out. I was very thirsty and clammy; everything went white. I needed to stand up and get some blood back into my head. I needed to go to the bathroom and lay down on the cold bathroom tiles.

After this experience, I couldn't put it all into words for weeks. I tried to explain it but just couldn't. I expected to have learnings and realisations like MDMA, but this was completely different. There were learnings but through experience rather than through realising. I was able to work and drive with no issues the next day. I slept okay too that night, which was different from MDMA. The following week I still couldn't articulate any of this. It was so profound. I knew I loved and trusted myself. I knew I had my own back and that I needed to do more of the things that the mushrooms had told me to do.

The enduring effects have been incredible. I now have an incredible amount of empathy, understanding and compassion. I give everyone more freedom to live their own lives. My partner says it all the time, he says, 'Wow! Your empathy and patience are so obvious.' For example, he was complaining about someone and my thoughts were, 'It's okay, they're doing the best they can and if you were them, you'd probably do the same.' And I genuinely feel that. Everyone is just doing their best. I do love me, trust me, and feel motivated. I spend all my time trying to optimise my life and find things to do that I love and enjoy: sport, beach, and diving.

I've done so much research into psychedelics. After just two sessions I'm changed and feel that there is still work to do. I'd love to microdose mushrooms to find how much it helps my athletic performance, and creativity. It will help my work, and also give me more time to be able to process difficult people in my life. I feel another mushroom and MDMA session would be valuable. Not everything is healed, but it's 70% there. I still have body dysmorphia, jealousy, insecurity and lack of trust in men.

I would strongly recommend this to others, and I do. I wish everyone could access this healing! Why would we withhold this from anyone! Why would anyone stand in the way of someone accessing this elevated life! This is healing I never thought possible. Having someone there to safely guide and support the experience is incredibly important. Honestly, I wasn't on this earth the entire time, but I felt safe to surrender because I had a therapist there.

Therapist note: A lot of people who participate in psychedelic therapy, don't take on board the importance of having a follow up integration session and may consider it a waste of money. Stephanie's story adds weight to the fact that even one follow-up (integration) session can help immensely to understand and integrate the medicine session. I always strongly suggest an integration session especially after psilocybin or ayahuasca, but ultimately, it's the client's decision.

Deborah, 26, Lawyer

Deborah was referred for Psilocybin Therapy by her psychologist, who knew from personal experience, the benefits of psychedelic therapy. She was suffering intense anxiety and low self-esteem which had caused her to withdraw and isolate. She was confused about her forward career path; a recently qualified lawyer, she felt she'd studied the wrong subject and now wants to study psychology and become a psychedelic therapist. Although Deborah has been twice diagnosed with clinical depression, she was not suffering depression at the time of her psilocybin session. She says she's always had mild anxiety symptoms, which she's been working through with her psychologist for a number of years.

She'd previously tried a number of psychedelics for recreational and spiritual purposes and credits them with changing the direction of her life; psilocybin mushrooms, LSD, ketamine, and 2CB (4-Bromo-2,5-dimethoxyphenethylamine). As a psychology student, planning to eventually move into Psychedelic Therapy, her motivation for this session was to experience psychedelics from a therapeutic perspective. Deborah requested a larger than standard therapeutic dose, as she wanted to experience a higher dose in a safe environment. It was given to her as an initial dose of 3grams then a gram 40 mins later then .8grams at about 75 minutes in.

Deborah - First Psilocybin Session (4.8 gms *P. Cubensis*)

Deborah's words

It took around an hour, including a second dose to come-on, because the first dose didn't quite let me get past the barriers in my head. Honestly, I felt terrified a lot of the time. I have always felt slightly at odds with my mind, like we battle each other for control. I felt as if my mind was trying to scare me enough that I wouldn't try to be so introspective again.

It showed me horrific images and grotesque, dark parts of my mind came into full view. It was truly unnerving at many points and there was a moment where I became so overwhelmed, I thought I was going to throw up. However, when I pushed through and kept digging, I was overcome by a sense that everything in life is utterly meaningless. That might sound depressing but for me it was liberating. Every worry I've ever had seemed useless. Why did I care what people thought about me when nothing mattered anyway? If nothing matters, why would you do anything other than what makes you happy? That is the feeling I got.

I also felt incredible sadness about things in my life I wasn't even aware that I was holding onto. I remember sobbing about my dad leaving me when I was a baby. It's something that I had never even thought about in my day-to-day life, as it happened before I even started to retain memories. It was incredibly cathartic to expel that kind of pain and I felt a weight lift off my shoulders.

I kept getting the message over and over again that nothing mattered. Everything is meaningless and my problems were insignificant in the scheme of things. I got the feeling that the Universe itself was screaming at me to just stop caring so much. I know this sounds bad, but I truly have never felt more liberated in my life. I worry so much about the tiniest, most insignificant details of my life. To have the entire weight of the universe pushing the message that none of it mattered, was incredible. It has stuck with me ever since.

After the session, to my surprise, I didn't feel very good. I was incredibly exhausted, like I'd run a marathon. I slept for a really long time the following night. This might sound strange, but I experienced amnesia for the next few days. I couldn't remember a lot of what had happened during my session which was really upsetting for me as I had really hoped to be able to take something meaningful from my time with the medicine. I felt let down by a medicine that I had so much faith in and had heard other people having magical experiences.

Looking back on it now, I think the experience was too traumatic for me to process in the days afterwards. I think I was too exhausted to begin to unpack what had happened, so I simply wasn't able to remember it. The following week, the feeling of disappointment around not being able to remember persisted for a while. I can't recall exactly how long or when I started to remember what happened. Eventually the whole experience came back to me, especially after I discussed it with close friends and was able to work through it in my own head. The more I thought about it and spoke about it the clearer my experience became, and I realised the profound affect it had on me.

The enduring effects have been phenomenal. I can't explain how much it has helped me. Once the memories of my experience returned, my confidence came with it. Prior to my session I had lost touch with who I was. I had always been confident and sure of myself but issues at work and home had turned me into a meek, unsure person with little to no confidence or self-assurance. The medicine changed all of that for me and set me back down the correct path.

I definitely would take it again. I went into the session feeling like I knew exactly what a mushroom trip was like, because I have had so many of them before. I was taken aback by how completely different it is in a therapeutic setting. I think I'd like to try it again with this grasp on what it is actually like, so it doesn't rock me emotionally as much and I can perhaps go deeper with a clearer mind.

I would recommend it to anyone who feels they are capable of it, but I'd recommend a strong base of consistent therapy beforehand. I don't think I would have been as aware of what I wanted to get out of the process, if I hadn't done a lot of soul searching with my psychologist for many years previously.

I loved the setting and facilitation. The facilitator was an incredible person and I loved spending that time with her. I felt safe and nurtured. The more relaxed homely environment really put me at ease and the ability to go straight to bed after, was so good for me as I was completely exhausted. Honestly, I think it's only in the last month or so that I've truly been able to digest the effect our session had on me, so I thank her a million times over.

Deborah's story is a prime example of why integration sessions are important. If she had done an integration session as advised, her integration might have gone much smoother; perhaps a valuable lesson for a budding psychedelic therapist.

Marie, 56, Social Worker

Marie had a host of diagnoses: Complex Developmental Trauma, CPTSD, Anxiety, Depression, OCD, and ADD. I initially felt that she might be too unstable for psychedelic therapy and was reluctant to work with her. But her desperation and persistence eventually won me over.

Marie hadn't worked in the previous seven years. She had left her job after some problematic relationships in her work place which had triggered her PTSD. She was under the care of a psychiatrist and had been for the previous seven months. He of course prescribed her medication: increasing dose of Ketamine for seven months; Baclofen morning and PRN afternoon; Quetiapine nightly. She'd been on Diazepam - as needed for sleep since 2003. She took Pseudoephedrine Hydrochloride which apparently helps her focus to drive safely after her usual three hours sleep. She drinks a nip of whiskey after dinner, or in middle of night if her mind is too busy to sleep.

It was requested that Marie come off all medications prior to doing any psychedelic therapy. Surprisingly she managed to do this over a period of two months, seemingly without much difficulty. All prescription medications had been ceased, three weeks prior to her first medicine treatment. Marie had no previous psychedelic experience, but had smoked cannabis semi-regularly from 1983 to the present.

Prior to this psilocybin session, Marie had done three MDMA therapy sessions which she'd found extremely beneficial. Marie keeps her intentions very broad, which I feel makes her sessions less focused. Her intention for this treatment was to further heal her childhood and adult trauma and hopefully break through resistance that arose after her first MDMA session. She desires access to repressed memories and to understand the significant barriers she'd experienced since childhood that stop her achieving vocationally and interpersonally and living a productive and rewarding life. She wants her obsessive fantasising to abate, something that has worsened since doing her first MDMA session.

Marie - First Psilocybin Session (3 gms *P. cubensis*)

Marie's words

During the active effects I felt happy at the very start of the session, and then anxious throughout most of the rest. I felt confused, impatient, angry at the words, actions and inactions of my parents, and at my broader realisations of the impact of their neglect and abandonment on me. I felt very sad for my childhood and teenage self, and angry and disappointed at the damage done to my psyche.

I processed the details and results of my abuse and neglect more deeply than in my previous MDMA medicine sessions. I cried four or five times - more than in the MDMA sessions. I felt my feelings about these old wounds much more strongly with psilocybin. I had a sensation of treading water, knowing I couldn't move, because if I did, I would bump up against, or see, what I was trying so desperately to avoid and acknowledge in myself and my life.

I felt the defeatist resignation of knowing I had to self-sabotage to stay safe from the jealous abuse of my brother. I felt pathetic in my self-sacrificing, self-effacing efforts that I sometimes made to appear hopeless - hoping that someone would notice I was hurt and needed help. I re-visited my adult times of suicidal ideation, fully knowing that, 'It doesn't matter what happens to me.' Try as I might, I couldn't find a way to matter and achieve much in this life.' I heard my mother say,

'Marie, you want too much!' I don't know what 'want' this is related to, but I laughed ruefully and cried in frustration and confusion. I wondered if this 'want' I had, was for higher levels of ordinary things like fair treatment, opportunities, and unjudged free expression of thoughts.

I fully realised that as a child I believed I was not good enough and did not matter. I was just an extra. It seemed obvious but devastating to me to realise that I was using the dissociation tools of daydreaming, TV, and reading to not just escape from my family circumstances, but from myself as well. I realised that I was treading water throughout my childhood, adopting a Pollyanna attitude of abuse denial, of how I felt about myself and my (mis-) place in the world.

I felt the direct links between my abuse, neglect, and abandonment and my feeling that I didn't matter, and my own self-neglect in areas of my life. I had the idea that maybe part of why I was judged by and rejected by others was because I could feel what was possible and wanted it to be; possibilities like better relationships, communication, ideas, and values.

The next morning, I felt a bit tired and spacey but fine. In the afternoon, I had mental energy to do life admin despite being physically tired. On Wednesday I had more mental energy, motivation and clear focus for life admin. I had a few short Auto-Negative Thoughts (ANTs). On Thursday I saw my chiropractor who was amazed and pleased that for the first time in three and a half years, my body was more stable and my hips didn't require adjustment. Friday, I felt tired but managed to attend a medical appointment and was in a good mood. From Thursday onwards, my obsessive fantasies started to abate. On Sunday there was no fantasizing at all; only passing brief thoughts that were not indulged.

Terry, 35, Veterinarian

Terry completed five MDMA sessions prior to his psilocybin treatment (Intro in MDMA section.) Although he had a very powerful and therapeutically beneficial response to MDMA, he wanted to access more emotion that he felt must be linked to his childhood sexual abuse.

Terry - First Psilocybin Session (3 gms *P. cubensis*)

Terry's words

Shifting to psilocybin was my attempt to break through differently than I'd been doing on MDMA. My intentions were to feel emotion, especially grief, hoping for relief from my stuck-ness and to revisit my final trauma once again.

COVID-19 Lockdown was a time of me just coping and getting by, the way I've learnt to do my whole life. Dissociating and burying myself in work helped mask things - frustration and disappointment that I wasn't making better proactive use of my time. I wished I'd been able to better myself during that time by reading, exercising, finding a new me, but instead I felt I'd gone backwards. I avoided writing up my last MDMA session for the longest time, particularly as it pertained to the final trauma that was still unresolved.

I haven't felt the full gamut of emotions I'd assumed would flow from realising my sexual abuse trauma. I'd cried in small fits and starts but had felt myself actively shutting down my emotions when the grief started to really envelop me. This is an involuntary self-protection mechanism that is stunting my growth and preventing me from properly processing it. I want catharsis, and hoped psilocybin could give me that. I felt apprehensive trying something new but hoped the risk would benefit me.

I still don't understand that final trauma. The memory was unclear, incomplete, hazy, and shrouded. I presume my brain is still protecting me from it. The memories I'd already recovered were shameful and I presumed this was why it still felt like a raw nerve whenever I attempted to remember it.

My psilocybin session was divided into three internal periods bracketed by some debriefing with the therapist before and after each: The Metaphysical Journey; My Traumatic Memory Recovery; and Reliving all my Nightmares.

The Metaphysical Journey.

This was incredible! It was a journey, a trip, transcendental, and all the other stereotypical things that psilocybin usually offers. There were various spirits, different from ones I'd met or who'd helped me before. Lesser ones, not the mother and father and not even my eternal spirit, just those who were not me, but who were like me. Gone before me. This is probably the section I remember the least detail of, but I've still taken away impressions, experiences, and realisations that will always be with me.

While the medicine was coming on, we talked for a while about how I was feeling. Then as soon as it came on, I went on a literal metaphysical journey that transcended bounds of time and space. It was much as you'd imagine from the countless depictions, but the difference was, I knew as it was happening that what I was experiencing was real.

I was given a tour by some spirits of the meta-verse. I was shown the vast internal structure of things. The way the perceivable universe is built and rests upon a spiritual and metaphysical lattice through which things can be seen and understood. I was shown inside the wave of an ocean for example, under the water, looking up, and seeing how it was put together on a subatomic level. I was shown this is what holds up the world and this is where the spiritual intersects with the physical - on this level.

By taking psilocybin I was effectively leaving my corporeal body behind so my spirit-body could melt and drift through the physical into the lattice where the spirits showed me how the universe was constructed. There was SOMETHING. Everything is connected. It was deeply reassuring, reassuring to my core. It affirmed what I felt in my spirit, felt and knew, but now my whole self could walk around in this physical domain with a degree of reassurance.

I had two guides. One who spoke, pointed, and showed me things, and one who was with us to silently transport us. To the one who spoke I asked many questions; at a speed and in a way that sometimes they were posed in language and sometimes posed in another kind of communication between my heart and theirs. Sometimes I got literal answers, sometimes I got a strong sense of something in my heart that I understood was a response from them to me. There were things that needed to be asked and answered that language wasn't fit for dealing with. That's the level on which we operated.

I don't know how long these stretches of 'the tour' lasted, but I kept doing sanity or control checks with the therapist. But mostly my very earth-bound consciousness and my actual body on the couch would just chime in and want to make sure I was in control. I would open my eyes and look around and assess that, Yes, I'm really in two places at once, but Yes, my body is here.

I think more than a couple of times I went to the bathroom. I would get up and walk and prove to myself that I was still present and real. This need to pee has been a constant presence in ALL my MDMA sessions. I've never understood why, but presumed it was connected to the fact that the trauma always happened in the toilets. Maybe one, or all those times I went to the toilets with him, I really did want to pee... but wasn't allowed. So now I always need to pee to reassure myself that I'm in control of things but most especially of my own body. In my literal vision, things were beginning to get a little melty.

To some of my questions I wasn't given answers that I was able to grasp and keep with me. Overall, I felt deeply reassured and tended to by my spirit guides. I gathered at the time that I was being prepared for what was to come. I kept being impatient with them, asking, "When should I turn my mind to the trauma?" And asking, "Why aren't we getting to that pressing issue?" They were endlessly, joyously, patient with me. They explained it was necessary and planned for me to have this tour first. This is the way this is done, so that I had something to reassure me and call me back when things became difficult. I think they meant both that day in the session, as well as in the months ahead. They were right on both accounts. I was shown these things and given this noetic understanding to make the next stage possible.

The immediate one of going to dark fucking places and re-experiencing dark things, this time without the fear of the un-knowingness of when it will end, as well as this longer-term slog that I'm in right now. In both cases I've needed and have been reassured to return to this noetic sense, a reassurance that there is SOMETHING going on. We're not just abandoned to chaos in the entropic sense (maybe we are technically in this universe), but that there is SOMETHING BEYOND.

One of the key things I saw, and why I think we went to the ocean, was a foam. It sounds ridiculous but I was shown how our universe bubbled up into existence in a quantum foam of universes, the meta-structure of which I was currently touring through. This revelation was some real quantum physics, string-theory, multiverse shit that I didn't expect. Rather than giving me a sense of pointlessness, it gave me a deep sense of optimistic peace. Knowing that we were part of something SO large and SO fleeting, and yet SO packed with such meaning and beauty and possibility left in me a deep and abiding sense of hope. It's so counter-intuitive. It's related to awe, wonder, and to the real and infinite sublime.

One thing I was shown while flying through a gigantic, spiral, lattice landscape in a vessel that held us, three spirits no less: a black void space at the far end of the spiral. I asked about it, knowing all along really, that this was the threshold of death. It wasn't a scary black, more like it was so deep and black that it was hard to directly look at. Like the opposite of the sun, but just as hard to look at. The brightest void. I knew there was even more beyond that threshold, so I asked about it repeatedly in numerous ways.

Initially my questions were waved away with a simple dismissal that death and the void was not a key part of the tour, except to acknowledge it as the later place. It was explained to me that my guides were not equipped or authorised to talk more about it. It wasn't the point of my trip, so I shouldn't spend time dwelling on it. Even if they could there was actually no physical way for me understand or comprehend the answers. It was explained that once you pass through that threshold, you're changed in a way that is so outside the paradigm of understanding that it's physically impossible to understand it in our current state of being. It was all just patiently and caringly explained that I was asking the wrong questions; I wouldn't understand the answers and that instead they had a lot to show me about my current present state. That other place was for the future.

One of the numerous things I got from this stage (apart from a gentle and loving preparation for the hell to follow), was that I don't fear death anymore. I certainly don't want to die. It makes me sad for the pain that my partner, family and friends might feel if I were to suddenly die, but I feel kind of prepared to just go into and through that threshold and find out more about what's next. I feel the reassurance not to fear the unknown-ness of whatever comes next. And the beautiful structure underneath gives me confidence that whatever comes next will be amazing.

I came back up out of this briefly to debrief X on the amazing experience. Then, almost as if I knew it was necessary, I moved from laying on my back on the couch, to laying on my stomach on the floor with a pillow as I went back in for the second stage, knowing it was now time to go back to the last trauma. The last time the abuse happened, to examine that experience for new insights.

My Traumatic Memory Recovery

He almost killed me. That's what it was. I knew I had to go back to that time. I thought it was because I was ashamed. I thought it was because I needed to see and admit what I'd done; how I'd acquiesced; how I'd thought I needed to. How, even when I was trying to do what I thought I had to do, my job, my responsibility, I had failed. That tangle of shame and disappointment was what I needed to unravel and set straight. But it wasn't that. It was worse. There was a reason I still hadn't remembered it.

At some point during that time, I wasn't doing it right. It didn't matter that I was trying. I was failing. It wasn't working for him. I tried to do the most horrible thing to the best of my ability and it still wasn't enough. I knew that. I'd remembered that. What I hadn't remembered until now, under psilocybin, was what he did at that point. That had always been a blank still for me. I don't think I'd been ready to cope with that memory before now. Maybe I couldn't have even got to it with MDMA, given how deep and serious it was.

I went back there. Firstly, I saw myself trying to do the 'right' thing. Then I went back into my little body at the time. The moment when it shifted. When he wanted more. He grabbed my head. He forced things further. He started grasping at my head and face. He went too far. In the moment I think he forgot himself. He choked me. It was violent. He needed that. He was an animal. He was trying to obliterate me. I don't think I was human at that point. I was just flesh. I saw white light. That's the memory I recovered. He choked me so far that I saw a white light. Nothing else. I was blacking out. I was dying. I was going to die. That's what I hadn't wanted or been able to admit or realise until now. I almost died. He almost killed me.

I don't know which thing made him stop. Did he see I was dying and stop? Or was it because he finished and so he didn't need me anymore? Was it a moment of clarity and fear for him? Or was it a coincidence that he finished in time that I didn't die? Will I ever know? Which would even be the preferred option? Is there such a thing? Am I out past the edge of things to a degree that these aren't even questions that are worth asking? Let alone answering.

I was inside my body again when I saw White. I saw it the way I saw it that day. It wasn't even scary at that point. It just was what it was. I was dying. Three near-death experiences are more than is good to have by age 35. I've had enough to know that there's three different kinds. In one you see a white light. I knew I could go to it. Maybe it even drew me in. In one it's happened before you even know what's going on, and then you think, 'Oh I'm not dying here after all.' It's very matter-of-fact. In one you know you're about to die. You see it coming. And then you just don't. It passes you by and you're left with the knowledge that's useless now.

He must have tossed me aside. I remember thinking later that he must have scared himself too. But I came too on the floor; The gross dirty floor. My face was on the tiles. Discarded and exposed. Facing away from him, into the wall, half under the bench. I was frozen in fear trying not to figure out what had happened, but purely instinctively what might happen next? I remember trying to listen and sense his movements. Hyper-vigilant, feeling dirty, exposed and alone. Like each other time I don't think I ever left that place either.

I lay there very exposed. I think I was prodded with a toe. I don't like being prodded now. I certainly don't like someone squeezing my nostrils together. That's a couple-more disproportionately hated things explained. It's very hard to know what to do with some of this knowledge. It just sits there now, explained, but not processed. How do you process that? What do you do with it? Do you need to do anything? Understood, and acknowledged.

The mushroom showed me this so I could appreciate why I've never been able to move past that mode. It's existential to the extreme. There's no way to leave that behind. Of course, I'm everything I've been since. On top of everything else, I had a near-death experience at age six and

I've been coping ever since. How could a kid be OK trying to carry that by himself? It's a miracle that I'm here. Whatever the fuck those are. However, I managed to get here, it was me that did it, before and after and despite everyone and everything else. Of course, that's going to take a toll. Of course, that's going to mean I've got some wrinkles in my psyche. Of course, six-year-olds aren't meant to have near death experiences, let alone like that, let alone deal with them alone. I've done incredibly well. The mushroom showed me that. I'm fucking awesome.

There was some paranoia in my debrief. I did have to talk this through with the therapist, my usually-unconscious-but-now-very-urgently-conscious fear that because he finished in me, that I was infected with who he was. What he was, I would be, or will become like him. We went in circles for what felt like a long time with me being deeply worried and finally relieved to be voicing that I might become like him. In my high, paranoiac-state, I even spent time worrying that perhaps if I can repress memories, I could be living a double-life that even I'm not aware of. Ridiculous I know, but in the moment, it seemed a very urgent need for me to account for my time. To run though the hours and test the likelihood that I'm secretly someone else doing other things. It felt possible.

Of course, it isn't. And I'm not. I was high, on top of which, yes, there's been an unconscious fear of being dirtily 'infected' by him. With him inside me – something I never had a chance to purge, clear up from, or rectify – it was lying dormant and bound to erupt at some point. It isn't, it hasn't, and it won't. I needed to finally say it out aloud.

Actually, there is a secret-life inside me, but it's not as an abuser. It's as a survivor. It's the little fractured-off senses of self that have been stuck inside me all along, dictating my thoughts and feelings, motivations and actions out of their fear and trauma my whole life. Yes, there's something inside me, but it's my core self, my true self. My adult self.

Somewhere in here, after I'd done a control check, and debriefed, I sobbed, on my knees with my face buried in a pillow, for the briefest of times; 10 seconds maybe; at the life I've lost, at the poor little kid I was, suffering so deeply, with something so fucked up. With no one to help him, and only himself to keep him going. Only me. I thought I'd cry more. I thought I'd want to cry more. I did want to cry more. But I didn't. I still don't really understand this. I went back in. Laid back down, face first into the pillow and the floor.

Reliving all my nightmares.

This was the absolute fucking worst. I presume this is what people describe when they have a bad trip. At numerous times throughout this hour or two (I'm not sure how long it was), I remember my conscious mind thinking, 'Fuck this is awful take me back to MDMA,' with variants of three main concerns regularly: Am I losing my mind? Will this be permanent and is this my reality now? And am I still in control?

Basically, in this section my brain was running through, maybe even purging, every horrible fear and nightmare I ever had as a child. What happened was that because as a kid, I'd done such a good job at repressing what happened, in my conscious waking mind, all the suffering and pain I had, was only able to be felt and processed by my sleeping or dreaming unconscious.

I think the reason I've never woken refreshed, why I never wanted to go to bed, and why I never wanted to get up in the morning, was because it was such a tortured experience. I never wanted to go to bed because I knew the terrors I'd dream about once I was asleep. I also didn't want to get out of bed in the morning because I was dead tired having had such nightmare-filled sleep and I wanted to rest. My whole life I'd never been able to reconcile those two seemingly incompatible ideas, and now I get it – sleep is a highly contested space for my fractured selves.

I've always remembered two recurring dreams I've had from childhood, but apart from that, through adulthood, I've never remembered any dreams beyond the first second of waking. This changed with PTSD after the car crash, when I'd wake very aware of the awful and constant experiences I'd had in sleep.

In the first nightmare, I was chased and threatened by a huge bulldog. Alone and afraid, this giant, hairy, dark grey snarling menace was terrifying and constantly trying to chase and attack me; it's slobbering mouth and jowls dripping and flapping about as it tried to devour me. Only now this very minute do I see the very clear connection. It was him. A gross and disgusting mess of flesh and wetness, with a horseshoe moustache hanging off his ugly furrowed face like the dangling jowls of a bulldog. Fucking hell.

The second nightmare I had was also of being chased. This time by an indigenous man with a spear or weapon, and in full traditional ceremonial corroboree dress. Dad was always with me, and we were running away together. Running, hiding, being found, and needing to run more. I don't remember ever being caught, just the endless, exhausting, terror-filled running. Dad never saved us - never saved me. But we were fleeing together.

I don't imagine my young brain was making some kind of racist decision but I do wonder if my little brain thought about his darker skin, or his facial features and made a leap. It's possible I thought he was indigenous, my Aunty certainly was, and I never really thought about it at the time. Given our family, it's possible he was and doesn't know. I'm not even sure it was symbolic or specific, him chasing us, as it was an imagined or projected and personified sense of danger in family history, genealogy, or legacy. I know I was continually upset that dad wasn't better able to save us from, or even face our pursuer. I do know I liked running away with him, but I wished he'd turned and fought.

Most of the time of this bad part of the trip however was a rapid-fire re-living of a maelstrom of nightmarish experiences. For some of the time, I was really scared that I was losing my mind and that I was trapped forever in this hellish experience. Even then though whenever I tested it, as with the previous sections, I found I was still in control, in fact, I believe the point of the first two sections was so I had the experience to know I was still in control.

A couple of times I stopped, rose from my face-down position, opened my eyes and tested what I knew to be true. I could at any stage stop the bad-ness of the trip if I wanted to. I even went and peed at one stage and each time I tested, I still willingly went back down, face into the pillow, stomach to the floor, to keep experiencing the nightmares. Somehow, I knew that for some reason, I needed it.

Somewhere in here I decided to ask for the *Singularity* album to be turned off. I'd requested it be played and it had now been playing for hours, I guess. It seemed the therapist had been hoping that would happen. Fair enough. She did remark that perhaps it hadn't been the right music for the moment, which I can understand. It's quite possible that in its highly repetitive, fast-looped, pattern-filled construction, it might have supported some of my tightly-wound circular thinking in the trip and certainly some of the more aggressive songs sound tracked the more awful moments of the trip. But having said that, not only do I think that those were necessary experiences, those same songs also very ably sound-tracked the transcendent part of the trip. So, it might just be also that their potential for anything to go bad or good depending on your intention, but also what the medicine knows you might need.

What was scary about the trip was how quick, grotesque, impressionistic, and unclear the memories were. What I realised now was that the other thing I learnt was how different it felt to recover repressed memories vs repressed nightmares. Unlike the specifics of all my traumatic memories, these re-dreamt nightmares were fleeting, with no solid details, only fears and anxieties.

Now I realise that they were ideas of what might happen not memories of what did. Feelings of my body being used, terror of what might happen to it and how it could be broken, endless anxiety about who might hurt me next. What felt like countless permutations. In the thick of it I was worried that these were all repressed memories. Given the number of them and the perpetrators involved, I was terrified. Was my world about to fall apart? If all of this was real, nothing and no one of my childhood was innocent. I had never remembered all of this before. If it was all real, there was no one who didn't hurt me; no time I wasn't being hurt; and nothing redeeming about my childhood at all. Were these real? Did this happen? Did anything? Have I lost it? Fuck this is too much, I'm scared, take me back to MDMA where I can feel nice. How can I come back from this? This is bad.

But then after some internal debate and reflection, I'd remember that actually, NO, I have control over this, and again I'd open my eyes, sit up, re-orient myself, and realise that whatever was going on, I remained in control. Of course, the other thing I learnt in going through this, was a renewed and deeper appreciation, love, understanding, admiration, and even pity for that little boy I was. Imagining myself stuck in that loop every night and getting up and tackling it again the next day. What a strong little trooper.

In retrospect, including immediately after this section in the come-down, I realised very clearly that all this maelstrom felt very different than my recovered memories. I kept picturing my childhood bedroom and realised, no, it's not that it was a site of abuse, but it and my bed, were where my little childhood brain attempted to defragment itself every night. Every night exhausted from a day of keeping myself together, I would retreat only to find my unconscious in turmoil until the next morning. This final section was finally releasing all the re-traumatising nightmarish shit back into my conscious experience in one almost-overwhelming tidal wave of fear and suffering.

It was also a gift; a way for me to experience the difference between recovered memories and recovered nightmares. Part of the endless torture of this trauma is the nagging voice that says it mightn't have happened. Maybe it was all concocted. Things from the screen, bad dreams amplified by bad chemicals. I 'knew' that wasn't true before. But I 'know' this isn't true now.

The mushroom gave me the experience to know the difference between the highly-specific, clear, somatic, and sensorial accessible memories and the hazy, fleeting impressions of a half-remembered nightmare. In the former I remember the places, the floor tiles, the geography, the smells, the sensations. In the latter I just have feelings. Vague fleeting impressions of something that defies logic, is situated in no place, and is given any structure at all only through the consistent fear of what if, what next? In my traumatic memories, I'm never worried about the future, only the very present. I know the difference now.

So, I think this purging was necessary. I think the mushroom needed to break that structure open. Maybe it was holding me back; Still doing damage. A piecemeal dam wall built with good intention but which needed to be broken down to irrigate everything downstream; To bring it to life.

Eventually I came up to debrief. At this point the therapists face took on very cat-like features, but I think that's just one of those things. I knew she wasn't a cat, but she looked like one. So I'll just look past that, knowing it's not real, as a way of moving towards the bigger, deeper conversations and reflections - that I'd just gone through hell to earn safety.

The next day I felt clearer, more considered. I could characterise it as time moving differently, but really, now, seven weeks on, I think more that my mind moves differently instead. My mind isn't racing the way it used to.

Tim, 32, Business Owner

Tim had a plethora of diagnoses: ADD (attention deficit disorder) CPTSD, OCD (obsessive compulsive disorder), Anxiety, Depression, Insomnia, Social Anxiety, and Agoraphobia. He was on Modafinil for his ADD, but came off it three weeks prior to his psychedelic therapy session.

Raised in a strict Korean Unification Church Tim had received little emotional support from his indoctrinated parents. He was sent to Australia a few years ago to marry a girl he'd never met - (an arranged marriage, organised by his family church.) He experienced a lot of bullying and racism while attending a violent school in England where stabbings and suicides were common place. He'd been assaulted at a church camp when he was nine, by an older, mentally ill woman. No one came to his rescue or defended him, they just stood by and watched her assault him. This all left him with profound feelings of powerlessness and abandonment.

Tim's intention for doing psilocybin therapy was to overcome his constant hypervigilance and alleviate some of the negative impact that his traumas have had on his life. This was Tim's first experience of taking a mind-altering substance. He participated in a small group with two other men.

Tim - First Psilocybin Session (3.5 gms *P. cubensis*)

Tim's words

When the medicine started working, I felt my mind was separating from my body - I was sinking deeper into something. I felt I was on a journey somewhere, but in my mind. My body felt tingly and the body aches I had from my sleep deprivation were intensified. My chest and stomach were aching and tingling but in an unusual way. I felt all my emotions much more intensely. Every thought and feeling I had was amplified a hundred-fold.

The main insights I received were: I witnessed my generational and ancestral suffering and felt the pain of the people of my race. I saw how I had been emotionally neglected. I felt the pain and loneliness of my physical abuse in South Korea. I saw scenes of racism that have happened to me throughout my lifetime. I felt the fear and hypervigilance of being bullied in high school. I saw how much the church cult I'd grown up in had influenced and manipulated me. I felt that I've never been seen or heard and saw a vision of my dad constantly talking, talking, talking to me, but not really talking to me - more talking at me. I deeply wanted to connect with him, but he was not able to connect with me. I saw a vision of my Mum and how she never talks to me and how I was screaming internally for her attention.

I had very clear visions of the movie 'Annihilation' with Natalie Portman and how the book and movie must have been inspired by psychedelics. The vibrant colours, the shine zone, the echoing, how all the cells connect with each other, and how people were going crazy. A lot of my experiences were centred upon the themes of this movie. The echo being my repeating thoughts and words.

I found myself talking out loud to myself a lot - which I realised was an alter ego; a way to comfort myself, as I felt very alone during the times of difficulty that I went through and felt no one was there to console me. I saw vivid, flashing bright colours when I was first starting to go deep into my session. I saw a vision of my dog and the anxiety and pain he experienced, always wanting my attention, which I could see was a reflection of my own suffering and how my dog was absorbing my pain.

I could see my partner and the pain that I caused her in our relationship, and the pain it had caused me being so uncertain and feeling trapped. I saw that I had been dealt some bad cards in life, being born into a cult that repressed who I was, being emotionally neglected, being physically abused, being bullied, having an arranged marriage, then moving to Scotland where there were barely any people that looked like me (racial fatigue), then again to Australia, where again, I feel so out of place.

I could see that my suffering was not to be taken lightly, that I have had some serious things impact me that I need to take it more seriously and allow myself to heal. From what I've been through, it makes sense that I've been wasting away and isolating myself. I could also see that I had incredible power within me. I am worthy of this space called life - like anyone else. My mind is very powerful, which can be used for amazing good or self-destruction.

The following day I felt very emotionally vulnerable and sensitive, as if my feelings were just below the surface. This felt very exposing to me and made me more sensitive in relating to others. I noticed that I would cry more easily and unprovoked than usual. Other than feeling very emotional, I felt pretty normal.

I would take it again - although I would probably do it in a one-on-one session to have more guidance and support throughout the experience. I would not recommend it to others just yet as I feel I have a lot more to understand about this process and it is early days. It is also very intense and is certainly not for everyone. Doing this in a small group setting, it's hard to get adequate support when there are other people who also need it. When you might be going through some really emotional and heavy things and can hear people in the room speaking or laughing, it can be distracting for your individual experience, so in that sense I think doing it one-on-one would have been better for me. In saying that, it was rather nice to share the experience with others. It can add another dimension and show you how different people can be during their session; and how your trauma impacts the way you relate to others, which is quite insightful.

The setting was great and I felt really safe; a nice house with a great ocean view and not too many distractions. The facilitation was great; I remember being held by the therapist and given tissues when I cried which meant a lot to me in that moment. I felt really supported in those moments. It was a very impactful experience and I'm grateful to have had the opportunity, despite it being messy and ugly. I feel I'm getting steps closer to the real me.

Shaun 52, Artist

Shaun, a committed Buddhist, had suffered prolonged periods of depression throughout adulthood. This has waned somewhat after a deliberate change in work and lifestyle, and participation in meditation and Buddhist learning in recent years. He describes his nature as compressive (as opposed to depressive). This manifests in him not living a fulfilled life. In his words; 'There's a little monster on my shoulder holding me back, so to speak.'

His intention for taking Psilocybin is to hopefully eliminate his depression and also to have a spiritual encounter and experience the feeling of divine love. Shaun's ex-girlfriend had experienced ayahuasca and encouraged him to try it. He didn't feel ready for ayahuasca but had heard from some Buddhist monks that psilocybin mushrooms were great for achieving enhanced spiritual states. His session took place in a small group of four men.

Shaun - First Psilocybin Session (3.5 gms *P. cubensis*)

Shaun's words

What happened during the active effect of the medicine is quite hard to describe. I was aware at all times of my experience. I don't believe I had hallucinations or visualisations so to speak. I had some periods of strong laughter which generally does not come so easily to me. There were also periods of feeling immense 'oneness,' a level of vibration that one only dreams of living with. There was a confirmation of the feeling of kindness and compassion and that offering these to others is the only thing that matters.

I have deliberately waited a number of weeks to write this post taking the medicine, as I was aware of amazing changes and wanted to see if they were just short term or were something deeper. I have used alcohol in large quantities at times and continued regular consumption to generally negate my depression. I drink beer daily and have done for years. Both myself and my partner have noticed rather dramatic but subtle changes since my therapy session. Most notably I have basically had NO desire for beer since this date. There have never been many days in recent years, before the session, where I was not buying beer each day. Drinking beer was an aid to me, to chill me out or to help me get some focus. This is quite a phenomenal change.

This mushroom journey also appears to have removed my procrastination and level of mind chatter that always attempts to complicate things, especially with the 'compressive mind.' I find myself just doing things now as opposed to having an internal dialogue and trying to negate activity, like going to the gym or starting a painting. I am also much more mellow with driving in traffic now. Driving and traffic has always been a nemesis of mine.

I would definitely recommend this to others. While I really enjoyed the small group setting and it was enjoyable to share the experience with others, I would be more inclined to work alone with the medicine in future – for now at least. I made some notes and set intentions before this experience, and I believe there have certainly been some dramatic shifts since then, in particular the need for alcohol.

Nic, 52, IT Specialist

Nic was diagnosed with anxiety, adult ADHD, and a form of dyslexia. He has seen psychologists previously for his issues, with little success. He was taking Concerta and Valdoxan, but had stopped for the two weeks leading up to his psilocybin session. He has never consumed any illicit drugs and drinks alcohol maybe twice a year.

Nic has a wife and two children and is soon to be in a position of having to apply for a new job. He has won national awards for his work and says he is brilliant at making systems and structures work more efficiently; despite this, his anxiety around applying for jobs is immense and incapacitating. He simply can't even fill out a job application or promote himself in any way. Understandably he is worried and anxious that if he can't apply for and get a job, he won't be able to provide for his family.

With regard to his childhood; Nic's German father was badly affected by the war, and had consequently cut off all his emotions. He had a 'just get on with it' attitude. Nic, a sensitive and creative child found it difficult to grow up in what he describes as a 'bogan' type family where the men idolised cars and drinking beer. His Mum, his only ally, died when Nic was 21 and he experienced this as a huge and terrible loss. Nic's older brother died shortly after his mum died, due to alcohol related complications. During his teenaged school years Nic moved interstate with his family and had to start at a new school where he was constantly bullied for being foreign and tall. His previous Steiner type school was a haven in comparison.

Having researched psychedelics thoroughly Nic eventually decided to give it a try. His motivation for doing psychedelic therapy was to understand and hopefully address his intense anxiety around applying for jobs so that hopefully he could break this debilitating chain and apply for and get a job.

Nic - First Psilocybin Session (4.8 gms *P. cubensis*)

Nic started with 3 gms, but after an hour asked to have the dose increased, then again twenty minutes later. This is a bigger dose than would typically be given for a therapeutic session, but all was fine and he managed well.

Nic's words

During the active effects I felt hyper mentally aroused and curious. I ruminated on many issues. Constantly swinging between simply experiencing the emotions and back to being super analytical about what was going on. I found my absolutely insatiable desire to analyse everything both annoying and highly amusing. I enjoyed the visualisations. The entire experience was quite pleasant.

I moved from the issues I'd been dealing with in succession and each time instantly came to the conclusion that each one of them did not matter. I had the sensation that my consciousness was simply a continuing sequence of sensations or thoughts that I would process momentarily - only for them to be replaced by another sensation or thought. Very often the replacement thought was my awareness that I was following this sequence again. This happened a massive number of times and was both very annoying and highly amusing.

I had a very cathartic experience when the therapist guided me back into my childhood. It really helped me to realise why I have difficulty promoting myself in a job interview. I grew up in a family where I felt very different, and on some level unacceptable. This was mainly due to my ADHD and being kind of spiritual and conscious, in a family of beer-swilling, blokey, bogans. I know my father wanted to love me, but he just couldn't understand me. On some subconscious level I felt unacceptable. The mushrooms really helped me to fully experience how I'd felt as a child and I had a big cry about this. The therapist helped me see that this is a programme that is still playing out subconsciously in my life and is probably why I can't promote myself.

My Mum died when I was 21 and, in a sense, she was my only real ally. I got bullied at high school when we moved to a new city. I was very tall and just didn't fit in with the mainly sporting crowd. My previous school had been so nurturing; it was similar to a Steiner school. The transitional shock was quite profound.

The next day, after my session, I felt extremely calm, content, and relaxed. I continued to feel that a huge number of issues I'd spent a long time worrying about previously, no longer bothered me at all - like a huge number of emotional stones had been removed from my shoes. I felt exactly the same person I was previously, just minus a load of emotional baggage. The anxiety I previously felt about many issues no longer seems to exist. This has continued.

I was finally able to respond to the email that I'd left unanswered for about six months, from a guy high up in my profession who understood my situation and had offered to help me find a job. I had ruminated over this for the previous six months. The therapist was excellent and extremely insightful. I strongly feel this has been an enormously beneficial experience for me. I really thank her for taking the risk she takes and doing such great work.

John, 24, Civil Engineer

John has suffered from mild anxiety, since he was 18. Luckily his doctor was switched-on and aware of the addictive potential of benzodiazepine – (anti-anxiety meds), and didn't medicate him for this. While he partied a bit in his teenage years, John no longer drinks nor takes any drugs. On the contrary, he is vegan and into sport and healthy living.

John's Mum died when he was only ten which impacted him hugely. His teenage sister made a suicide attempt shortly after, but this was more a cry for help than a serious attempt. John felt angered by this, seeing it as a selfish act. His father drank quite a lot back then but is now into health and fitness. John has good memories of his maternal grandmother who helped them out a lot after his mum's death, despite the fact that she was alcoholic and in and out of rehabs.

John currently has a good job and a fairly stable and loving relationship. They have just bought a house together. She's also doing psychedelic therapy to deal with her own childhood issues. Early in their relationship John had a bit of a pornography habit. She caught him out once and unfortunately, he lied to her about it. She now has trust issues as a result because similar honesty issues had occurred in a previous relationship. Although John says he has definitely stopped this behaviour, she is having trouble letting it go.

John's intention for doing this medicine therapy session was to heal residual pain around his Mum's death and other family troubles that happened throughout his teenage years. He hopes to heal relationship issues with his partner around his shutting down emotionally and inability to share his feelings.

John - First Psilocybin Session (2 gms *P. subaeruginosa*)

An initial dose of 1.5 grams then a half gram a top up after an hour. It took about 75 minutes to take effect. Subs seem to take longer to take effect and for this reason, they're not as ideal for the timeline of therapeutic work. But they were all that was available at the time.

John's words

I felt a lot of anxiety and fear initially, in fact, I was very scared. These are typical feelings I have for the unknown; my initial reaction is always fear. I realise now that I had to break through that fear myself and not rely on others to help me stay calm. I still think about that initial feeling today, as it was very disturbing and worrying. However, the therapist mentioned five words to me, which has changed my life since. They were: 'You are your only healer.' I learnt and realised emphatically that I could let go and get myself through that initial stage. I realised I have complete control over how I respond to fear and anxiety – and not to let it control my entire experience in life.

Finally, I let go and allowed the mushrooms to guide me through my experience. There was this little ball of light, which I now realise is this star in the sky (which my Nana used to say was Mum looking down on us, as it was the brightest in the sky every night). I kept waiting to see my Mum but she never came and during the session it clicked. She was always there; she was the Star, and she was with me for my entire session. I was following my Mum and she was taking me to where I needed to go, to show me how to love myself, respect myself and how to heal.

I kept asking the guide, my Star, why we weren't focusing on my Mum as that was what I thought I needed to heal. However, we never went there; we never touched on it at all. I now know that I don't need to heal anything with my Mum; she doesn't want me and any of my siblings to focus on her death, or to never let her go. I thought I needed to make amends to her. I thought I had let her down. But she doesn't want that for any of us – she completely loves us and misses us to death, but there is no way she is coming back.

Realising this was extremely important to me because I now know that my self-healing isn't about my Mum. Now I could let that go and explore all the other possible ways to heal - focusing on mum was just holding the rest back as it wasn't needed; it has already happened. I didn't want to honour my Mum in any negative way. She deserves so much more than that – being negative to other people, due to what I thought was pain over my Mum, was no way to honour her.

I realised that the way I treat and love other people as well as myself, is a reflection on how my Mum and Dad raised me. They didn't raise me to do anything less than treat others and myself with compassion, respect, love, honesty, and generosity. They deserve that to be reflected in how I act.

The 'middle' section of the session - I don't know how long it went for - however it felt like the majority of the session - probably 70% of it. The initially stage around my fear (explained above) was about 20%. The other 10% I'll get to later, was focused on my partner. But this middle 70%, was just like a compilation of my life experiences; a bit like watching TV and changing the channel - however it was me going up an elevator, controlled by the Star (Mum). It would stop for a bit and another experience would be relived, from either the same perspective as it happened, or from different angles and stand points. I could see the happiness, and love I felt.

With each experience, my love for myself grew - the feeling of happiness and complete joy just continued to increase. I have never felt so much joy before. It was showing me how to feel these things again and where to find them. Some went for longer than others; some were very short. At every 'level' or door opening, the love increased and got stronger and stronger. These scenarios were mainly times with family, especially my twin brother. One experience was from when I was two to three years old, and seeing my Mum and Dad raise me.

It then moved on and I got to see the hurt and pain my dad felt when my mum died. The huge amount of empathy I felt for him was amazing. I felt a bond between us grow from just seeing it. It showed the effort my dad put in when my Mum died to give all us kids everything we wanted – the genuine love I felt for my dad was unexplainable. It showed me the pain my brother is currently in and how I need to be there more for him and be a better brother. It showed experiences with my partner that really emphasised how much she loves me, how much of an asshole I can be, and all the hurt I have caused her.

With all these experiences that this elevator stopped at, I could not only see these things, but most importantly I felt the emotions the people felt. It also focused on how I felt, from knowing their pain, sadness, depression, and anger. I know now how critical the order of these experiences was, it allowed me to see my own love for myself, and the happiness that comes from that. With these feelings it allowed me to love others and empathise with others. It showed me not to be selfish and self-centred, but to experience the pain of others, and the pain I inflict on others by my actions.

This went on and on - the elevator went up and up, and just continued until I really loved myself. I really know how painful my actions have been and how I need to be a better partner, brother, uncle, son, and grand-son. Not that I need to be for other people, but because I absolutely WANT to be for my own happiness and enjoyment in life.

The last section of my journey was the most incredible. I literally felt my partner's energy in the room, and I undoubtedly knew it was her straight away. The Star sent me straight to a place, which is not describable at all. It was just an existence of the purest love, care, compassion, and a few other emotions I still can't explain. Just mainly, that this person was the most important person in my life and my soul's life – my soul is my partner's soul. It all was for my partner. The music that was playing increased these emotions until my experience finished. It was extremely overwhelming.

There were no come down effects, however, I am not sure what they feel like. I felt light; no depressive feelings. Joyful and free. Free was the big one, I felt free from what others thought. The following week I felt a huge increase of my love for myself and my partner due to the strong emotions I felt during my session. I had the urge to reach out to my grandfather who I haven't spoken to for almost eight years and asked to catch up for coffee, (which couldn't happen due to the border restrictions.) I had the best sleeps I have had in my entire life for the next seven days. They are still great, due to being able to let go and relax, as I feel more in control.

The enduring effects are that I love myself completely, I respect myself and look after my physical body as well. These things are helping with the growth of my relationship with both my partner and my family. I would absolutely, 100% recommend this to others. I've already recommended my brother and father to look into it.

The therapist was fantastic, during that first period of when the medicine started becoming active, I couldn't let go and let it guide me. She said something to me that has stuck with me ever since and is 100% correct, which was; 'You are your only healer.' The reason she mentioned that was due to me asking her to text my partner and get her to come up. She could have easily said, 'Yes,' but she said those words to me. They were very powerful for me and critical for the session to go as well as it did. It is completely true. The music playlist was amazing.

Shannon, 46, Sales Representative

Shannon took part in several MDMA and ayahuasca treatments prior to her psilocybin session. (Intro in MDMA section.) Her intention for the session was to heal more of her childhood trauma and hopefully gain access to some more repressed memories.

Shannon - First Psilocybin Session (2.5 gms *P. Cubensis*)

Shannon's words

About forty minutes after ingesting the mushrooms, they kicked in like a freight train - no warning. I'm thrust unceremoniously into the distant past, into a place where I'm feeling intense physical pain. My back is breaking. Something bad is happening to me. Someone is hurting me. I'm very young and frightened. I don't know what is happening. I want it to stop. I'm groaning and wailing - trying to get away. My adult self knows it's something sexual. But the child doesn't know what is happening. Every journey lately, I seem to go back here - MDMA and now mushrooms. I seem to be stuck in this place.

The therapist touches me on the arm and I startle in absolute terror. She speaks and I cower and back away. I'm hypervigilant to the max. I collapse in a heap on the floor, my limbs flailing around. I accidently knock something over. The crash startles me and I jump in fear. This eventually stops and I surrender to grief and wail... a lone and bereft child... crying how a child cries, face crumpled and loud. I'm not worried about how I look. I have my back to her. I'm pretty much oblivious to her or the room. This thing has taken over me. The therapist speaks and I'm aware she is there - but I am not there.

I lie in surrender - spent and stunned. I need to move away from here. I wrap the blanket around me. When the therapist moves away, I think, 'She doesn't want to play with me.' The mushroom tells me that it doesn't matter. Fuck everybody. Don't care what anyone thinks. You can look after yourself now. You don't need anyone, 'Dancing Queen.' I feel this was a decision I made when I was a teenager. But I don't know where the 'Dancing Queen' came from; I'm certainly no dancer.

I close my eyes again - the hallucinations come - bright orange and red - undulating waves of fractals with black eyes in every corner - coming towards me. When I open my eyes, the hallucinations stop. The bamboo leaves on the balcony reach out to me, their bright green fingers fluttering in the breeze. It comforts me to know that I can open my eyes and make it all stop. I fight the visions; I don't trust the mushroom. The therapist asks if I'm ok and looks at me with sincere compassion. I close my eyes and take the ride.

I feel strongly to move to the daybed now. I'm ordered by the mushroom to close the door. It wants my undivided attention. It says I need solitude to learn to listen. It wants to give me some lessons. It promises to always be gentle on me; that I can relax from here on in. But I don't trust it. I've heard all this before.

It shows me how as a child I always thought the sexual abuse was over, but it kept on happening. I was so exhausted. My lessons - locked away in a room with the door shut. I could hear the other kids playing outside, laughing, and I just wanted to go out and play with them. But I couldn't get away. And even when it was over and I eventually did get away, they avoided me. They knew something weird was going on and didn't want to play with me.

I felt dirty, full of poison, and ugly. I needed to keep myself clean, hide the messy ugliness - pull myself together. I still do this. Don't let anyone know. I needed to be clean, presentable, made up, because I felt so dirty inside, so full of shame. I truly believed that nobody liked me. The mushroom said that people, 'DO' like me, but I've got to stop caring about what other people think and start liking myself.

The hallucinations start again – red and orange undulating fractals coming towards me, black eyes in every corner. I say, 'No, fuck that, enough of your shenanigans. I don't want to play anymore. Leave me alone. I'm over this.' I turned against the world then. I rebelled. I was tired and I didn't want to be here. I've carried this all through my life, ambivalence, unable to commit to life. I'm still doing it.

I was put in a Psych Ward when I was 14, because I was so depressed. Too many years of fear and despair. I had no interest in school. Everything was destroyed. The horse I got, after many years of begging, was the only thing that kept me going. It was taken off me when I ran away from home and given to my sister. I was put in a Girls-Home for juvenile delinquents. That's me.

I don't know how I've lived this long. Sometimes I still don't really want to be here. I'm just kind of filling in time until I die. When I ask the mushroom, 'WHY, why me, why did all this happen to me?' It said, so I could help others - so I'd have empathy.' I said 'FUCK THAT - THAT'S NOT FAIR. I don't want to help others. Why me? Fuck that. No one should have to go through that in order to help others.' The mushroom said I need to ease up on the attitude a bit - be a bit nicer. I then began to swear at my father and call him all sorts of fucking swear words. I have to let this anger out - take it out on him - not others.

The mushroom said that I am an artist and should paint bright things with dark hidden meanings underneath. It said I am a Dancing Queen. (a bit cryptic) It said I should stop asking 'Why' and start asking 'Where' Where should I be? Focus on the future. I am to stop saying sorry and being sorry. Stop worrying about making a mess. It's ok to be a bit messy. I should stop thinking that people don't like me and stop caring if they don't. But they do.

The mushroom said that I'm in control now. I could open the door and go out and play. So, I did. I did just that. I just want to play with the happy people, to have happiness in my life. I deserve it. So, I opened the door, went out and talked to the therapist. She gave me fruit and we ate it together and it tasted divine and we laughed. People DO like me. My father told me that nobody liked me and that I was dirty and bad. I'm not. I'm fucking not. The mushrooms start to wear off.

This healing is painful, exhausting and harrowing - but you definitely feel much better afterwards. Connecting with this girl child me, helps me to admire and love her and hence myself. When they're not smashing you with intense and painful reality, the mushrooms can be quite humorous. They incite my rebellious, teenage, 'wild child,' persona and give me a weird sense of humour.

Shannon – Second Psilocybin (1.5 gms *P. Subaeruginosa*)

Shannon's Words

My intentions for this session were to try and understand why I don't have many friends and why I generally don't trust people.

When it kicked in, the mushroom took me straight back to the childhood neighbourhood where I grew up. I sort of flew over my neighbourhood and with this global perspective, saw and named everyone I knew, who lived in each house. I saw all the houses we lived in. I saw all the people. This went on for a while. The mushroom was emphasising that I grew up in a community - we all played together, we all knew each other. Our parents knew each other too and socialised together sometimes as well.

After this tour of my neighbourhood ended, I was taken back to and started reliving a horrific night when I was attacked and severely beaten up by two V8 girls; (tough girls, who hang out with a group of tough guys, who drive powerful American V8 cars - sort of a gang but not quite.)

A blue Chevy V8 pulled up alongside me. I was sitting on a bench seat in the main street of my town. I was fourteen and still at high school. I don't know exactly what I was doing there – probably waiting for someone who didn't show up. The car was driven by my next-door neighbour's boyfriend.

Two girls leaned out of the window and asked me up if I wanted to go to a party. The guys in the car were my neighbourhood guys, two were friends of my brothers. I'd gone to primary school with most of them so I didn't think for a minute that anything bad would happen to me. In fact, I was excited that these two tough girls would even bother with the likes of me. I'm not sure why my neighbourhood boys were in this car with these older girls: one - a tall, strong Maori; the other - a rat faced skank with dark liquid eyeliner. The girls were 21 and 22 – (it said so in the court news) the guys were not much older than me. I got in the car feeling very excited.

We drove some miles to the 'party,' arriving at a small wooden house in a dark, bush ensconced valley. There were no cars outside. It sure didn't look like much of a party. We leave the car and go inside. The doors are locked. Once inside, the girls turn on me. Rat face starts screaming at me, calling me a fucking slut and accusing me of sleeping with her boyfriend. (Not true.) They both start laying into me - beating me with their fists, punching me in the face and head. I am stunned and bewildered. What the fucking hell.

They then drag me into a bedroom where they continue hitting me. The Maori Amazon throws a large beer bottle at my head. I duck and it smashes through the bedroom window. When they eventually tire of beating me up, one holds me down on the bed, the other undoes my belt and jeans and pulls them off. I'm mortified. I have my period. They order the guys to put me on the block, (gang rape me) slam the door, and leave the room.

Fucking, fucking hell. I am hysterical. My neighbourhood boys just stand there. They watched me getting smashed to a pulp and did nothing – nothing – they just stood there watching and did nothing. Now they look at me and for a terrifying moment – a terrible moment – I think they will actually do it. I scream at them in my terror. 'Why did you let that happen?' 'Why didn't you help me?' 'Why didn't you do something?' They look a little ashamed and scared. They speak to me in whispers. They are scared of the girl's boyfriends – they are scared of the V8 boys. Oh, my fucking god - what heroes. They whisper amongst themselves and come up with a plan. They will sneak me out through the bedroom window and drive me home. But the damage is done. The damage is done. Abandoned again.

By the time I get down the steep driveway to the front door of my house, I am hysterical and crying. Probably a delayed reaction to my terrifying encounter. My family are all sitting in the lounge watching T.V. Through tears and gasps, I tell them what happened.

Not moving from his armchair, Dad looks at me with a sneer on his face. I am crying, bloody and bruised. He laughs at me and sneers, 'Serves yourself right for getting around with scum.' Fuck him. I hate him. I am so truly devastated that my father can hate me this much. Something ominous shifts in me – a terrifying penny drops. I have no protection - not even from my own father. Nobody will fight for me. Nobody will protect me. He hates me.

Mum takes me into the kitchen and through my tears I manage to tell her a short version of what happened. She calls the police. They arrive and take me away with them. I go alone - not even my mother accompanies me. I am alone. The cops get me to show them the house where it happened, then they take me to the hospital. The police were kinder to me and seemed to care more about me than my own family.

The bitches were arrested and charged with assault. They got their day in court and each received three months in prison. Bloody good job. I received two black eyes, a swollen lip and looked like a monster for a week or so; but the damage ran far deeper. I was devastated by my neighbourhood boys, who just stood there watching me - devasted by my own family who didn't seem to care. I lost more faith in humanity that night. I could trust no one. I was truly alone in this world. Alone and broken.

On this mushroom journey, it was quite surprising to me to realise that the worst part of that whole night, was the betrayal of my neighbourhood guys – the guys who did nothing to protect me. This felt far worse than any pain those girls inflicted upon me. That was one of the scariest nights of my life.

Far out - it's no bloody wonder I don't trust people. I'd forgotten about all this. I remembered the event of course - it was in the court news. But among all the other terrible events in my life, I'd somehow forgotten the details – the feelings – the betrayal - the devastation. Now I understand. I understand myself so much more. The mushrooms did that for me.

Ayahuasca Therapy

Natalie, 30, Medical Doctor

Natalie's anxiety was so extreme she recently had to leave her job at a busy hospital. Responsibility, long hours, lack of staff support, and the stress of making life and death decisions, finally undid her. She had ruminating, fearful thoughts, battled agoraphobia and struggled to even venture out to the shops. Reluctant to take antidepressants, she had resorted to occasionally self-medicating with benzodiazepines.

Some family history: During Natalie's childhood her mother was a practising but reasonably functional alcoholic (she's now clocked up twenty years sobriety in AA.) Two years ago, her mum attended an ayahuasca retreat in Costa Rica and had raved about it ever since. This sparked Natalie's interest who had already tried LSD and psilocybin, finding them both spiritually and mentally profound.

Her dad, once a successful businessman, became seriously addicted to Oxycontin when he was prescribed it for pain relief after an accident. This extremely potent painkiller lures many unwitting recipients into its daunting and addictive handcuffs. Addiction is big business for Big Pharma. Like so many others in its dire grip, her dad eventually resorted to heroin - it was cheaper and easier to get. Natalie was only informed of her dad's death, two years after the fact; he'd moved to Canada and remarried and his new wife hadn't bothered to inform his family. It completely shocked and confused Natalie to discover that her dad had died in such a terrible way - and two years after the fact.

Apart from the considerable stress of her fairly demanding job there seemed no obvious reason for Natalie's extreme anxiety. Growing up with an addicted parent was obviously not ideal, but there was no serious abuse or neglect.

Natalie - First Ayahuasca (3.5 gms *Syrian Rue* + 20 gms *Acacia Courtii*.)

Initial dose of 15 gms of Acacia and two small top up doses took the total to 20 gms. This is a strong therapeutic dose and made for an intense experience, but certainly achieved the desired purpose.

Natalie's words

Previously in my life I'd taken magic mushrooms and LSD. I took mushrooms during a time I was going through a depression in 2017. It was a deeply profound experience and my first mystical experience on psychedelics. I have taken LSD over the years since 2015, sometimes at home for therapeutic purposes, sometimes with friends to facilitate bonding and connection. My main purpose when taking any psychedelic is to expand my mind and push the limits of reality. Ever since my first mushroom trip, it became clear to me that these medicines can change your life.

I wanted to take ayahuasca because for most of this year, I've struggled with debilitating anxiety. I was having regular panic attacks and really not coping. The constant anxiety was leading me into a depression. I ended up having to quit my job, but the anxiety still remained. After a six-week stint at a job away from home, I came back completely broken. My anxiety was the worst it's ever been. Even small tasks like going to the grocery store was giving me anxiety. I was constantly in tears and felt I had no control over my mind or emotions. My mind was in a constant state of worry and panic, and on high alert for the next threat. I catastrophised everything. My mind was stuck in ruminating thoughts and unhelpful ingrained patterns that never let up; no matter what I did, meditation, yoga, breathing, exercise - nothing seemed to bring me relief. I was so close to starting antidepressants but ultimately decided against it, knowing in my heart they weren't the answer. I knew it was time to hit the reset button in my brain and I felt called to ayahuasca to help me do that.

I took my first dose around 7 PM and then another dose about 40 minutes later. That's when the visual hallucinations started. I started seeing fractals and geometric shapes. I felt like I was slipping in and out of a dream. I recall the plant introducing herself to me and inviting me to come along with her on a journey. I felt curious and excited and let my mind go.

I felt an overall sense of peace and love. I recall a point of entering what was a dusty old computer lab where there were old machines running. I realized that this place was my mind. I had all these background programs that had been running for years on autopilot. I remember the plant showing me this and guiding me to turn off the switches. It felt great to turn off these programs; they were no longer serving me. They had in the past but now it was time for an upgrade.

I also acknowledged all these separate parts of me. I came into contact with parts of me that were anxious, sad, and scared. At first, I wanted to ignore them. But then the plant told me to love them, acknowledge them, and thank them for all the hard work they had been doing for me. They really had been trying to do their best to keep me safe. I embraced all these parts of me and felt myself becoming whole.

Every time I felt scared, the plant told me to just shower those feelings in love and it would all be OK; and that worked - it was beautiful. I felt deep gratitude for myself and all that I'd accomplished. I realized that

I'm extremely hard on myself and have impossible standards. Nothing is ever good enough. I am always striving for something else to make me happy. I do that to my partner as well. I realized that I am perfect and whole just the way I am. I don't need to keep trying so hard. I am complete in this moment.

One of my intentions was to connect to my body and be fully present in the moment. I finally felt that peace. I remember thanking all parts of me, of feeling such joy for my body, and all that she does for me. At one point I purged and that felt really therapeutic. Releasing all that built up emotion. And when there were times, I felt a bit panicked, I just asked the plant to be gentle and she listened.

I also had an experience of feeling my father's struggle with addiction and death. I found peace and comfort in that and a deep sense of forgiveness. Up until that point everything I faced, I faced with such a sense of love. I remember having moments where all sense of reality melted away. Where what we know as reality had no meaning. Time didn't exist and my mind had dissolved. Even though I was losing touch with reality, it was bliss.

Around 9 PM, I had the option to take another dose. I remember being reluctant because I was in such a great place. I recall asking the medicine if I should take another dose. She told me I could end it there and I would be in that bliss state or I could go deeper. A part of me wanted to end it there but another part of me wanted to see where the medicine could take me. Up until that point I had been having beautiful visuals. I felt as if the medicine was rewiring my brain and upgrading all the hardware.

I took the third dose and in what seemed to be a short amount of time, I began to slip into a state where reality didn't exist. It was like earlier in the journey but a lot more intense. I became extremely uncomfortable in my body. My heart was racing. I felt like I couldn't breathe. I was hot and sweaty and my mind began to unravel. I felt the most panic I have ever felt in my entire life. My heart was racing so much that I thought I was surely going to die. That's how it felt, as if I was going to die. All language and words lost meaning.

Normally on any other psychedelic, I still think in English but this time, all I heard were sounds, harsh terrible noises that were unrelenting. I remember feeling as if I had gone mad and that I would never feel "normal" again. My body was so weak. I felt as if it was going to give up. I still felt as if I couldn't catch my breath. I went outside to get air, but I still felt like I was suffocating. I was absolutely terrified.

At one point I felt as if I was giving birth; to maybe myself. It felt like I was simultaneously dying and being born. I believed I had actually overdosed. There was a very small part of me that knew I hadn't, but I was sure I was going to die. It wasn't a blissful death, but a terrifying, suffocating death. My mind was completely jumbled. I never thought I'd be the same again. I begged the medicine to ease up, but nothing worked. It was absolutely the worst feeling I have ever had in my entire life. I was not only physically unwell, but felt as if I had truly broken my mind.

The challenging part after the third dose, I later realized, was my birth. I had been born with my umbilical cord wrapped around my neck and in foetal distress. What I was experiencing was my birth, in which I did come very close to death. I was pre-verbal so I couldn't communicate what I was feeling to the facilitator. I was alone and had no way to make sense of what was going on. I believe that this is where my anxiety stems from. I was born into this world in a state of panic and terror and this has been my default for my entire life.

The next day, I felt extremely tired. It is exhausting work. I slept most of the day. But overall, I felt a sense of calm and peace. I feel like the worries I have are gone. The following weeks, I felt really good. My anxiety has been low to almost non-existent. When I do have moments of anxiety, I have been able to recall the insights I had during my ayahuasca journey and the anxiety does not escalate further. I have felt calmer and present in my body. I have an overall sense of calm and peace. It has quieted my racing mind and has helped put things into perspective - like things that would normally send me into a panic don't seem as overwhelming.

The main insights I got from the experience were that I realized that I'm extremely hard on myself and am my own worst enemy. I learned to integrate and love all parts of me. I truly felt that I am enough. I went into my mind and turned off all these old, outdated programs that I had forgotten were even there. I felt a sense of peace knowing that I am connected to something greater than myself. All of this is a construct of my mind and I have the power to change it. I let go of worry and doubt and felt a deep sense of trust.

It was an extremely intense experience and, in the moment, I said, 'I'd never take it again,' but now that I'm out of it, I would definitely take it again. I'm blown away by what this medicine can do. Truly life changing. I have more healing to do and believe ayahuasca is going to play a big part in that.

The facilitation was great. The therapist was helpful and really comforting especially during the last part when I seriously thought I was dying and asked her repeatedly to take me to hospital. Luckily, she didn't. I did end up taking 5 mg of Diazepam because it became too much for me. I really did try to surrender to it but the level of panic was unbearable. I don't think this diminished my journey or the healing.

I believe that I experienced exactly what I was meant to. Now I know that I can handle anything.

Therapist note; It's not that uncommon for people to think they are dying or going mad on some psychedelics. In such an instance the therapist just needs to calm the person as much as possible. Strongly dissuade them from taking a sedative as this will disrupt the experience so it doesn't reach its natural conclusion. Because the session occurred at her home and as she is a doctor with a drawer full of medication, it was difficult to dissuade her. The therapist relented towards the end of the session, but stayed the night close by to assure she didn't take more.

Lily, 45, IT Specialist

Lily was diagnosed with depression and non-purging bulimia nervosa some years ago. She is stuck in a pattern of attracting unavailable, non-committed men and admits to having codependent relationship issues where she ends up being the caretaker. Self-hatred, bad relationships and low self-worth are her self-described issues.

Lily previously worked in palliative care and as a prison chaplain and has been a committed Buddhist of twenty years. As an only child, Lily's mother was neglectful of her needs and emotionally absent. Her father left the family home when Lily was eight.

Her intention for this therapy is to hopefully gain some insight into what is blocking her spiritual growth and development as a practising Buddhist.

Lily - First Ayahuasca (3.5 gms *Syrian Rue* & 18 gms *A. Courtii*)

The Acacia was given as initial dose of 15 gms and later a small top up dose.

Lily's words

There was an entry doorway where I had to go through the crazy psychedelic visions before entering the deeper realms of the self. This was really hard as it was super intense and opening your eyes didn't help much as my vision was quite distorted. After this passed, I moved deep into my mind. The first thing that became apparent was that the thinking, everyday mind was a thin veneer atop a vast, vast internal landscape. A landscape not considered by the thinking mind as it doesn't use words.

The experience was very much a dialogue between myself and an unheard voice. I asked questions and answered them in my own internal voice - that was also not my voice. Then I moved into an awareness of my self-hatred. I am deeply visual so there was a lot of imagery. The medicine also informed me not to be silent anymore and to talk about everything - which I did. I talked constantly to the therapist, reporting everything I was experiencing. That brought the internal into the external, and in a way, made it more real and more tangible.

The first impressions were of the self-hate, dripping like treacle from the mind into the body and filling every cell. Then I saw it dripping into a vast cavern in my body centre. In the middle was suspended a three-year-old girl child, wrapped in the foetal position. She couldn't cope and was wrapped around a tiny diamond of compressed hate. As if that both protected her as well as being the cause of her suffering. It showed me again my self-hatred but showed me the way out this time. This was a big win for me, and I have been doing what was asked. I have found it enormously helpful and no longer feel like I hate myself.

The next day I felt very sensitive to kindness as this was one of the messages of the journey: Be open and receive kindness. I had three nights of waking during sleep in some sort of sticky confusion. It felt like I was still under the ayahuasca until a week later. I have so much to work with and integrate. It will take some time before I can dig down another layer.

Therapist Notes: Lily experienced carnivalesque visuals that were very intense. She talked continually through the entire session, to both myself and mother ayahuasca. The main themes that arose were around her intense self-hatred, missing a sense of family and worry about the state of the world. She accessed her inner child and got clarity around both past and potential relationships and said they were all now over – that they had given her nothing.

When I saw her again about a year later, Lily told me that the session had helped her immensely in her life.

Gina, 62, Business Advisor

Gina is a strong, assured business woman, heavily into New Age spiritual practices. She is in long term sober recovery from alcoholism. Her motivation for drinking ayahuasca was more exploratory than for healing purposes. She had researched ayahuasca and hoped to have a spiritual experience - preferably a death experience. She had participated in both MDMA and psilocybin therapy sessions and on both occasions had needed quite large doses.

Gina was drinking a smoothie when the facilitator arrived at her house at around 6pm. When asked about this, it was discovered that Gina had misunderstood the recommended preparatory dietary requirements (no food after midday). This possibly prolonged the time it took for the medicine to fully take effect; it took four hours to fully kick in and her session was still going strong at 3 a.m. By this time the facilitator could no longer stay awake. As things were going smoothly, they agreed she would nap on a nearby couch in the same room - close by should anything problematic occur.

Gina - First Acaciahuasca (3.5 gms *Syrian Rue* & 20 gms *A. courtii*)

The dose was given as initial dose of 15 gms and 2 later top up doses.

Gina's words

I heard a squawking outside and there was a cockatoo sitting on the fence and felt that my dead father was right there with me. I felt the effect in my body pretty quickly with a distinct pulsing and buzz. The images came and went and were of no real interest. I felt disassociated from them and stopped looking for the significance of the images and just surrendered to them.

The facilitator gave me the second dose but nothing much changed and then she later gave me a third dose. Again, nothing really changed. I felt I dozed off a couple of times, but I didn't. The images continued. The images were very similar to those experienced in the alpha state just before sleep, but they were continuous. They were cameos of all sorts of everyday scenes like a man with his four grandchildren, a man eating with his mouth open, dolphins lined up watching a woman going into her apartment - not so every day.

I could go into these cameos if I wanted and I did a couple of times but they held no interest for me. I think it was showing me that the externals were just that, externals - to be loving but disinterested. I can choose to get involved or I can choose to let it pass. I felt removed from all of these and they just didn't spark any interest. However, during this time I felt nauseous on and off and vomited a couple of times. The yawning which I also had in my mushroom session started almost at once. Both of these are forms of purging, so I knew I was letting go of stuff. One of my intentions was to let go of any build-up of residue in my body and I knew that was happening. Plus, there were lots of tears but without any emotion attached. I just felt them flowing.

The facilitator offered to give me a bit more, but I decided that the experience was what it was and I didn't want anymore. I felt a bit disappointed. I knew I was in a really good place and I was surprised that my experience felt so ordinary. This went on until 11pm. I asked what time it was and we both thought I was coming out of it but I actually had my second vomit and from there, it all started.

Throughout, I noticed that the sounds and the music were exaggerated. Even though it wasn't music I liked, from that point on, everything became about the music. It was in a way like the continuation of a Rupert Spira meditation I'd done that day and various others I'd done throughout the week. It was the dissolving of the density of the body and the music mixed vibrationally with that and allowed the body to disperse. There weren't images with this. It was more conversations and understandings.

I talked to Mama Aya and asked her what the earlier experience was all about. She told me that I was being rewired in a way. I was letting go of all the chatter and mindless noise from my body and that this was an easy way of doing it. There were no emotions felt in this. I saw a graphic of a face all contorted by time and knew that I was letting go of that old patterning. I asked Mother about experiencing the true nature of Self. She made it clear that I was experiencing it on and off all the time. The peace, happiness and love of my true Self was there all the time and I know that I just need to recognise the moments more and more. Mama was incredibly loving and gentle and kind. I thanked her for nurturing me and loving me. I curled up in her vibration and felt pure love. It was like an energetic day spa where I was immersed in so much love.

The facilitator and I talked about the music at that point. I said I was over the electronic synthesised music and found it quite jarring. She put on a playlist she uses for MDMA and mushrooms. Immediately I was transported to my previous mushroom journey, with her, even though I had not really been aware of the music in that session. It was a feeling of euphoria and coming home without the visions. It was wonderful. I felt like I was soaring in the music and again lots of tears were flowing. Then I went to my first MDMA session and felt the love that I felt in that session. This time that love was for me and Mama wrapped me up in it. I had a sense of the people that had appeared in my MDMA session, that I was able to flow love to - but this time it was all about me.

Mama showed how I could be softer and gentler within myself and how that energy would heighten my knowing of myself. All through this, the music was an experience in itself. The facilitator was great as I would ask for certain songs to be replayed. Darpan in particular really resonated with me. His voice was like the dad in the Lion King talking to Samba. It was beautiful and his song about closing the circle had the same effect on me although I didn't realise it was the same guy. I knew that sound was a big part of my journey. A few days ago, I had done a Holotropic breathing session, and on my out breath came a noise that went between a guttural sound to a type of tribal singing or maybe chanting. I had the same feeling then that sound was important for some reason.

At 3am the poor facilitator had had enough. She was tired, which I totally get. It's a long night for her holding space in the dark. She did it so well and again it was so lovely to have this experience with her. So, at 3 AM we made the decision that I'd be fine to continue and she was going to have a sleep on the nearby couch. She was there if I needed her. I was fine with this.

I put on my headphones and listened to some chanting and had a lovely journey back into my childhood. I saw that Mum and Dad did the best they could but were often distracted and I felt the struggle of trying to get their attention and love by striving to be the best in everything but really living a double life. Mama Aya came on the journey with me and re-mothered me by filling in the gaps. The places where I felt unseen for who I really was. She was able to give me that love that I craved and I had the real sense of changing my past. I saw my sisters as little girls with me, and I saw our vulnerability and our trying to navigate it with the nuns and Mum and Dad. She gave me the encouragement and sense of worth I was looking for from Mum and Dad.

After the session I felt more able to meditate and rest in the feeling of peace and happiness. Sound integration is wonderful; taking me to all sorts of places. I have a new appreciation for music and sound.

Shannon 46, Sales Representative

Shannon shares three ayahuasca experiences. Her first two were done in a group setting, the third in a solo session. Ayahuasca was her introduction to psychedelic therapy but she's since done several MDMA and psilocybin treatments. (Intro in MDMA section).

Shannon - First Ayahuasca (*B. Caapi*, + *A. acuminata* 15 gms.)

Shannon's words.

I cannot lie, the taste was shockingly vile; a rust-coloured swamp liquid, reminiscent of an ancient witches' brew. The price one pays for healing! Forty minutes later it kicked in with a power nothing could ever prepare you for. The shock when this powerhouse medicine introduces itself, is nothing short of astounding. A spirit seemed to invade my body; then it owned me; it owned my mind and body for the next five long hours.

The first thing I noticed was complete body anaesthesia, like something had pinned my body to the ground. It was terrifying. I could barely breathe from the shock of it all. Then my body started jerking. The facilitator startled me by putting a tuning fork on my heart and telling me to breathe. 'The jerking is just the medicine clearing blocked energy,' he told me. He later said that no one had ever looked at him with such fear in their eyes.

There were constantly moving visions with a carnival circus theme, like being on a roller coaster and merry go round at the same time. This continued for quite a while then it all suddenly changed. Three objects from my childhood home appeared - superimposed over each other and spinning; a brown ashtray, a plate with birds on it, and a chair. Suddenly, I was back in my childhood bed, reliving a traumatic memory. My father was getting into my bed. Something terrible was about to happen and no-one was going to save me. I experienced my small child's feelings of complete and utter abandonment. It was devastating and heartbreaking. I simultaneously witnessed this event from my adult observer's perspective and felt so sad for the little girl who was me. The feeling of utter abandonment was palpable and devastating; a life defining moment - the night my family abandoned me.

The facilitator was busy and didn't seem to be helping me much. His helper appeared and started talking, which was distracting because I couldn't talk back; too much was going on. He departed to help someone else and I returned to my terrible journey.

Two Asian guys from across the room looked at me and connected telepathically. They seemed to know I was in despair. They somehow managed to get up and come over to me. I don't know how they could even walk; I couldn't have if I'd tried. One sits down, cross legged, side on in front of me. He suddenly transformed into a meditating monk, sitting there silently supporting me. The other sits down beside me. He transforms into a Maori warrior with white aboriginal face paint. He looks into my eyes with such deep compassion - my face crumples and I start crying like a child. Their presence was so comforting and healing. I wasn't alone anymore. Mother Ayahuasca was giving me a different ending to my abandonment.

Those three symbols kept repeating in a loop, taunting me; brown ashtray; plate with ducks; and a chair. A girl from my primary school pops into my consciousness. I couldn't figure out why she was there. I'd never hung out with her at school. My only memory of her was that she beat me in a school running race. I came second. Her father was a photographer for the local newspaper, and we got our photos in the paper. But I couldn't figure out what those symbols meant or why this girl was in my trip.

The facilitator turns Shrek green and morphed into a praying mantis. I smile and turn away, trying not to giggle. I look again; yep, definitely a praying mantis. The music was indescribably beautiful and the lights outside amazing. Flashes of lightning crackled across the night sky. But those symbols kept repeating and I was stuck in this exhausting loop. I couldn't make it stop; not the visions, not the abuse, not the feeling of utter abandonment. I vomited.

Things seemed to ease up a bit. I can't remember much more, but it went on for ages. Certain songs stood out to me. Some were simply beautiful. When the medicine finally wore off, I felt like I'd survived a nightmare of monumental proportions. I was surprised to return to baseline so fast with no residual trace of where I'd just been and no hangover whatsoever. I was speechless at my journey beyond words – beyond the limitations of human language.

The following day, I asked the two Asian guys why they'd come over to help me. They said that Mother Ayahuasca had directed them to. Astounding! I've heard ayahuasca referred to as Telepathine; people can tune into others psychically and know what they're going through. Frankly, I couldn't have tuned into anything other than myself.

Shannon – Second Acaciahuasca (*Syrian Rue, A. Acuminata* 15 gms)

Shannon's words

After last night's intense session, I felt pure trepidation for what lay ahead. I asked for a smaller dose. I prayed to God, Mother Ayahuasca and anyone else who would listen, for mercy, as I drank the bitter brew.

Strangely, the theme followed on from last night but it was a bit gentler and more focused on TRUST, or my extreme lack thereof to be exact. I sat up and looked suspiciously around the room, feeling paranoid, defensive and threatened by everyone. Ayahuasca seemed to be showing me how my extreme lack of trust plays out and how it resulted from my childhood abuse and abandonment.

Then I became a snake. I literally got to feel like what it felt like to be a snake, which was sensual and sardonic. I began to quietly hiss at people. I'm not sure if I actually did this or whether it was just in my mind. But it felt kind of cool and probably symbolic of what I do in real life. Ayahuasca seems to work on multiple levels simultaneously; my fear of snakes and my fear of people; it was confounding, mysterious and powerful.

The girl beside me had her arms up in the air making strange intricate twirling movements with her hands. It was distracting and exhausting to watch but I couldn't stop watching her. She was like the girl in the magic red dancing shoes who couldn't stop. Finally, I broke the mesmerising spell, sat up and perused the room. I felt strangely like I'd peed my pants but couldn't be sure if I was imagining this or not? I certainly hoped so. I fixated on this for a while, feeling immense shame. I vomited.

A guy who'd arrived late today came over and took my bucket, replacing it with a clean one. 'Good work sister.' This struck me as a beautiful gesture. He returned to his mattress and sat down beside his beautiful partner. She smiled at me then suddenly transformed into a high priestess. These archetypes were truly fascinating to me, but I wasn't sure what to make of them. Ayahuasca is so strange and I wish I knew what some of this stuff meant.

Sunday morning, we had a sharing circle to discuss our journeys. Words kind of failed me - my experience was profound and indescribable; it would take a while to process all that had happened. The kind people who helped me were memorable and helped me feel connected to people for the first time in ages. For this reason, I'm really glad I did it in a group, even though some of what happened was very personal and it was intense to have others witness this. The theme of my first night was definitely ABANDONMENT and my second night was TRUST.

When I returned home, the changes in me were instantly noticed. My mother was truly amazed. She couldn't believe how much calmer I was. I was no longer reactive. Mum was astounded at the difference in me and so was I. My hypervigilance had completely downregulated. I'd lost the need to enforce my opinions. My PTSD symptoms had pretty much disappeared. Even people in AA commented on the difference in me, though most didn't know what I had done. The feeling of calm has endured, as have other changes. I feel more connected to nature and my life feels like it's in some kind of synchronous flow - like I'm connected to a higher force that is conducting profound and magical things to happen. Things seem to line up; connections are made, wishes are granted and things come to pass. I've reengaged with music and the smells of incense and candles. My diet has improved; the desire to eat meat and sugary foods has diminished.

Ayahuasca is completely mysterious; challenging, profound, frightening, but massively life changing. The journey is epic - a hero's journey - the person who embarks on this voyage is not the same one who returns. It takes you to psychological places that no amount of counselling could ever reach. Ayahuasca is a life demarcation point – one I'm extremely grateful I had the opportunity to do. I was suicidal before this and maybe it saved my life. It certainly upgraded it.

Shannon – Third Ayahuasca (B. *caapi*, & A. *courtii* - approx. 17gms)

Shannon's words

I quickly understood that I was in for a thrashing. It came on fast and strong. At about thirty minutes in, I started purging; loud, gut wrenching, vomiting which continued for quite a while. Then ayahuasca smashed me into a high definition, full on feeling experience where I was made to fully remember, feel and experience all the immense shame, depression and exhaustion I'd felt as a child. I was shown how I'd carried this shame all through my life; how it seeped out everywhere like poison, stopping me from connecting to people.

My journey of shame looped over and over relentlessly - there was no escape. I was back fully feeling it as my child self - literally squirming with shame. Shame, Shame, Shame...looping over and over. All the shame I'd carried from the sexual abuse inflicted upon me as a child and the physical and emotional abuse that pervaded my childhood home. Powerless to stop it back then, I don't know how I survived, but from a very young age, I wanted my life to end. I begged God for help but he never answered the phone so I lost faith pretty early.

Brown ashtray, plate with birds, chair; superimposed over each other and spinning around. The same familiar symbols I've seen on every ayahuasca journey, spinning around and taunting me - looping and looping. I can't figure out what they mean. Brown ashtray, plate with birds, chair. The meaning feels so close and significant, but just so out of reach. Shame, shame, shame. It's exhausting.

Towards the end of my journey of shame, the medicine entered a different phase. When I asked Mother Ayahuasca, 'How am I meant to live after this?' She replied, 'You have to find things you like and do them.' But what do I like? I've lived life in survival mode so long; I didn't have a clue what I like.

Then my journey took me back to my childhood, to see the things I'd liked back then. I loved animals – especially horses. I had one for a while. Dad must have felt guilty for all the horrible shit he did to me, or just finally succumbed to my many years of begging. But he used my horse to control me and eventually took her off me and gave her to my sister after I ran away from home. I rebelled after that. I went totally wild. I'd lost the only thing I loved - the thing that kept me going. I hated my sister for taking my horse. Divide and conquer - every tyrant's tool.

The killing of all my pets.

Ayahuasca then takes me on a journey where I get to feel all the powerlessness and despair I felt as a child. Ayahuasca takes me through the killing of all my pets. He killed them all - my father - and in little vignettes I get to witness and feel it all over again - as a child and an adult simultaneously.

First - I'm taken back to a Sunday night in our lounge. Mum is complaining to dad that my dog has ripped up some washing. She had locked him in the basement laundry, and he'd ripped up a sheet. Dad is angry. He says he's going to shoot my bloody dog. I plead with him not to and even threaten to call the RSPCA. But he just sneers and smirks. When I arrive home from school the next day, my beautiful dog doesn't race up the drive to greet me, wagging his tail like he always did. My heart sinks, my body freezes and I know. I never see my dog again.

Second - We were just little kids and thought it hilarious when dad put our cat into the station wagon to take us on a Sunday family drive. He stops on a quiet country road, gets out of the car and opens the back of the station wagon. He removes his shotgun. He takes the cat out of the car and puts her on the ground. He shoos her away by throwing a stone at her. I'm so confused. What is going on? Our cat runs off a little way into a paddock then turns around and looks back looking as confused me. Dad takes aim and fires and slaughters our cat in front of us. I freeze in a silent scream of horror and shock. My tears are laughed at. My cousin, who was with us that day, buys us a framed print of a sad eyed cat which still hangs in my mother's house today – ever a dark reminder. Mum told us later that the cat was sick but dad was too stingy to have her put down.

Third - Another Sunday while we are eating a family roast lunch, Dad smirks at me and asks me how I'm enjoying the lamb. I tentatively say it is nice. He starts laughing uproariously, then tells me I'm eating my pet lamb. I almost vomit and flee the table crying.

Fourth - I'm in the backyard. Dad is chasing my pet chicken around with an axe. He eventually catches it and decapitates it in front of me. I'd raised it from a fluffy yellow chick that they gave out at my school every year.

I could never comprehend why my father was so cruel. I loved animals and his acts of gleeful annihilation devastated me. He seemed to derive some sick pleasure from it and the unspoken message was clear – anything I loved could be taken away – maybe even me.

To my utter relief, the medicine finally stopped. That would have to rate as one of the worst nights of my life. I sit up and survey the nightscape feeling like a holocaust survivor. The night is iridescent and still, with myriad stars and a full champagne moon. I lie on the deck for a while listening to the distant hum of a truck passing through the sleepy country town. I wander inside like a sleepwalker - have a shower and go to bed - feeling sad, alone, devastated.

This medicine session was traumatic and intense - far worse than my first two. I felt broken. Ayahuasca is definitely not some rocket ship to Nirvana. To heal is to feel, but feeling is intense. There's no way you'd ever get addicted to this stuff. It's a slow form of relentless torture with no escape; once ayahuasca has you in her clutches, you are her hostage and there's no going back. You are confronted. But you definitely feel much better in the long run.

Honestly, I felt depressed for quite a long while after this. But now I have so much more love and compassion for myself. My childhood was really quite brutal; psychological torture. My father was deranged and possibly sociopathic. I never actually realised this. I just thought I was a bad and horrible kid and that there was something really wrong with me. I'm so grateful to the people who facilitate this medicine work. It has opened my eyes and definitely saved my life.

Part Three

For Therapists and Facilitators

CHAPTER ONE

First DO NO Harm

"At some level, this is the essence of psychedelic therapy. As therapists, we have to be able to meet our clients in those mysterious realms that both open from within and also blast into outer space. We have to know how to access these mystical territories within ourselves in order to connect with our psychedelic clients who are exploring these otherworldly worlds. We have to know in our bones what they are talking about. It's the mystical traveller in ourselves that we must bring to the therapeutic relationship." Rachel Harris, *Ayahuasca and Psychotherapy*.

A therapist administering psychedelics absolutely needs to have considerable personal experience with the medicines they work with. This is incredibly important. You can't guide people without an internal map of the terrains they are likely to visit. You need to understand the effects of different doses and the different medicines. The first person I allowed to facilitate an MDMA session for me was a psychologist friend who wanted to learn the ropes. When I regressed to a small child under MDMA's effects, as can commonly happen, she appeared visibly shocked, and I saw that shock unfold on her face, which made me feel ashamed. It was a long while before I allowed someone else to hold space.

An open mind as opposed to rigid thinking, is a psychedelic therapist's friend. I've heard earnest would-be psychedelic therapists ask, 'What existing therapy models can best be used in psychedelic therapy?' In my opinion the therapist role requires a whole new paradigm, one that shifts away from standard therapeutic practice. You can't fit a client into your box and must be willing to stay open, flow with the situation, and use your intuition. Psychedelic medicines are the greatest teachers of being present in the moment. Try to treat each experience as an adventure unfolding; be in the presence of the experience but ready to steer should intuition guide you.

In terms of models, I liken a good version of psychedelic therapy to the 12-step model of AA—contemporaries helping each other. A psychedelic therapist needs to be genuine and willing to get down in the trenches with the client. You will potentially be reliving the client's trauma with them. You may bear witness to a client's sexual abuse as if being present—an extremely personal and vulnerable experience for the client that needs to be respected as such.

A psychedelic therapist should be willing to offer a genuine corrective experience to the client's trauma by being the way a loving parent might have or should have been: sincere, loving, empathic, willing to stroke, hug, or hold the client's hand if that's what they wish.

When dealing with sexually abused clients, in-depth knowledge of sexual abuse and PTSD is advised. A psychologist once commented to me that she found it 'perplexing' that some of her sexually abused clients seemed to have multiple perpetrators. I found this comment somewhat understandable for the uninitiated but also a little staggering. I considered that this person wasn't able to comprehend or was unwilling to believe that a sexualised child is easy prey. A sexualised child has no boundaries. A sexualised child knows his or her worth as a body. A sexualised child is often neglected by alcoholic or emotionally absent parents and left in unsafe situations with unsafe people. Perpetrators detect abandoned, lonely, vulnerable children a mile away.

That said, it's also important to know that not all memories revealed under the influence of psychedelics are true. If they seem too fantastical, unlikely, and hard to believe, they probably are. Some clients develop a propensity for fantasy from an early age as a means of escape from their unbearable situations. It can sometimes be difficult to believe some of the emerging stories. The boundaries between fantasy and reality can blur. Psychedelic-induced false memories potentially comprise a whole field of research. Usually, an authentic memory is accompanied by the expected feelings and somatic reactions. Accessing a genuine memory, as opposed to a fantastical one, usually helps the client make sense of their behaviours or symptoms. They liken it to an 'a-ha moment' or pieces of a jigsaw puzzle fitting together.

Terry, a long-time client, explains the difference quite well (see Part Two, Terry Psilocybin for full story).

> 'The mushroom gave me the experience to know the difference between the highly specific, clear, somatic, and sensorial accessible memories and the hazy, fleeting impressions of a half-remembered nightmare. In the former I remember the places, the floor tiles, the geography, the smells, the sensations. In the latter I just have feelings. Vague, fleeting impressions of something that defies logic, is situated in no place, and isn't given any structure at all only through the consistent fear of, what if, what next? In my traumatic memories, I'm never worried about the future, only the very present. I know the difference now.'

Any therapist worth their salt must largely have dealt with their own 'stuff'. One psychologist said—to our mutual client, in relation to his emerging sexual abuse memories under MDMA—that he'd be better off not opening that particular can of worms as it would be never-ending. I happen to know that she hadn't dealt with her own sexual abuse and sadly, was projecting her own denial onto her client. Luckily, he ignored that advice.

Good boundaries are essential. Psychedelics can open up vulnerable spaces beyond the realms of normal therapy and create an intimacy beyond the usual therapeutic alliance. A psychedelic therapist should be open to a level of intimacy beyond their usual practice, which might involve nonsexual touching, holding hands, and hugging or stroking an arm, but they must honour the ethics and boundaries expected of a registered therapist and not enter into intimate relationships with clients. Having a supervisor or another therapist whom you are answerable to is a good safety precaution. Finding one however, can be difficult in the current legal environment.

Though this might sound obvious, only work with people you like and resonate with. Under psychedelics a client becomes hypersensitive to energy and even quite psychic, so they'll likely pick up on dissonance, transference, or judgement. Occasionally I've ignored my own advice because of a person's desperation, but it usually backfires. Lastly, it's essential to provide a clean, comfortable, quiet space; a relaxing environment conducive to therapy; and an atmosphere of safety, integrity, and compassion.

CHAPTER TWO

Psychedelic Therapy—a Three-Stage Process

The three-stage model first proposed by MAPs is a good rough guideline for psychedelic therapists to follow: Stage 1, Assessment and preparation - Stage 2, Medicine treatment session - Stage 3, Integration.

Stage 1: Assessment and preparation establishes whether the client is a safe and suitable candidate for psychedelic therapy, and if so, what medicine might best be suited to help them. The assessment starts establishing the necessary rapport and trust needed for deep medicine work. It provides an opportunity to answer client questions about the medicine treatment. Preparation might involve helping and supporting a client to detox off prescription medications before a medicine session. (I have provided an Assessment Form as an Appendix).

Stage 2: Medicine Treatment is the actual ingestion of the chosen medicine and whatever else unfolds.

Stage 3: Integration is the post-medicine counselling process that supports the client in processing any emotions and memories that have emerged so they don't feel too overwhelmed. Integration will help them understand the meaning of the visions and messages they received and how best to incorporate insights into everyday life and reinforce behaviour change.

Stage 1: Assessment and Preparation

Assessment

Before psychedelic medicines are offered, a therapist/facilitator should undertake a thorough assessment of the client's psycho/social/medical and trauma history. At a minimum, a one-hour session is suggested to gather enough information to check client suitability for treatment. The assessment will establish rapport and trust and bring to highlight potential issues, misunderstandings, inappropriate expectations and knowledge of traumas that may arise during a medicine session.

The client's past and present medical history needs to be understood, particularly regarding heart or blood pressure issues. A history of heart disease or high blood pressure is an immediate heightened risk. Some psychedelic substances raise blood pressure and place a strain on the heart. Prescription medications should be noted. Antidepressants, benzodiazepines, painkillers, antipsychotics, beta-blockers, and some asthma meds are contraindicated and potentially dangerous with some psychedelics or may diminish their effects to the point where they just won't work effectively.

Mental health issues, diagnosed, self-diagnosed, and suspected, need to be ascertained. Psychedelics can trigger manic episodes in bipolar people, psychotic episodes in schizophrenics, and unravel people with DID (dissociative identity disorder). Some psychiatric diagnoses are incorrect and may have been made due to the effects of substance abuse or due to withdrawal symptoms from prescription medications. Diagnoses, therefore, must be fully explored.

Family history in relation to addiction, dysfunction, mental health, and physical, sexual, and emotional abuse should be explored. Bullying, car accidents, domestic violence and war trauma should be noted. Past and present relationship history will reveal a lot about relationship patterns and is important to understand.

Personal addiction history, whether involving alcohol, drugs, food, work, relationships, sex, gambling, pornography, self-harming, or codependence, should be known. If the client is actively addicted to alcohol or drugs, a period of total abstinence is recommended before addressing trauma as it can be destabilising. I usually recommend 12-step programmes such as AA or NA for substance addictions. Personal commitment to ongoing recovery is important to avoid the chance of relapse.

The client's intentions regarding psychedelic therapy and what they hope to achieve, help guide the medicine session and uncover unrealistic expectations. It's unrealistic, for example, to think they will solve all their problems in one four-or five-hour medicine session. It's important they understand that the most current and most pressing issues generally arise before subconscious material is revealed. And that occasionally mushrooms and ayahuasca don't work the first time, especially if they've just detoxed off medication.

A thorough assessment provides an overall picture and astute therapists will use this information, along with intuition, to ascertain client stability and suitability for medicine work. Given that psychedelic therapy is illegal, precautions must be taken to eliminate potential risks related to client safety as well as therapist prosecution or other types of harm. Underground psychedelic therapists have a duty of care to both the client and themselves.

The client must be psychologically sound and unlikely to be too overwhelmed with the emotional content that can emerge. You don't want them presenting at Emergency Psychiatric Services, where they'll be asked what precipitated their psychological meltdown, thus endangering the therapist. They are also likely to be medicated, which in some cases is best avoided.

Preparation

Many traumatised people are medicated and will need to detox off medications prior to engaging in psychedelic therapy. My booklet, *Beating the Benzo Blues,* is an easy-to-follow guide for detoxing off Benzodiazepines while maintaining regular activities. A strong piece of advice: don't try to rush this process. It will end in despair. For information about antidepressant withdrawal, you can find various online detox programmes, or a doctor can assist in this process.

Providing Information: One facet of preparation is to answer questions and concerns regarding the upcoming medicine session. I suggest providing an information sheet that addresses the following: preparatory diet, things to bring (eye mask, water bottle, electrolytes), how to set an intention for the medicine session, the fact that they won't be able to safely drive afterwards and should organise someone to pick them up or plan to stay in a nearby hotel. It might suggest documentaries, articles, or books to read, such as this one, where relevant information can be obtained.

Stage 2: Medicine Session

Length of the Session: A medicine treatment typically lasts four or five hours with MDMA, five or six hours with psilocybin. Ayahuasca lasts five to six hours and usually requires an overnight stay in a remote or rural location. The medicine may still be gently working after these timeframes, but the client is usually good to go.

MAPS medicine sessions use a top-up dose and last eight to twelve hours. The client sleeps in the clinic overnight. This is not usually feasible in underground therapy as it would be too expensive for the average client and too long a session for one therapist to handle. MAPS lengthy sessions, in my opinion, would provide too much information for a client to process and integrate. The MAPS treatment model is a funded research model and not a financially viable treatment option for many.

Dose: MDMA dose is between 100 - 135 mg with no top-up dose. Immediate dosing considerations are the person's previous psychedelic use and anxiety levels. Regular alcohol or marijuana consumers seem to need the higher doses as do people who have recently detoxed from psychiatric medications.

Psilocybin dose is between 2.5 and 3.5gms of dried *Psilocybe cubensis* or 2 to 2.5gms *P. subaeruginosa*. Mushrooms vary widely in strength, so it pays to know the ones you are using and to have a regular and known source.

Acaciahuasca dose is approx. 15 grams of dried *Acacia courtii* and 3 to 3.5 grams of *Syrian Rue* or 75 to 100 grams of dried *B. caapi*. This is quite a strong dose. In ayahuasca groups the dose is often kept lower so that facilitators can keep things sailing smoothly. Deeper work can occur at higher doses, but it requires more input, care, and energy from the facilitator.

Notes about dosage; Most people when referring to Acaciahuasca or Ayahuasca doses, measure the dose in mils rather than grams. This is usually because they don't make their own medicine hence, they don't actually know how many grams of Acacia went into the brew per dose. Measuring doses by mils essentially means little, as different people simmer the brew down (dehydrate) to differing amounts of liquid per dose. When you make the brew yourself, you measure the 'grams' of Acacia you allow per dose. Fifteen grams of Acacia Courtii is an average therapeutic dose.

When Syrian Rue is used as the MAOI component, it is best made as a separate tea and given to the participants 40 minutes before the Acacia brew is given. This allows its MAOI effect to kick in first - thus allowing the Acacia to work faster, stronger and last longer. This is a far better method than brewing the two together, which some people do.

Therapist dose: Some therapists take a half or full dose of medicine while conducting their group or solo sessions, while others feel the need to be fully present. It certainly wouldn't be feasible to take MDMA that frequently as you need a four-week break in between treatments to get a decent effect and to restore your serotonin.

Ceremony and ritual: When working with entheogenic medicines, I feel that some ritual shows respect to the medicine, cleanses the space, and sets the scene. I feel an affinity with the Lakota Sioux of North America due to past sweat lodge ceremonies I've had with Lakota medicine man Wallace Black Elk. I was also gifted a Lakota medicine pipe. You might start a medicine session by smudging (cleansing) the space and the participants with the smoke of either - sage, palo santo or mapacho and saying a protection prayer. Maybe burn pure incense resins on charcoal discs at different times throughout the session; frankincense and sandalwood are some of my favourites. Avoid synthetic incense sticks and stick to natural products.

Intentions: The client is strongly advised to set a clear intention prior to their medicine treatment and focus on it before arrival. What do they hope to achieve from the session? What do they want to resolve or change? What guidance do they need? Prior to ingesting the substance, they might state their intention, which should help guide and focus their session. Once the medicine is consumed, they are asked to let their intention go and ride the wave of whatever presents itself; to observe without engaging, and to surrender. It is in the state of surrender where the magic happens.

Music: Choosing music for a session is an art form in itself. Music can be used as both a catalyst and transformation tool. The medicine playlist should largely avoid music with lyrics although it can include some at the start and end of the session. Songs with lyrics can be cathartic if they trigger emotions and childhood memories, but as a rule it's best to use music that can't be misinterpreted, is directive, or distracting.

A combination of classical, atmospheric, electronic, world, indigenous, and some music that includes vocals is commonly used in psychedelic therapy. The medicine playlist is structured to peak with the most common intensity curve of the medicine. In other words, as the medicine increases in intensity so does the music. This helps to carry the session and potentiate the effects of the medicine. Music has immense power to affect mood and invite thought. Its profound impact is obvious to anyone who has been moved to tears by a song. When directed in a meaningful way, music is a complex and powerful communicator that conveys ideas, thoughts, and emotions. It transcends human language and shifts the mood of a space. The music played during medicine sessions will have a profound impact on the way emerging material is supported.

During traditional Peruvian ayahuasca ceremonies, music takes the form of icaros—songs sung by a shaman. These songs have a threefold function: to provide reassurance and guidance to participants, indicate the passing of time, and catalyse the ayahuasca itself (through vibration, they can stimulate and intensify the effects of ayahuasca). A participant will notice that the songs interplay with the medicine experience almost as if the ayahuasca can be controlled by the songs. In Australian ayahuasca ceremonies, music is usually pre-recorded or live, with the facilitator or designated musicians playing instruments and singing.

Talking or staying silent: There are conflicting ideas in the available psychedelic therapy literature regarding therapist/facilitator involvement during medicine sessions. The amount of verbal interaction will largely depend on the medicine being used and whom you choose to listen to. I tend toward Friederike Meckel Fisher's method as this has achieved great results for clients. She delves into the client's traumas while they are under the influence. But there is also a time to step back and remain silent.

With the information gathered in the assessment phase, you should know enough to understand what might arise under the effects of the medicine. Find a way to tune in with the client to understand where they are. This can be an intuitive process or you can directly ask questions then help them focus more deeply to gather details and insightful information. Encourage them to look further and deeper while they feel safe and supported. Accompany them to face the events from which they dissociated in terror when they first happened. They can endure it now—with the help of soothing words, touch, and empathy.

Talking or staying silent – MDMA: The medicine-experienced therapist is intuitively guided. Sessions usually alternate between some trauma exploration and time spent in quiet. A lot is gained by mining traumatic events for details, clarity, and insight. Guiding is almost a channelling process that comes with practice, self-trust, and wisdom gleaned from your own medicine work. Knowing when to talk, delve, encourage, or calm and when to stay quiet comes with experience.

Countdown: The first twenty minutes before the MDMA takes effect is usually conversational, with a focus on the client's intention—what they want to address or explore. This usually influences the direction the medicine session will take. Twenty minutes after substance ingestion have the client lie down and don their eye mask, then help them to relax by doing slow, deep breathing through the nose. Music is now played.

Blast off: The point when the medicine is about to take full effect, usually forty to sixty minutes in, is signalled by a deep sigh, a smile, an obvious sinking or surrender, or in some cases, increased anxiety. Ask the client whether the medicine has kicked in. Often, they will just smile and nod.

During the second and third hours the medicine is at its most intense. Most clients will now go internal and flow with where the medicine takes them. This is also the time when suppressed memories are the most accessible, so you can maybe help them access repressed trauma. If this seems appropriate, get them to visualise the place where the trauma occurred then ask some delving questions: How are they feeling? What can they see? Who else is there? What are they doing? The act of confession, of telling and being heard, releases shame and can be profoundly healing.

Remaining silent so as not to interrupt the flow of things is also vitally important. Check in quietly with the client as to what they prefer. Ultimately, it's their session. Clients who have trouble surrendering may prefer you to guide them somewhere. Some may want to talk right through the session, while others want to stay totally quiet and stay internal. Definitely encourage some specifically internal time.

Under the effects of MDMA, clients are extremely receptive to a therapist's verbalised suggestions and observations. This is true both directly before and while they are under the influence of the substance. A therapist needs to be aware of and respect this and not try to influence the client unduly with their own opinions or agenda unless this might facilitate the change in a dysfunctional perspective or thought pattern. It's usually better to ask questions so that the client can access their own wisdom. It's truly no wonder that in the 1950s psychedelics were researched for mind-control purposes by MK Ultra and the CIA.

Talking or staying silent – psilocybin: Talking takes place in the first and last thirty minutes of the session. The psilocybin session is more guided by the medicine; conversation is usually minimal in the active phase. Some clients, however, may want to talk, and you can successfully explore traumas for insights.

Talking or staying silent – ayahuasca: Generally speaking, minimal talking occurs during the active phase of an ayahuasca session. The facilitator/therapist's role is to be an anchor, to calm the client if the effects become overwhelming, to offer a safe space in which to surrender to this truly mystical medicine. Also, to help them physically if they need to purge, drink, or visit the bathroom—unless, that is, you know how to work with energies. The therapist/facilitator talking role is more pronounced before and after the medicine session to aid in the preparation and integration of this life-changing, paradigm-shattering experience.

Touch: The presence of another human can be very comforting in a medicine session because the original trauma, particularly sexual trauma, was usually faced alone and in secret. The client might feel the need for physical contact during big revelations (a hug, holding hands, stroking an arm). Touch should be discussed at the start of the session and permission sought.

Distraction: You learn with experience when a client is using distraction to avoid surrendering and going within. Common distraction techniques are compulsive talking, compulsive body movements, removing the eye mask, saying the medicine isn't working. One client sat up, removed his mask, and insisted that the mushrooms weren't working, then he suddenly gasped in shock, started weeping, and said that the therapist had transformed into his dead mother. Body movement usually indicates somatic trauma release, but compulsive body movement might also serve as a distraction, particularly when surrender is an issue (see Bridget Part Two). Deep, slow breathing and focusing on the music will help with surrender.

Example of a Typical MDMA Session

During the first hour, the client may enter a phase of mild uncertainty and the feeling that nothing might happen. At some point they become aware of a shift and an expansion of awareness. The most pressing subconscious material starts to emerge into awareness for processing. This may increase anxiety as the subconscious guard that kept the material hidden from everyday awareness starts protesting.

The therapist helps disarm the guard by encouraging surrender through deep breathing and emphasising that the client is safe. As suggested by Jung, the unconscious contains all the repressed, unfelt, and blocked off pain and confusion that couldn't be safely felt or processed at the time of the original trauma. Provided the client feels safe and breathes regularly, the guard will stand aside and allow access to the traumatic material. [1]

---

[1] Some of this information came from the Castalia Foundation website.

The next phase may involve a release of some kind—sadness, crying, questioning, sweating, rhythmic jerking, somatic release. Then a realization might start to occur whereby the client discovers that they may have made mistaken assumptions about themselves. These assumptions might orbit around the sense of responsibility they took on for a trauma they experienced. It's common for children to blame themselves for what was done to them, and this may be encouraged and exploited by perpetrators. But the client now sees the situation from an adult perspective, not just as the child who experienced it. Realizations of these false self-beliefs stemming from the trauma typically feel like a huge weight has been lifted. This feeling persists into everyday life. These new realizations are followed by the excavation of more trauma. And the cycle of revelations repeats until the session ends.

Concluding the medicine session: Twenty minutes before the medicine session is scheduled to conclude, most clients will indicate they are back by talking or removing the eye mask. If this doesn't happen, maybe bring them back by gently talking, then ask them to sit up and remove their eye mask. Maybe stop the music and encourage them to start talking about what occurred.

If you have the time and are happy to let it end naturally, do so, but some therapists work to the clock and have other clients to see. You might come to some arrangement with the client beforehand about what to do if the session goes overtime. It's best not to disturb the session, but sometimes it can't be avoided. The timeframes given are pretty accurate but occasionally a highly sensitive client will be affected more strongly.

Before leaving, they should be able to communicate and walk easily. Ideally, a friend, partner, or driver will be waiting. This is a great time for them to sit somewhere quietly and process and write down what emerged since memories and insights are still vivid. Advise clients not to plan social activities, work, or commitments directly after a session.

Stage 3: Integration Sessions

Integration essentially means understanding, embodying, and applying the new information to everyday life. Integration takes place before, during, and after the medicine session. Setting an intention is part of integration. Getting insights and cathartic release during the medicine session is part of integration as it's helping the client understand where their dysfunctional behaviour patterns stemmed from. Writing or journaling after the medicine experience is part of integration, as is follow up counselling.

Maybe send out a follow-up questionnaire after the medicine session to help with the integration process. Documenting the insights gained will help to consolidate the arising material and provide a written record of sessions. Most of the information in Part Two of this book came from follow-up questionnaires.

Encourage the client to commit to at least one follow-up integration session, particularly if traumatic memories arose along with strong emotions. They may not heed this advice, but those that do will be able to integrate information and invoke desired behaviour changes much faster. Some won't understand their medicine experience at all until they verbalise it. Even discussing the experience with a friend can help integration. Some try to figure it out on their own, which is usually an old, self-reliant survival programme (see Natalie and Deborah, Part Two).

In this new paradigm of psychedelic therapy, espoused by the likes of MAPS, and others, the focus seems to be on lots of integration sessions. Whether this is necessary depends on the medicine used and the experience that occurred. An MDMA experience is not hard to integrate as it usually induces biographic information; however, it can elicit overwhelming emotions afterwards, and this is what the integration sessions would support. Psilocybin and ayahuasca operate on a more mystical, transpersonal level and may require more help to understand and integrate.

Sometimes things just happen where no easy explanation can be proffered or understood with our limited human knowledge. After Shaun's psilocybin session (Part Two), with no conscious intention, he suddenly stopped drinking alcohol (he had been drinking daily for years). Try to explain that! Not everything needs explaining. Sometimes mysterious outcomes just need to be accepted as profound gifts from the medicine gods. However, to ensure this behaviour change becomes permanent, systems are best set up. I know from experience that it's one thing to stop drinking but quite another to stay stopped.

Certainly, psychedelics can reveal things that need changing in our lives and even give us a helping hand, or a gentle nudge to start with, but humans are both blessed and cursed with free will and ultimately must decide whether or not to incorporate lessons learned into their lives. Some changes can involve taking big steps that a person is just not willing to take right now—or ever—such as ending an unhealthy relationship, leaving a job, going to a 12-step recovery programme, or moving to a new country. On this note, I always advise people to not make life-changing decisions or have potentially radioactive conversations for a week or two after the medicine session. Time is needed for the cosmic dust to settle or flowers to gently blossom.

CHAPTER THREE

States That Can Occur During Psychedelic Therapy

The trajectory of any transformative psychedelic experience could be described as Entry, Immersion, Reflection, Emergence, and Integration. There's no generic state or typical psychedelic experience; however, at therapeutic doses they are not too unpredictable. Psychedelics can trigger experiences, such as regression to childhood traumas or confrontation with unresolved grief, fear, anger, shame, or guilt, that have significant value in accelerating therapy. But if one is unprepared for this and tries to control or escape from these emerging inner demons, it can culminate in panic, paranoia, confusion, and emotional distress.

Resistance: Opposition to the therapeutic process. A way of pushing back against suggestions even when they could be beneficial. Not surrendering to the medicine. A way to avoid self-knowledge so as not to have to face disturbing feelings like disgust, anxiety, anger, envy, and shame.

Dissociation: Feeling detached from the body, the environment, or the people around. Disconnection and lack of continuity between thoughts, memories, surroundings, actions, and identity.

Regression: Regressing to an earlier age, state, or time. The person may regress to a younger age and make the sounds, cries, and movements of a child. They have accessed the unconscious and are essentially reliving an old and possibly traumatic memory.

It's important to know that both regression and dissociation can manifest either during or directly after a medicine session during which the client has re-experienced repressed memories. A dissociated or regressed person is unsafe to drive or to participate in normal activity. They will need to be looked after until they properly return. An extreme example of this was related to me by psychedelic therapist Friederike Meckel Fischer. One of her clients couldn't actually walk or talk for twelve hours after her MDMA session. During the session, she re-experienced repressed sexual abuse as a toddler. Grounding exercises, like walking barefoot on the earth, a bath, bodywork, or eating earthy foods, may help.

Transference: A situation in which a client associates the therapist as their good or bad parent. They redirect their emotions to a substitute person, usually the therapist. This parental projection may be due to emotions, originally felt in childhood, that needed to be repressed. As an example, during a psilocybin group session, one client felt the therapist was trying to control her and felt the need to rebel against both her and the safety rules established for the group. In such instance it's best to use a bit of reverse psychology and give the client freer rein, within reason. Through later therapeutic integration the client was able to recognise that she was reacting to how her controlling father had treated her and transferred it onto the therapist.

Projection: a common phenomenon whereby a patient attributes to the therapist, or others, characteristics they don't like about themselves. This is one of the reasons why MAPS have two therapists present during their research medicine sessions as a safety measure.

Hallucinations or visions: Hallucinations are what people typically associate with psychedelics, but the visual content of the experience can vary a lot depending on the medicine used, and it may not happen at all. While few people have visions while on MDMA, occasionally someone does (Louise, Part Two). It's comparatively more common with other psychedelics. Psilocybin is associated with enhanced colours and visual imagery, moving fractals, geometric designs, and eye-based images. If hallucinations happen at all, it's usually during the earlier phase of a session. Ayahuasca or DMT visions are often associated with circus themes, clowns or jesters, entities or strange beings, alien beings and their vehicles, machinery and Escher-like buildings. Visions, rather than hallucinations, can occur on ayahuasca, in particular, archetypes: religious or mythological figures such as Ganesh or Buddha. Shannon (Part Two) saw various group members transform respectively into a monk, an indigenous warrior, and a high priestess.

Animals and animal totems: Seeing or becoming animals. Snakes are common on ayahuasca; the snake is the manifest spirit of the vine. Shannon experienced becoming a snake. Some people experience being entwined in snakes. The medical caduceus symbol or the DNA double-helix symbol made of snakes is also common. Various people have told me that during their psilocybin sessions that the therapist transformed into a cat, a leopard, a bird, a Native American, and various dead relatives.

Traditional shamans believe that spirit animals or totems are revealed to guide and protect their charges throughout a journey and that they offer influential insights and meaningful messages for those who listen. They bring attention to parts of life that need acknowledgement or exploration. Snakes are symbols of healing powers and represent life force, unconscious drives, and primal instincts. Snakes can symbolise spiritual guidance and transition and often appear when you are stepping into the unknown.

Spirit guides: These may take the form of dead relatives or pets, animals, indigenous medicine people, light or energy beings. They usually come to guide the person to other dimensions, show them the workings of physics or the galaxy or universe or to give them messages, advice, or predictions.

Somatic experiencing/physical release: In, *The Body Keeps the Score*, Bessel van de Kolk famously states that trauma is stored in the body. It's common for people to shake, shiver, convulse, or have rhythmic body movements. This is trauma being released from the body or the body re-experiencing sexual abuse or violence. The body plays out the experience as if it's happening in real-time.

Purging: This can take the form of vomiting, yawning, diarrhoea, sweating, screaming, crying, convulsing, shaking, or hyperventilating. It's essentially a way of clearing stuck traumatic energy from the body. Purging in the form of vomiting or diarrhoea is more likely on ayahuasca and unlikely on MDMA or psilocybin.

Past-Life experiences: Some people relive past lives while under the effects of psychedelics. Two clients experienced being witches. One saw her friend being burnt at the stake. Another witnessed the death of a beloved benefactor; her emotions whilst reliving this experience appeared very authentic and raw.

Pre-natal or post-natal birth trauma or rebirthing: Stan Grof, the father of psychedelic therapy, created a model called the *Perinatal Matrices*. This framework recognises four distinct patterns related to crucial moments in the birth experience. Natalie (Part Two) relived her birth experience while on ayahuasca. She was born with the umbilical cord wrapped around her neck, nearly choking her, so she was literally born dying. The sensation of strangulation caused her to feel she couldn't breathe and was dying. She asked to be taken to hospital. Because she was preverbal while reliving the experience, she couldn't say what was happening to her. An appropriate response would be to gently blow on her, administer touch, and help her focus on her ability to breathe. A facilitator must know how to handle these situations or it can lead to re-traumatisation.

Retrieval of repressed memories: It's common in psychedelic therapy to gain access to enhanced or repressed memories and to the emotions that go with them. This may feel traumatic depending on the medicine used. On MDMA the trauma experienced is minimal because memories are accompanied by a feeling of profound relaxation. Memory retrieval on ayahuasca and psilocybin can be experienced as more intense.

Experiential learning. Just as you can't truly understand the experience of sexual abuse by reading about it or heal from it by talking about it, ayahuasca and psilocybin can offer an experiential learning encounter whereby you relive something vividly, including the emotion and pain you felt at the time. Or you may get to experience something from another's perspective: A rapist might experience being raped; a man may experience being a woman; a rich person might experience poverty. Chris Bache's amazing book *LSD and the Mind of the Universe* offers some great examples of this. Chris experienced the drudgery and monotony of being a poor, low-class woman, which he found rather diabolical.

Preverbal trauma: A return to being a toddler or a baby. Usually, the client can't verbalise what is happening at the time, but may have a full sensory experience of what is occurring. They can feel the toddler's emotions—and may cry, wail, grunt, and groan the same way a toddler does. They may re-experience physical sensations. It may be sufficient to let these preverbal scenarios play out for the insights that come, but without intervention and assistance, a client could potentially get stuck here. They might need help to invoke their adult perspective.

Oceanic boundlessness, ego dissolution, or death experiences: A sense of leaving the body, disintegrating and that they will not be able to return. This is more common on higher rather than therapeutic doses; however, it occasionally occurs with sensitive folks. Resistance to this can be frightening, and the key is surrender, which is easier said than done! Discussion around the potential of this happening should occur prior to the medicine session so the client has in the back of their mind that they will return. Touch and talking during this phase help to ground them so that on some level they realise they're still here.

Euphoria: A sense of complete relaxation, bliss, and surrender. An experience of being right in the present moment, resting in the hands of God. Healing comes in various forms and doesn't have to be experienced as painful or traumatic. The medicines are intelligent and will generally meet you where you are and give you what you need. And this might be just what you need.

Paranoia: A sense that the therapist/facilitator or group members has intentions to harm them, steal from them, poison, or kill them, or that they're not safe in some way. One client doing his first psilocybin treatment was convinced that the therapist planned to steal his wallet. His anxious son, who'd driven him to the session, had planted this seed in his head by remonstrating with him about taking 'drugs' with a stranger. This had only served to freak him out.

As his wallet and phone were in the other room, the therapist simply bought them to him, which seemed to calm him down. An anxious guy to begin with, he'd never taken an illicit drug in his life but had recently detoxed off antidepressants. Maybe the medicine was showing him how lack of trust plays out in his life. Soothing words, encouragement, and assurance that the experience will come to an end can help.

Fear of going insane: This is more likely on high doses, but infrequently also happens on therapeutic doses if the client is medicine-sensitive. Reassurance is the key. Maybe turn the music off or change it or encourage them to change position, sit up for a while, and take their eye mask off.

Looping: A particular process, emotion, thought pattern, or event that feels like it's happening over and over again. It can be accompanied by the feeling that the situation can't be escaped. There's not much to do but ride it out and trust that the medicine has a purpose for this. Maybe it's showing the default network in action. Long, monotonous music tracks can make this experience feel relentless. Changing the music or lighting sage, mapacho, palo santo, or pure incense can create a shift. Don't interfere with this experience too much unless it's overwhelming.

A Voice: It's not uncommon to have a conversation with a Voice that transmits directions, observations, or advice telepathically. This is more likely to happen on psilocybin, ayahuasca, mescaline, or iboga. Debate occurs about whether this is an auditory hallucination, the subconscious mind, or the spirit of the plant or fungi.

Return to exactly where they left off on the last trip: A bizarre but common phenomenon that can occur even when using different psychedelics with very long spans of time in between. During an ayahuasca ceremony, I began hyperventilating in terror. My process was cut short by the group helper, who was worried I might disturb the group. This disrupted my process and it felt incomplete as if the trauma hadn't left my body.

Some months later, after taking psilocybin, I was immediately thrust back to where I'd left off, and began hyperventilating again. I allowed this process to play out until it ended naturally. This released the trauma from my body, much like an animal shaking after an accident. Although there were no accompanying memories, it seemed the process had to fully play out. Amazed that on two completely different medicines I was able to catalyse this completion, I also learned an important lesson about not short-circuiting people's experiences.

Chris Bache describes a similar occurrence in *LSD and the Mind of the Universe*. He halted his seven-year, personal LSD experiment for two years, and when he resumed his experiment two years later, the medicine took him straight back to the trip he'd had when he'd paused. This phenomenon is utterly fascinating and shows the profound intelligence of these entheogens.

CHAPTER FOUR

The Road to Hell is Paved with Good Intentions

'True initiation is a response to an inner calling. It requires that you face personal challenges heroically and experience a genuine rebirth into a new way of being.'—Alberto Villoldo.

The path of an underground therapist or medicine facilitator is an inner calling and is by no means all light and love, instant miracles, or a blissfully easy road, so to speak. Besides all the positive stories of profound and beautiful healing in Part Two of this book, it's important to balance this out with a look at the dark side. No book on psychedelic therapy would truly be complete without a look at the things that can and do go wrong; though few will dare to mention this.

Typical issues facing underground therapists is the constant stress caused by the fear of being busted. You can get a little paranoid that a new client is a potential cop or that a client might turn on you if something doesn't go their way. Hearing the constant horror stories of what humans are capable of inflicting on each other can start to destroy your faith in the human race; though I stopped being shocked a long time ago. Being the subject of unwell people's transference and projection can also take its toll. But clients' miraculous healings, instant relief, and/or expulsion of long-held demons more than trumps any of this.

Supervision is generally hard to find in this illegal profession, so things can build up and you can feel quite alone. It's important to find support and also to take some regular time out to do more self-work or just have some fun.

Unlike traditional therapy, psychedelic therapy does not tend to be a long-term relationship. Clients may move on quickly because they actually get well. Shaz left her seven-year therapeutic relationship with her psychologist after just three MDMA sessions. So, I'm curious to know how traditional therapists will handle this new business model. It's definitely not one they'll be used to.

Few will dare to mention negative events when it comes to working with psychedelics. They fear being judged, found wanting, or maybe just sounding a bit crazy if supernatural events unfold. They also wish to avoid bringing disrepute to a profession struggling to find its legal feet. But the fact is, things don't always go so swimmingly well. In fact, things can occasionally devolve into a downward spiral of hell - but hopefully a lesson is learned.

Acaciahuasca: Initiation and Trial by Fire.

If you have the fortitude to embark on the medicine-healing path with ayahuasca, an initiation is probably inevitable. You will be tested. Are you a worthy channel, healer, or intermediary for this plant? Can you navigate through stormy seas or are you just a fair-weather sailor? Will you bail water from the sinking ship or simply jump overboard?

What could possibly go wrong you might ask! Truthfully, if a good assessment is done, you should avoid most issues. But occasionally, even with a good screening, you simply cannot pick the person who is going to cause you trouble. They may have no obvious indications.

Those desperate for relief may lie to you. The message to clients should be clear: PLEASE DON'T LIE! For in so doing, you endanger both yourself and the therapist, who is already taking a great personal risk to help you.

A great level of care, respect and experience is needed when serving powerful medicines like ayahuasca, in fact most people just shouldn't. But if a client is suicidal or needs a massive psychological shift, ayahuasca may be their best option. Ayahuasca saved my life, and I wouldn't deny the same opportunity to someone else in a similar situation. I believe that people are 'called' to drink ayahuasca, so it's usually the client who'll suggest it first. If anything, I'd tend to steer them away from it and suggest MDMA or psilocybin, which are far less likely to cause issues for a facilitator or client.

There is ongoing debate within the psychedelic community about who should or shouldn't facilitate ayahuasca. There are those who believe that 'the medicine' should only be administered by jungle shamans. Then there are others like J.P. who disagree. While I have all due respect for shamans and their knowledge, wisdom, and training, not everyone can make it to the South American jungle, particularly people with PTSD. Money, Covid, mental health issues, and fear are some of the obvious reasons, not to mention the deterrent of the numerous reports of sexual assault, robbery, murder, and sorcery taking place in the jungle. The bottom line is this: Ayahuasca ultimately calls the shots and it seems she's entwined her healing vines around the world. She's certainly made it to the land of Oz and it's not looking like she'll be leaving anytime soon.

You often learn through your own mistakes, and we're also dealing with people's damaged psyches. In the Amazon they go through many, many years of training before they ever serve ayahuasca. If you are approaching this from a non-traditional perspective, then drinking the medicine many times, being a helper at other people's ceremonies, learning how the medicine works with people and how to support them is pretty much par for the course!

Australian acaciahuasca can seem stronger than the South American brews. Well, not necessarily stronger—the strength is in the dose—but it can take people by surprise; it can be more visionary and have wilder more unexpected effects. People can freak out. In fact, I don't think a lot of people realise quite what they are getting themselves into with ayahuasca. I've heard the odd horror story. This medicine is not to be taken lightly. A client must come to ayahuasca with respect and good, honest intentions. If not - the best-case scenario is that the medicine won't work at all - the worst-case scenario is that it will kick their arse.

Ayahuasca drinkers should adhere to the dietary restrictions particularly with regard to high tyramine foods like red wine and blue vein cheese. A client should not drink red wine or eat blue-vein cheese a minimum of forty-eight hours before and after their medicine session; they are both strongly contraindicated with ayahuasca. Red wine and blue-vein cheese contain high levels of tyramine, which stimulates the release of epinephrine in the bloodstream. The MAOI component in the acaciahuasca brew blocks the absorption of epinephrine and this can cause medical issues. The other problem with red wine is serotonin syndrome: people have been known to go to hospital in Australia from drinking red wine twenty-four hours before or after a rue and acacia tea.

A facilitator must be extremely discerning about who they give ayahuasca to - as well as 'where' they give it. Always follow your intuition. No matter what, if your intuition tells you not to proceed for any reason – listen to it. Not to do so is inviting trouble. The setting is extremely important. Ayahuasca should be served in a rural setting with no neighbours around. Things can indeed get noisy as people release pent up emotions that may have lain dormant for years. The facilitator must be fully in their power—solid, grounded, calm, calling the shots. I would imagine that some freakouts occur when a client senses that you can't hold solid space.

MDMA and Dissociative Identity Disorder

Martin, 50, Social Worker

Martin's story is in Part Two, so I won't repeat it. During his assessment it was suspected that something was not quite right. He seemed a bit manic and something felt a bit off. Although it hadn't come up voluntarily in his assessment, he was asked outright if he'd ever been diagnosed as bipolar. He said no, he'd never been diagnosed as such.

The therapist didn't listen to her intuition, mainly because Martin was suicidal—he actually had a plan for carrying out his own death—and she felt obligated and pressured to help him. They conducted an MDMA treatment session, and it seemed to help Martin immensely. In fact, he was over the moon as he attests in his story in Part Two.

As they were doing ongoing integration counselling, the therapist noticed that his behaviour was getting increasingly more bizarre and manic. She rang his partner, who was aware of the work they were doing together and the partner agreed that he did seem to be getting a bit manic and out of control but the partner had attributed it to his enthusiasm for how much better he was feeling post MDMA.

Martin eventually admitted himself to a psychiatric ward. The therapist felt awful, thinking that maybe the MDMA treatment had something to do with his unravelling, although nothing remotely like this had ever happened before. She questioned him intensively and told him she felt terrible about what had happened and felt somewhat responsible. He must have felt guilty and finally admitted that he'd recently gotten the flu and started quaffing bottles of cough mixture. DXM, an ingredient in cough mixture, is a dissociative.

Whilst in the psych ward, Martin was diagnosed with dissociative identity disorder (DID), the new name for 'multiple personality disorder.' His partner told the therapist that she suspected he'd probably had this for years, but it had gone undiagnosed. The DXM from the cough mixture would have exacerbated his DID and made it more obvious, and hence easier to diagnose.

Martin was in the psych ward for a couple of weeks but is now out and doing well. At least he knows what he's dealing with now. They probably won't do any more medicine work together although he totally believes that the MDMA session was nothing short of miraculous. MDMA has the potential to help people with DID, but it would be far safer if administered in an inpatient environment where the person can be safely monitored.

Psychedelic therapists working with recovering addicts need to be aware of the potential for them to relapse. MDMA would more likely be the medicine to trigger a relapse as it's the one that predictably feels good. And addicts like feeling good. Its addiction potential is possibly mitigated by the fact that its effects diminish if taken continuously, but that's not to indemnify its addiction-triggering potential for recovering folk. For this reason, be careful when working with people in recovery and generally avoid doing so, unless, despite a stable recovery period, they are staring into a dark abyss. Mushrooms are probably a better option for addicts.

Underground psychedelic therapy can be a minefield and at times impose a steep learning curve—not helped by the lack of training available. But, truly, even training can't prepare you for some of this. This work is definitely not for the faint of heart. Enter at your peril – or, more precisely, enter only if you are called and even then, consider it very carefully.

CHAPTER FIVE

Reviewing the Psychedelic Resources

Whether you wish to undertake psychedelic therapy for your own healing or you are a practising underground therapist or considering becoming one, then research is your best first step. Listed below are some helpful resources, besides this book, some essential reading for would-be therapists.

Within the 'Underground' a growing number of books are appearing on how best to conduct psychedelic therapy, this one included. Though thoughts on best practices differ widely, most agree on this point: no therapist should conduct psychedelic therapy unless they have had extensive personal experience with the medicines they work with. I endorse this absolutely.

While the following resources reveal differing ideas on what constitutes good psychedelic therapy, keep in mind that some authors may have self-serving interests. The people seeking to control the looming legal psychedelic therapy field may have vested interests in maximising their incomes. This may emerge as a focus on lots of integration sessions or extremely long medicine sessions with two therapists present.

Personally, I find that one or two integration sessions help after a difficult medicine session but most people don't require more than that. MAPS model of having two therapists present for a solo MDMA session is in my mind, totally unnecessary, and long 8–12-hour medicines sessions would potentially provide too much information to process. At the other extreme, some authors believe that no therapist is needed and the individual can progress alone. Somewhere on the middle path lies the golden key.

Books on Psychedelic Therapy

Therapy with Substance: Psycholytic Psychotherapy in the Twenty-First Century, Dr Friederike Meckel Fischer, 2015, Muswell Hill Press.

This book has been very helpful to me, as have my Zoom discussions with Friederike, whom I'm grateful to consider as one of my mentors. A German doctor and psychotherapist living in Switzerland and now in her 70s, Friederike trained in holotropic breathwork with Stan Grof in the late 80s. She also trained in psychedelic therapy with Samuel Widmer. With thirty-odd years of psychedelic therapy under her belt, I doubt many others have as much academic and hands-on experience as she does. She is also a stellar and humble human.

Her method of practice was quite hands-on, delving into the client's issues and traumas and whatever else arises while they were under the influence of a psychedelic substance, MDMA, LSD, 2CB, psilocybin, and ayahuasca among them. Her medicine work was done in groups, and she combined psychedelic therapy with the Internal Family Systems model, an approach that involved group members role-playing family members for the client doing the focused work.

The Psychedelic Explorers Guide: Safe, Therapeutic, and Sacred Journeys, James Fadiman, 2011, Park Street Press.

Fadiman is often called 'America's wisest and most respected authority on psychedelics and their use.' He's been involved with psychedelic research since the 1960s. In this guide to the immediate and long-term effects of psychedelic use for spiritual (high-dose), therapeutic (moderate-dose), and problem-solving (low-dose and microdose) purposes, Fadiman outlines best practices for safe, sacred entheogenic voyages, from the benefits of having a sensitive guide during a session to the importance of the setting and pre-session intention. Fadiman reviews the value of psychedelics for healing and self-discovery as well as how LSD has facilitated scientific and technical problem-solving. He reveals how microdosing (ultra-low doses) improve cognitive functioning, emotional balance, and physical stamina.

Listening to Ayahuasca: New Hope for Depression, Addiction, PTSD, and Anxiety, Rachel Harris, 2017, New World Library.

Rachel Harris is a clinical psychologist and psychedelic explorer. Her book describes how ayahuasca is being used in a Western psycho-spiritual context. She says that the underground ayahuasca community has a level of sophistication far beyond most therapists. The book supports the observation that ayahuasca can have an almost immediate anti-depressant effect. As a therapist, Harris brings the reader into her office for an intimate glimpse into how people are using ayahuasca to aid both psychological healing and spiritual development. Her experience of working with people using ayahuasca is that the medicine is like a rocket boost along the psychospiritual path, helping them to heal from childhood and traumatic events as well as to explore spiritual states of being. Harris shares her own experiences of ayahuasca ceremonies, including receiving advice from Grandmother Ayahuasca to do the research and write a book.

Psychedelics and Psychotherapy: The Healing Potential of Expanded States, a collaboration edited by Tim Read and Maria Papaspyrou, foreword by Gabor Mate, 2021, Park Street Press.

This book appeared while I was finishing this one, so I haven't gotten all the way through it, but it's on-topic and written by credible authors. It includes a superb chapter by Rachel Harris. It examines the therapeutic potential of expanded states, underground psychedelic psychotherapy, approaches for healing individual and collective trauma, and training considerations. It addresses challenging psychedelic experiences, spiritual emergencies, and the central importance of the therapeutic relationship. It details spiritual exploration with LSD, microdosing with iboga, and MDMA-assisted psychotherapy for PTSD. It explores the latest developments in modern psychedelic therapy and shares practical experiences and insights from both elders and newer research voices in the psychedelic communities.

Trust Surrender Receive: How MDMA Can Release Us from Trauma and PTSD, Anne Other, 2017, Lioncrest Publishing.

Ann Other promotes a hands-off approach in which a facilitator is present but acts as a quiet bystander and anchoring source, essentially a trip-sitter who allows the medicine to do the work. For that reason, this book is not greatly helpful from a therapeutic perspective, but it has a lot of client stories, so it will be helpful to clients looking to participate in therapy and to read about other people's MDMA experiences. There is some good information on CPTSD and how psychedelics work to access repressed traumatic memories.

LSD Psychotherapy: The Healing Potential of Psychedelic Medicine, Dr Stanislav Grof, 2008, 4th edition, MAPS.org.

A Czech psychiatrist and transpersonal psychologist, Grof is one of the founding fathers of psychedelic therapy and has written several books on the topic. Drawing on his previous work, Grof outlines a new cartography of the human mind, one which accounts for experiences such as shamanic trance, near-death experiences, and altered states of consciousness.

Psychedelic Psychotherapy: A User-Friendly Guide to Psychedelic Drug-Assisted Psychotherapy, R. Coleman, 2017, Transform Press.

Presents practices for safe and successful psychedelic voyages. This book also details the benefits of having a guide and offers information about how to be a guide.

How to Change Your Mind: The New Science of Psychedelics, Michael Pollan, 2019, Penguin Press.

Diving into the world of psychedelics, Pollan explores it from a client-focused perspective. He writes a compelling portrait of his own experience, using underground psychedelic therapy.

In the Realm of Hungry Ghosts: Close Encounters with Addiction, by Gabor Mate, 2018, Vermilion.

Based on Gabor Mate's two decades of experience as a medical doctor and his ground-breaking work using ayahuasca with the severely addicted on Vancouver's skid row.

Books on Trauma

Here is essential reading for therapists who are considering working with traumatised clients. It's imperative to have a basic understanding of PTSD.

Trauma and Recovery, Judith Herman, MD, 1992, New York Basic Books.

A treatise on PTSD and its symptoms and effects. An oldie but a goodie.

Warriors of Truth: Adult Survivors Healing from Child Sexual Abuse, Kim McGregor, 1993, Otago University Press.

Powerful and easy reading. Provides great insight into the incestuous family system and how victims are treated, isolated, and scapegoated within the family system.

Healing the Fractured Selves of Trauma Survivors, Janina Fisher, 2017 Routledge.

Unpacks CPTSD as a lower-level type of multiple personality disorder. An academic book with a strong focus on the neurobiology of trauma.

The Body Keeps the Score, Bessel van der Kolk, 2014, Penguin.

Kolk is considered an expert in the trauma field. In this book he discusses case histories of trauma clients and the related neuroscience. Kolk has recently discovered MDMA therapy and even participated in a MAPS MDMA trial; hopefully, his next book will include more on this.

Psychedelic Training Institutes and Networks

MAPS – Therapist Training Manual. For those wishing to learn about or conduct psychedelic-assisted therapy, this might be a good starting resource. The MAPS website also contains other relevant resources (https://maps.org/).

While MAPS certainly have credibility due to their thirty-five-year history in the psychedelic field, their therapy model is research-focused, funded, and very hands-on. A typical MAPS session has two therapists present at all times, for eight-to-twelve-hour sessions, with overnight stays. There are fifteen preparatory and integration counselling sessions involved. When legalised, this treatment model will be extremely expensive and beyond the means of many.

Mind Medicine Australia (MMA) (https://mindmedicineaustralia.org.au/). Though a relative newcomer to the psychedelic therapy space, this organisation models itself as the Australian equivalent to MAPS. MMA is owned by an entrepreneur couple, both of whom have tried legal psilocybin therapy in Europe. MMA currently offer a 'non-accredited', Psychedelic Therapist Training Course, where no personal medicine experience is deemed necessary to become a qualified therapist. While this is likely due to legal restraints in Australia, it is, in my mind, a concerning position to hold. The course cost is circa AU$7000, plus the cost of several trips to Melbourne.

MMA are pushing for psychedelics to be legalised to use in medically controlled settings only, but they're not promoting blanket legalisation. They seek to have MDMA approved on compassionate grounds for treatment-resistant folk. It would be administered by doctors, psychiatrists, and psychologists connected to their organisation. Their progress in this area thus far has been slow. They hold free webinars, and have free website-based resources on mainly clinical trials.

The Castalia Foundation (https://castaliafoundation.com/). The organisation continuing and promoting the work of Timothy Leary (1920 – 1996) and others. The website offers free resources and information, particularly about MDMA, self-guided sessions. Leary was a proponent of going it completely alone and maybe that's why he recommends potentially 100 MDMA sessions for healing trauma. Leary didn't seem to have much faith in therapists and believed that a 'truly healed' person would never conduct psychotherapy for others.

As already stated, I believe more is achieved in a shorter timeframe with the aid of a good therapist. The challenge of undergoing long-term, solo MDMA work consists in confronting and integrating the parts of yourself that will inevitably seek to stop, side-track, or sabotage your healing process.

Australian Psychedelic Society (https://www.psychedelicsociety.org.au/). A passionate organisation that provides a lot of free resources as well as social gatherings and other meetings in most main centres. They have a Facebook group where you can ask questions and have discussions with 'the others' as long as they are discrete and non-incriminating.

Documentaries

A Trip of Compassion (2017) on Vimeo. An Israeli documentary, directed by Gil Karni, about MDMA-assisted PTSD therapy at Beer Yaakov psychiatric hospital.

From Shock to Awe (2018) (https://www.fromshocktoawe.com) and on Vimeo. Directed by Luc Côté, this is an intimate story of two war veterans who undergo psychedelic therapy with ayahuasca and MDMA.

Way Out There. By 60 Minutes (2020, Nine Digital). Story of ex-policeman, Nick Watchorn, who survived the Port Arthur Massacre in Tasmania, Australia. After losing his job and marriage because of his PTSD, he flew to San Francisco and participated in a MAPS MDMA-research trial. Consequently, he was healed and avidly promotes this therapy.

CONCLUSION

Who's Really in Control?

"A man living outside the circle of delusion which imprisons most men has a question of everyone he meets, usually asked silently. 'Can you get outside of yourself for even a split second to hear something you have never heard before?' Those who learn to hear will enter a new world."
—Kahlil Gibran.

The Part Two stories presented in this book came from predominantly professional and trustworthy people who, desperate for relief from their debilitating symptoms, had to break the law in order to receive effective therapy. The results were instant and profound and the relief they experienced after just a few hours of psychedelic-assisted therapy shocked and later angered them. They felt shock and disgust at a medical system that had betrayed them. A medical system that robs traumatised people of numerous functional years of their lives, wasted years of unnecessary, unbearable suffering.

Research conducted in the 1940s, '50s, and '60s revealed the efficacy of these medicines, yet legal psychedelic therapy and research were bought to an abrupt halt in the late '60s. One must question whether the influence of the global pharmaceutical companies had something to do with that. The gigantic profits Big Pharma enjoys are dependent on traumatised people consuming daily doses of assorted addictive pharmaceuticals for extended periods of time, often reaching into decades. The laws against psychedelic medicines have left suffering people to struggle and die, often at their own hands, because there's minimal profit in a cure.

The Global Pharmaceutical companies fund political parties during government election campaigns and lobbies parliamentarians in order to maintain influence over health care legislation. They offer financial incentives and grants to researchers who skew, manipulate, or withhold research. They offer perks to doctors and psychiatrists who promote and push their dodgy drugs. This compromising situation diminishes these respected professionals and brings into question their intentions[1].

The public are largely oblivious to the huge amount of their tax money currently being wasted on drawn-out, ineffective therapies for mental health disorders. According to the Australian Institute of Health and Welfare (AIHW), between 2019 and 2020, 4.4 million people received mental health–related care. Between 2018 and 2019, $10.6 billion was spent on mental health. One in eight Australians are on antidepressants, and 1.5 million were prescribed benzodiazepines in 2018 (Australian Bureau of Statistics). In 2020, 3,134 people took their own lives in Australia, and that's just the ones we know about. Many suicides are wrongly labelled as car accidents or drug overdoses.

With a serious mental health crisis on our hands and soaring suicide rates, particularly from within the war-veteran community and among sexual abuse survivors, governments can no longer justifiably withhold the psychedelic solution. It constitutes a travesty of justice and is morally and ethically wrong. This book and a growing number of other books,

---

1   Who Caused the Opioid Crisis? The Sackler Family – A Secretive Billion-Dollar Opioid Empire. https://youtu.be/zGcKURD_osM

prove without any doubt that psychedelic medicines WORK to heal mental illness and far more effectively than anything else currently available.

As you read this book, the tide appears to be turning, and the race is on to profit from the 'psychedelic renaissance.' Big Pharma, entrepreneurs, and venture capitalists are positioning themselves for control of the approaching legalisation of psychedelic medicines. As we see in the recent Australian Therapeutic Goods Administration report (September 2021)[2], 'MDMA and psilocybin may show promise in highly selected populations but only where these medicines are administered in clinically supervised settings and with intensive professional support.' It would appear that special interests are being arranged to enable control so that MDMA and psilocybin may become hostages.

Another reality is this; Legal or otherwise plant medicines call us, particularly ayahuasca. It finds us. It certainly found me. It invaded my consciousness and haunted me until it became an obsession. It seems to target atypical people with out-of-the-box characteristics, intelligent and creative people, socially and environmentally conscious people. Questioning people who are not easily fooled by the status quo, rebellious people unafraid to stand up, stand out, or stand alone. People with courage and conviction. Broken people with a story to tell. So there appears a higher purpose in this pathway. This awakening or renaissance seems far bigger than state, national, or international regulations. I feel we are being called upon to maintain the light, to heal humans in crisis and contribute to societal healing before it's all too late.

---

2 https://www.tga.gov.au/evaluation-therapeutic-value-benefits-and-risks-methylenedioxymethamphetamine-mdma-and-psilocybin-treatment-mental-behavioural-or-developmental-disorders

We find the world in crisis: COVID-19, biological warfare, environmental collapse through man-made climate change, social and religious terrorism, the continued threat of nuclear war, rampant, fear-driven greed resulting in unaffordable real estate and homelessness for many. I'm no conspiracy theorist but plenty of evidence abounds that Big Pharma has infiltrated governments, research universities, media, as well as our minds and bodies with some of their destructive and addictive pharmaceuticals.[3]

Darpan, one of Australia's early facilitators of ayahuasca, refers to ayahuasca as an intelligence agent, and I agree. With the ingestion of psychedelic medicines, particularly ayahuasca, something profound and seemingly other-dimensional occurs—a transpersonal experience unfolds. When one returns from an ayahuasca journey, a common phenomenon that occurs is an inability to articulate the experience, perhaps because they've touched upon something transcendent, otherworldly, mother nature herself—God perhaps. Some heal spontaneously from physical ailments, immune disorders, addictions, or psychosomatic illness. Some attest to alien-like encounters where an operation occurs, a brain defrag or software upgrade; others develop an interest in things of an alien nature, ancient history, indigenous wisdom.

So, despite how studiously Big Pharma and the venture capitalists seek to capture the essence of mother nature and market her in a pill, I'm not so sure these Gaian spirits want to be captured like genies in bottles and controlled by greed. Most grow freely all around us and are accessible without prescription. Mother nature holds dominion with a powerful mind of her own. If you come to her with a humble and true intention, she can and will heal you—that I'm sure of—the how and why are a mystery and may remain so. Another thing I feel certain of is that, despite what the scientists say, this is not just all about neurobiology. Something greater is upon us, something far removed from our 21st century lives in Western civilisations is healing us and calling us to expansion.

Entheogenic medicines do more than heal our trauma - that's step one. They heal our souls, highlight our lost tribal humanity, and connect us with nature and spirit. We become better, more integrated, more loving people. Plant medicines wake us up and make us more conscious. Conscious people feel driven to challenge an unjust system. The awakened resist a system that seeks to control and enslave them. There are many ways to enter the fray; you are holding one in your hand, this humble book. I hope you will benefit greatly from it.

Bibliography

Books & Journal Articles

Bache, Dr Chris, LSD and the Mind of the Universe; Diamonds from Heaven, Jan, 2020, Park Street Press.

Beckley/Maastricht research team; *LSD as a Non-addictive Pain Medication*, Journal of Psychopharmacology, Published 25th August, 2020.

Carruth, Dale, *Beating the Benzo Blues,* 3 Feathers Books, 2021.

Castalia Foundation, Website Articles, 2021.

Cogley, Father Jim, *Legacy of Sexual Abuse Denial can be Traced back to Freud*, Irish Times, May 26th, 2003.

Fisher, Janina, *Healing the Fragmented Selves of Trauma Survivors,* Routledge 2017.

Grof, Stanislav, *LSD Psychotherapy*, 4th edition - MAPS,1978.

Harris, Rachel, Listening to Ayahuasca, New World Library. 2017.

Herman, Dr Judith, MD, *Trauma and Recovery*, New York Basic Books, 1992

Hoffman, Dr Albert, *LSD My Problem Child*, Oxford Uni Press, 1979

Julianne Holt-Lunstad, Timothy B. Smith, Mark Baker, Tyler Harris, David Stephenson *Loneliness and Social Isolation as Risk Factors for Mortality: A Meta-Analytic Review*, First Published March 11, 2015, Research Article, Pub Med.

Kennedy, Robert F Jr, The Real Anthony Fauci; Big Pharma's Global War on Democracy, Humanity, and Public Health, Skyhorse Publishing, Nov 2021

Kurtz, E. (1989). *Drugs and the Spiritual*: Bill W. takes LSD. In The Collected Ernie Kurtz (1999). Wheeling, West Virginia: The Bishop of Books, pp. 39-50.

MAPS (Multidisciplinary Association for Psychedelic Studies) *Therapist Training Manual*, MAPS, 2021.

Mate, Gabor, *In the Realm of Hungry Ghosts*, Penguin, 2010.

McGregor, Kim, *Warriors of Truth; Adult Survivors Healing from Child Sexual Abuse*, Otago University Press, 1993.

Merkel Fisher, Dr Friederike, *Therapy with Substance*, Muswell Hill Press, 2015.

Muraresku, Brian C, *The Immortality Key: The Secret History of the Religion with no Name*, St Martin's Publishing Group, 2020.

Other, Anne, *Trust Surrender Receive*, Lioncrest, 2017.

Palmer, Julian, *Articulations: On the Utilisation and Meaning of Psychedelics*, Anastomosis Books, 2014.

Pollen, Michael, *How to Change Your Mind*, Penguin, 2018.

Sun, Nic, *Microdosing Iboga Root Bark,* Medium article, Dec, 2020.

Van der Kolk, Bessel, *The Body Keeps the Score*, Penguin, 2015.

<u>You Tube</u>

Who Caused the Opioid Crisis? The Sackler Family - A Secretive Billion Dollar Opioid Empire. https://youtu.be/zGcKURD_osM

Appendix

Client Assessment Form

Date:

Personal Details

Name:

Address:

Phone:

Email:

Partner Name:

Children:

Emergency Contact details:

Employment:

Age:

Nationality:

Referral Source:

Medical History

Prescription Meds:

Existing or previous physical disorders/conditions:

History of Psychological Disorders/diagnoses/admissions:

Family of Origin: Addiction, Mental Health, Relationship Status

Grandparents:

Father:

Mother:

Brothers:

Sisters:

Children:

Family Trauma History:

Emotional Abuse:

Physical abuse:

Sexual Abuse:

Other Trauma History

Sexual Abuse:

Physical Abuse:

Emotional Abuse:

Other Traumatic Events:

Partner Relationships History:

Spiritual/ Religious Beliefs:

Drug & Alcohol use:

Alcohol use frequency:

Drug use & frequency:

Previous use of Psychedelics:

Addictive or avoidant behaviours; Sex, food, work, gambling, money, exercise, co-dependency, self-harm.

Presenting Issues and Intentions:

Dates Booked:

www.ingramcontent.com/pod-product-compliance
Lightning Source LLC
Chambersburg PA
CBHW020315010526
44107CB00054B/1858